Hamilton Fish

*Memoir of an
American Patriot*

Hamilton Fish

Memoir of an American Patriot

Epilogue by Brian Mitchell

REGNERY GATEWAY

Washington, D.C.

Library of Congress Cataloging-In-Publication Data

Fish, Hamilton, 1888–1991
Memoir of an American patriot / Hamilton Fish : Epilogue by
Brian Mitchell.
p.   cm.
Includes index.
ISBN 0-89526-531-1
1. Fish, Hamilton, 1888–1991.   2. Legislators—United States—
Biography.   3. United States.   Congress.   House—Biography.
4. United States—Politics and government—20th century.   I. Title.
E748.F5A3   1991
328.73'092—dc20   91-31881
CIP

Published in the United States by
Regnery Gateway
1130 17th Street, NW
Washington, DC 20036

Distributed to the trade by
National Book Network
4720-A Boston Way
Lanham, MD 20706

1991 printing
Manufactured in the United States of America

Dedicated to the Memory of All Those Who Served in Our
Nation's Armed Forces Who Paid the Supreme Sacrifice,
and to All Veterans.

Hamilton Fish

Acknowledgment

I acknowledge with gratitude the loyal and diligent assistance of Anthony Troncone, Lydia Fish, and Jo Anne Mecca, whose efforts on behalf of my memoir will always be appreciated. Also deserving of thanks are John Toland; Brian Mitchell; the Hoover Library, West Branch, Iowa; the American Legion Archives, Indianapolis, Indiana; the FDR Library, Hyde Park, New York; and Rutgers Library, New Brunswick, New Jersey. I owe a special debt of gratitude to William Miles for recording in a great film, "Men of Bronze", the glorious history of the "Harlem Hellfighters" of the 369th "Rattlesnake Regiment".

Contents

Hamilton Fish

Memoir of an
American Patriot

Preface

The ends I serve shall be my Country's, my God's and truth's. I was born an American, I will live an American, I shall die an American, and I intend to perform the duties incumbent upon me to the end of my career. I mean to do this with absolute disregard to personal consequences.

DANIEL WEBSTER

This book—my memoir—covers my family's history, my education at St. Mark's School and Harvard, my football reminiscences, my period in the New York State legislature as a Progressive, my service as an officer with the 369th Infantry—a unit made up of black Americans—during World War I, my twenty-five years in the United States Congress, and much else that I hope will be of interest to a variety of readers.

I have devoted my life to serving the American people by doing what I could to secure for them their civil rights, regardless of the color of their skin, and by protecting our country against her enemies, both foreign and domestic. From 1929 to 1930 I was chairman of the first congressional committee to investigate communism and the work of communist operatives in the United States and I continued to fight against communism throughout the 1930s, as the ranking Republican member of the House Foreign Affairs Committee, I was actively involved in congressional efforts to maintain American neutrality. My experience in the First World War made me skeptical of the wisdom and the morality of shedding American blood in European wars.

I do believe that the United States has an important role to play in world

3

affairs. For instance, I introduced and secured passage for Congress's 1922 Palestine Resolution endorsing the creation of a homeland for the Jewish people in Palestine—one of the most important pieces of congressional legislation I ever introduced—and I have always been a firm believer in the Monroe Doctrine, which defined the legitimate national interests of this country. The advice of Washington, Jefferson, and Monroe, however, that we should stay out of foreign wars seems to me infinitely sound. One of my favorite passages from Thomas Jefferson, in fact, is this one:

> I have ever deemed it fundamental for the United States never to take an active part in the quarrels of Europe. Their political interests are entirely distinct from ours. Their mutual jealousies, their balance of power, their complicated alliances, their forms and principles of government are all foreign to us. They are nations of eternal war. All their energies are expended in the destruction of the labor, property and lives of their people. On our part, never had a people so favorable a chance of trying the opposite system, of peace and fraternity with mankind, and the direction of all our means and faculties to the purposes of improvement instead of destruction.

When we were attacked at Pearl Harbor, I was the first congressman to speak over national radio and call for a declaration of war against Japan. I had emphasized in all my previous speeches that we should keep out of war unless attacked. When that happened, I urged the more than 25 million Americans who were listening to me over the radio, to rally behind the president, regardless of political affiliation, and support the war effort. It was only later that I discovered that FDR had deliberately tricked the American people into an unnecessary war.

FDR and Churchill wanted war with Japan in order to get the United States into war with Germany. The president and his so-called war cabinet contrived to deliver a secret ultimatum to the Japanese ten days prior to the devastating attack on Pearl Harbor. When they did not hear from the Japanese immediately, FDR even considered sending a second stronger dictum. In an open letter to FDR, Arthur Krock of the *New York Times*, said: "From the time of the quarantine speech in 1937 you have done everything possible to antagonize Japan and force it into the Axis. . . ."

The Japanese alliance with Germany and Italy in 1940 was a bombshell to the administration's opponents. Senator Nye declared:

> Our foreign policy has succeeded in driving Japan into the arms of those

who were the last ones we wanted her to associate with. Japan claimed it was due to the blunders of the United States State Department.

It was not simply bureaucratic blundering that precipitated war between the United States and Japan. Roosevelt and his six-member war cabinet were fully aware that they were deliberately provoking Japan into war.

I will go into the details of all these matters later in this book. I only wish to note at this point the price that all of us paid for the Second World War—the war, recall, that even Winston Churchill referred to as "the unnecessary war." It was a war in which 412,000 Americans were killed and 700,000 wounded fighting for freedom and democracy, only to have Central and Eastern Europe delivered to the totalitarian Soviet Union at war's end.

Because of my own war experience and my deep involvement in veterans' issues—I have been an active member of the American Legion since its very first caucus in 1919, was chairman of the committee of three that wrote the preamble to its constitution, and introduced the legislation in Congress that helped create the Tomb of the Unknown Soldier in Arlington National Cemetery—the cost of war has always been much in my thoughts. I honor and appreciate the sacrifices of all American soldiers; as a consequence, I strongly believe that they should be sent to war only when the national interest requires it. Similarly, my hatred of wanton destruction has made me a long-time supporter of verifiable worldwide nuclear disarmament.

But I will deal with all these issues in their proper place. Now it is time to turn to the family into which I was born.

Chapter One

Born into a Political Family

I came into this complex and interesting world on December 7, 1888, in Rocklawn, my father's old brick house in Garrison, New York, located on the Hudson River's east bank, just opposite the United States Military Academy at West Point. I was the fourth child of five, and the only son. In a letter to my grandfather, written the night I was born, my father noted, "The boy has very capable lungs, dark hair, not in profusion, and at first sight has not good looks; but then, he is the looked for boy."

The arrival of the "looked for boy" was no doubt a cause for special celebration to my father, for at last he would have a son to carry on the family name. I was the third in the line to bear the name Hamilton Fish, which has since been passed on to my son, now a congressman from New York, and to the oldest of his three sons.

The Fish family is deeply enmeshed in New York State's political history. My father, Hamilton Fish, Jr., was born in the governor's mansion in Albany in 1849. He attended Columbia University and graduated from Columbia Law School in 1872. After serving a year as private secretary to his father, who was then secretary of state in the administration of President Ulysses S. Grant, he ran on the Putnam County Republican ticket for state assemblyman and was elected at the age of twenty-four. Up to that time, Putnam County had been predominantly Democratic. He served

7

eleven terms in the state legislature and was elected speaker in 1895 and 1896. At the 1896 Republican State Convention, he was one of the leading candidates for governor, but at the eleventh hour Boss Tom Platt's political machine defeated him in favor of Congressman Frank Black of Troy, who was elected governor.

My father was an able and independent public official, and a high-minded and scrupulously honest citizen. He returned to politics in 1908, when he was elected to the U.S. House of Representatives. Defeated for a second term by a few hundred votes in 1910, he was appointed by President William Howard Taft to serve as assistant United States treasurer in charge of the old Sub-Treasury Building in New York City, an important position at that time. Though retired from active politics, he always remained interested in the local Putnam County political situation.

My mother, whose maiden name was Emily Mann, died when I was ten, but I remember her as a charming and beautiful woman with a sweet disposition who was loved by everyone. Her family was political as well. Her father was a distinguished judge and three-time mayor of Troy, New York. Her brother Elias Mann also served three terms as mayor. Her mother, Marquise de Lafayette Norton, was a direct descendant of Thomas Hooker—the man who settled Hartford, Connecticut, in 1636 and participated in the formation and adoption of the "Fundamental Orders" (the Constitution) of Connecticut in 1639.

I am also directly descended from Peter Stuyvesant, the courageous and constructive administrator who built New York into a beautiful town. Elizabeth Stuyvesant married my great-grandfather, Colonel Nicholas Fish, in 1803. My great-grandmother was originally given one-quarter of the vast Stuyvesant property from her father and later inherited another quarter from her brother, in addition to more accumulated property. As a result, the Fish family inherited a very large part of the lower East Side of New York City up to 23rd Street. But my family realized so little rent from the Stuyvesant properties that we sold them in 1919. Had the family kept the properties, I would be one of the richest men in the world today, as there are no male Stuyvesants left, and I have automatically become the head of the Stuyvesant family. I thank God I did not inherit the Stuyvesant properties because I would never have been able to resist all that money and all the pretty girls that come with all that money!

Colonel Nicholas Fish—who is responsible for this—was born in his father's house on Wall Street on August 28, 1758, the son of Jonathan Fish and the former Elizabeth Sackett (another well-known Hudson Valley family). Nicholas's parents were both ardent Tories and supporters of King George III. But young Nicholas, at age seventeen, went to work at the law office of John Morin Scott, a leading lawyer and founder of the Sons of Liberty. While working for Scott, Nicholas established his lifelong friendships with John Varrick, later mayor of New York, Robert Troup, later a federal judge, and Alexander Hamilton. Fish, Varrick, Troup, and Hamilton all served with distinction as officers during the Revolutionary War.

Nicholas Fish was commissioned a major in the Second Regiment of the Army of the United States on November 21, 1776, by order of Congress, signed by John Hancock, president. He fought in the battles of Brooklyn, White Plains, Saratoga, Monmouth, and Yorktown. He acted as division inspector under General von Steuben, headed a corps of light infantry under Major General Lafayette, and was adjutant to General James Clinton during the campaign against the Indians in 1779. Governor George Clinton made him the first adjutant general of the state of New York, and George Washington appointed him the first supervisor of revenue in New York. Nicholas Fish was also president of the Dutchers and Drovers Bank and chairman of the Board of Trustees of Columbia College from 1823 to 1830.

His son, my grandfather Hamilton Fish, was born in 1808, and embarked on a political career that included service as a congressman, governor of New York, United States senator, and secretary of state for President Grant's two terms. Grant offered him an appointment as chief justice of the U.S. Supreme Court, but he turned it down because he did not consider himself qualified, having not practiced law for many years. He was considered by some historians as the power behind the throne of the disorganized Grant administration, and he was once voted the third best secretary of state by an association of college professors of history and government.

Needless to say, the distinguished public service of my great-grandfather, grandfather, and father left its mark on me. But I was also much influenced by a Fish I never met, a cousin also named Hamilton Fish, who was the first American soldier killed in the Spanish War. It was because of this Hamilton Fish, whose father's name was Nicholas, that I was christened Hamilton Stuyvesant Fish. Naturally, I had nothing to say about this, but when my cousin died, my father arranged to have me legally drop my middle name, which pleased me greatly, as I was only ten at the time and had difficulty spelling Stuyvesant.

I knew my cousin only by reputation because he was much older than I was, but I admired him greatly. He was a glamorous figure, born into a famous family. He attended Columbia College, where he was captain of the championship intercollegiate crew of 1896, which in those days held regattas in Poughkeepsie, New York. The outbreak of the Spanish War found him in San Antonio, Texas, where Theodore Roosevelt was recruiting for the Rough Riders. My cousin joined up and was made a sergeant in Company L. Roosevelt described him then as an "eastern 5th Avenue dude," a fact I learned while attending the 1987 American Legion Convention in San Antonio with my fourth wife.

Cousin Hamilton led the advance guard at Las Quasimos, soon after landing in Cuba, and was killed at the head of his squad. The *New York Times* described the incident:

> Sergeant Hamilton Fish, Jr., was the first man killed by the Spanish fire. He was near the head of the column as it turned from the wood road into range of the Spanish ambuscade. He shot one Spaniard, who was firing from the cover of a dense patch of underbrush. When a bullet struck his breast he sank at the foot of a tree, with his back against it. Captain Capron stood over him, shooting, and others rallied around him covering the wounded man. The ground this afternoon was thick with empty shells where Fish lay. He lived twenty minutes. He gave a small lady's hunting watch from his belt to a messmate as a last souvenir.
>
> With the exception of Captain Capron all the Rough Riders killed in yesterday's fight were buried this morning on the field of action. Their bodies were laid in one long trench, each wrapped in a blanket. Palm leaves lined the trench and were heaped in profusion over the dead heroes. Chaplain Brown read the Episcopal burial service for the dead and as he knelt in prayer every trooper knelt around the trench. When the Chaplain announced the hymn "Nearer My Soul to Thee" the deep bass voices of the men gave a most impressive rendering to the music. The dead Rough Riders rest right on the summit of the hill where they fell. The site is most beautiful. A growth of rich, luxuriant grass and flowers covers the slopes, and from the top a far-reaching view is had over the tropical forest.

My cousin's body was removed and placed in a grave in the Fish family burial ground at St. Philips in the Highlands Episcopal Cemetery, Garrison, New York. He died as he had lived, a fearless fighter, and he made the supreme sacrifice as a volunteer in defense of his country. There are Veterans of Foreign Wars posts named after him in Philadelphia, the Bronx, St. Louis, Chicago, Minneapolis, and El Paso. As his cousin and namesake, I am proud of his courage, adventurous spirit, and final sacrifice for America.

Many years later, when I was testifying as a former member of Congress before the Senate Foreign Relations Committee in 1955, I was asked about my cousin's service in the war and about his time at Columbia. I told his story briefly, explaining how I changed my name after his death. Then I said:

> He was a very extraordinary fellow. He was as tall as I am, but in those days they were a little wilder, and he went up to my district when they won the races at Poughkeepsie and arrested the police force and tore up the bar, cost his father two or three thousand dollars, and they always thought it was me. I don't know whether it got me votes or not.

And the truth is, I still don't know.

Chapter Two

My Early Years

I received my earliest education before the age of eight from our German maid who looked after me and taught me a little German. My formal education began in 1896 with a trip to Europe. I was enrolled in a Swiss school, Chateau de Lancy, near Geneva. My father had attended this school in 1860, and it was one of the best-known schools for non-Europeans living in Europe. I remember fellow students from as far away as Egypt and Siam. At Chateau de Lancy I learned French and spent most of my spare time playing soccer. I was short then, but strong and left-footed, which was an advantage. Once when a British team came to play in Geneva, I was invited to fill a vacancy on a Swiss team at age ten, but my father would not permit it, much to my disappointment.

My family usually spent the summer months in southern Bavaria at Paartenkoerchen near Garmisch at the foot of the Zutzspitzer, the highest mountain in the German Alps. There I took long walks and was able—one day when I was twelve—to convince my father to hire a guide to take me to the top of the mountain. In those days, many well-known world leaders, like Theodore Roosevelt, were climbing the Alps, and even at the age of twelve I wanted to follow in their footsteps. Later, during the summers of my college years, I would embark on other vigorous pursuits such as working in the coal mines near Calgary, Canada, and camping in Alaska. I tried hunting once, too, but found I had no stomach for killing.

My remaining education was at St. Mark's in Southborough, Massachusetts, which is still one of the best preparatory schools in the United States. In my lessons, I was only moderately successful—a B student—but I excelled at anything athletic: tennis, football, boxing, the high jump, and the high kick. My roommate at St. Mark's, and also my classmate at Harvard, was Peabody Gardiner, who became a top tennis player and was on Harvard's baseball and hockey teams. His aunt owned the famous Gardiner art museum in Boston. "Peabo" and I remained friends for life.

The following is a transcript of a letter I wrote while at St. Mark's to my father and sister Rosalind:

ST. MARK'S SCHOOL
SOUTHBOROUGH

Monday

Dear Father & Rossy,

It was very kind of you to send me so many shirts but there is only one dance.

I have decided to keep my old tuxedo.

We had only ¾ of a holiday, but I managed to have a very good time.

I am going to dance the cotillion with Agnes Landon.

My dance card
1st. Agnes Landon
2nd. Natalie Howland
3rd. Dorothy Dexter
4th. Miss Lippit
5th. _____
6th. Cousin Marg
7th. K T Weed
8th. Miss Rice of j'en sais pas

Please allow Rossy to *inspect*.

A great many girls have backed out. Ruth Windsor and about six Philadelphians. There are 29 acceptancies and ten more have been asked. Appie, Weary Coleman, and Hutch have not yet got partners.

May Tuckerman and Dorothy Grunnel also have backed out.

The dining room is extremely pretty.

We had a Latin and English exam today. It is not bad fun now, no one studies for these darn exams.

My cash deposit is running low. A relief expedition of $ would not hurt matters. I had to buy some nice shirt studs. If possible, any plain white vest procurable at Aiegel & Cooper or Rogers & Peet, six 35 extra long would neither hurt matters.

With love, Affec/

It was just before the start of my last year at St. Mark's that I made my debut as a newsmaker in the pages of a local newspaper. My father and I, along with my sister Rosalind and Miss Margaret Roosevelt, a member of the local Roosevelt clan, were out for an afternoon drive in a horse-drawn carriage near our home in Garrison, New York. I was holding the reins and we were moving along at a good clip when an automobile came chugging down the road from the opposite direction. As it was about to pass us, the horses bolted to one side and I lost control. Try as I might, I couldn't stop the horses from taking off down the road at a frenzied gallop, which ended for us when the carriage swerved into a fence and lost a wheel. We were all dumped out in a heap by the roadside, tussled but otherwise unhurt. The horses kept on for another couple of miles, and the carriage was a total wreck. "HAMILTON FISH IN SMASH," read the headline, referring to my father. The rest of the story left no doubt as to my part in the smash.

After graduating from St. Mark's in 1906, I entered Harvard, intending to study history and play football, which I did. Among my classmates were T. S. Eliot and John Silas "Jack" Reed. I liked Reed very much and appointed him cheerleader of the football team. He was a very interesting character, and though a radical socialist—Lenin later honored Reed by having him buried at the Kremlin—he never joined the Socialist Club at Harvard, which was headed by Walter Lippmann, another classmate, who went on to enjoy a very successful newspaper career with the *New York Herald Tribune*.

Jack was impressed, as many socialists were, by the promises of the new Soviet government in Russia. He wrote a famous book about Lenin and the Russian Revolution, *Ten Days that Shook the World*, which so impressed Moscow that he was given a position in the Communist party. But Jack quickly soured on the communists when he discovered that they were killing everyone who disagreed with them. It is my conviction, in fact, that Jack was one of their victims—poisoned by the communists when they discovered that he intended to return to New York with communist funds.

When I visited the Soviet Union in 1922, as a member of Congress, I placed some flowers on Jack Reed's grave. His wife was allowed to leave the Soviet Union after Jack's funeral, and years later she married William

Bullitt, our former ambassador to Moscow. When they married, he was our ambassador in Paris. Bullitt eventually divorced Reed's widow.

It was in football that I really made my mark at Harvard. At 6'4'' and 200 pounds, I always played tackle, but a play devised by Harvard coach Percy Haughton made me eligible to receive forward passes. Yale coach Walter Camp once said I was the best receiver of the forward pass yet to play the game. I was twice picked for Camp's All-Time All-America Football Team, in 1910 and 1915, and I am also in the College Football Hall of Fame at King's Island, Ohio. One of my greatest honors was to receive the first Walter Camp Foundation Football Award in 1968. The presentation of this award to a former Harvard player was an act of the highest sportsmanship on the part of the committee, and I am sure it was welcomed and appreciated by many thousands of Harvard alumni.

In my junior year I became acting captain of the Harvard team after our all-American guard, Francis Burr, suffered an injury early in the season. The 1908 team had an undefeated season and went on to win the national championship by beating the tough Carlisle team in our final game of the season. Carlisle's team was coached by Pop Warner and featured Jim Thorpe, the best football player I ever saw. Before playing us, Carlisle had beaten Syracuse, one of the year's best teams, 12 to zero, but they had done so through a clever trick. Pop Warner had sewn the covers of old footballs onto the jerseys of his backs and ends so that the Syracuse defense would have trouble figuring out who was carrying the ball. This didn't violate any rules. But in those days, the home team was responsible for providing the football, and when Carlisle turned up at Harvard, we painted it Harvard crimson. And we beat Carlisle 17 to zero. To the best of my knowledge it was the first time Jim Thorpe didn't score; and I tackled him more than anyone else.

Football is a rough game, especially in my day when a player played offense and defense and could be tackled before he had a chance to catch the ball. We did not have all the protective equipment they have today, and there were not so many rules to prevent unnecessary roughness. Fatalities were not unknown. In the 1909 game between Harvard and Army, an Army player, Cadet Eugene Byrne, was fatally injured. Some people blamed me for his death. I had tackled him three times during the first half of the game, but I was nowhere near him in the second half when he was caught in a mass tackle that broke his neck.

The game was called on account of Byrne's injury, and Army cancelled its schedule for the remainder of the season. Later, an investigation determined that an exhausted Byrne should have been removed from the game earlier, but had he been removed, the rules required that he sit out the rest of the game, which he did not want to do. As a result of his death, the rules were changed to allow players removed from play to return to play at the beginning of any quarter.

As captain of our team, I visited West Point to express our sorrow, and I attended Byrne's funeral. There were no hard feelings there, and I was invited in 1912 to come over the Hudson River from Garrison to coach the West Point tackles before Army's game with Yale. This I did, and I am pleased to report that Army beat Yale that year for the first time ever.

I also helped coach Army in 1913, and it was then that I met a West Point cadet named Dwight D. Eisenhower. Actually, I don't remember meeting him at all, but he remembered. I think it was in 1961 at a Football Hall of Fame dinner, at which President Eisenhower was the guest of honor, that he told me he remembered me showing up for football practice in my big coonskin coat. I was flattered that he remembered me, but I was embarrassed because I still could not remember him. After all, he was then just a substitute halfback on the Army squad. But I do remember my coonskin coat.

I am a firm believer that football is a great teacher of lessons and that football players hardly deserve the stupid and untruthful attacks on their intelligence. Harvard's 1908 national championship team included men who would become able lawyers (three), highly successful private bankers (three), a coal magnate, a well-known doctor, a chairman of the Portland, Oregon, Chamber of Commerce, and a congressman (me).

I like to tell the story of the course I took in my junior year at the Harvard Theological School along with Burr, our injured captain, and Mort Newhall, a former quarterback. It was a very interesting course taught by a very good professor. We three football players received full A's and none of the twenty divinity students did, all of whom were intelligent and probably made fine ministers of the gospel. When the college heard that three football players had gotten A's, the course was flooded with applicants thinking it was a cinch; they soon found out it wasn't.

The Harvard of my day required all its football players to be both gentlemen and scholars. One player on the 1908 team, a sophomore named Charlie Crowley, was upbraided by the dean for poor marks. Crowley responded by calling the dean an s.o.b. and was consequently expelled. For the next three years, he played end for Notre Dame—the opposite end to Knute Rockne.

On February 1, 1979, I donated $5,000, through the Harvard Club of

New York Foundation, for three trophies. One was to be awarded to the most improved Varsity basketball player during the season terminating March 1979, and annually thereafter; a second to the most improved Varsity soccer player during the season that ended in the fall of 1979, and annually thereafter; and a third, in memory of Percy D. Haughton, to a Varsity football lineman (I later indicated that I wished it to go to the tackle who had shown the most improvement during the season). The funds were to be used to purchase three trophies with the income from the balance used each year to furnish each winner with a small replica of the trophy and the cost of inscribing the winner's name on the trophy and on the replica. Any surplus income was to be used for scholarship purposes. I added: "My purpose is to strengthen Harvard support of both soccer and basketball, each of which I played seventy years ago, and also strengthen Harvard support for the football team of which I was Acting Captain in 1908, and Captain in 1909."

All these trophies are kept in the NYC Harvard Club and are available for inspection by members from time to time.

I sincerely believe that football teaches players more about life than any academic course possibly can. Football requires a great deal of mental concentration in addition to strength, speed, courage, endurance, cooperation, self-discipline, and quick reactions. A good player must be able to get knocked down, get up, and fight all the harder to succeed. If life teaches anything, it is that character counts and inner strength is necessary for success. Football is a great builder and tester of character and strength.

But you don't have to take my word for it. In a speech at the Harvard Union on February 23, 1907, President Theodore Roosevelt said:

> We cannot afford to turn out college men who shrink from physical effort or from a little physical pain. In any republic, courage is a prime necessity for the average citizen if he is to be a good citizen and he needs physical courage that endures. The courage that will fight valiantly alike against the foes of the soul and the foes of the body. I emphatically disbelieve in seeing Harvard or any other college turning out mollycoddles instead of vigorous men. I may add I do not in the least object to a sport because it is rough.

I am proud to have known Theodore Roosevelt well. He was one of our ablest, most courageous, and most popular presidents. And we agreed on most issues. But I'd also like to quote Richard Mulcaster, the first headmaster of Merchant Taylor's School, who said in 1582: "The footeball strengthens and brawneth the whole body. It helpeth weak hames by much moving and simple shankes by thickening of the flesh no lesse than riding doth."

I graduated from Harvard in 1909 at the age of twenty with a cum laude degree in history and government. Unable to leave football behind, I helped organize the Harvard Law School team composed of varsity players from Harvard, Yale, Princeton, and other schools. During breaks in the school year, we toured the country playing teams made up of former college players. We played purely for fun, though the games were sometimes just as brutal as regular college games. In a way, we were a predecessor of professional football, which began in 1919.

I was offered an appointment to teach history at Harvard but declined out of lack of interest. Though I did well in school, I never took my studies seriously enough to have been a good teacher. Besides, the salary was too low, and I had already been offered a very well-paying job in John C. Paige's insurance office in New York City—a firm with which I was to be associated for thirty years.

In 1914, I entered politics by being elected a member of the New York State Assembly, and another chapter of my life began. My football career moved into the past. While I was at Harvard, being captain of two winning football teams meant something to the debutantes, who often would ask for my autograph. But I can assure you, after a few years of marriage, a man's college football glory just does not mean anything at all. Someone once asked my wife what position I played on the Harvard team, and she thought for a moment and said suddenly, "Oh, yes, I know. He played captain." It is difficult for me to account for this except to say that she used to be a Democrat.

Chapter Three

The New York State Assembly

When I entered the New York State Assembly, it was as a Progressive follower of Theodore Roosevelt. I had come to know his son, Theodore Roosevelt, Jr., at Harvard where we were both members of the Porcellian Club (I was also a member of the Signet Society and president of the Hasty Pudding Club). I was very friendly with Theodore Jr., who was one class ahead of me and who later had a brilliant career in the army, rising to the rank of brigadier general. Tragically, he suffered a fatal heart attack after participating in the D-Day Normandy invasion during World War II.

My father had known and admired Theodore Roosevelt and it was only natural that I, too, would become a Roosevelt man. In 1912, when I was twenty-four years old, I attended the Republican presidential convention in Chicago, expecting to see former President Roosevelt handed the Republican nomination. Instead, I was amazed, disappointed, and disgusted to see the Republican National Committee steal the nomination from Roosevelt and give it to the incumbent president, William Howard Taft. Taft was a fine man personally, but there was no denying that popular sentiment favored Roosevelt who had won 1,157,397 primary votes to Taft's 761,716.

Roosevelt was so enraged by the deceit and underhanded tactics of the Republican National Committee that he bolted the party and decided to run for president as an Independent on the newly created Bull Moose platform, which forged a coalition between progressive Republicans and disaffected Democrats.

Although Roosevelt failed to win the 1912 presidential election, there is no doubt he would have won had he been nominated by the Republicans. Roosevelt lost to Woodrow Wilson by approximately two million votes, but he received a million more votes than Taft, who came in a distant third. If the Republican National Committee had not stolen the nomination from Roosevelt, most, if not all, of the votes cast in favor of Taft would have gone to Roosevelt, giving him a decisive victory over Wilson and making him president. A look at the final tabulation of votes confirms this: Wilson—6,296,547; Roosevelt—4,118,571; Taft—3,486,720.

Politics was in my family's blood, so it was no surprise when I entered the field myself. In 1912, I was appointed chairman of the Putnam County Bull Moose party (the Progressive party). Two years later, I ran for a seat in the New York State Assembly on a fusion ticket of the Progressive and Democratic parties. The incumbent, John Yale, the so-called "boss of Putnam County," decided not to run against me, selecting instead one of his handpicked cronies, a man named Weeks. I defeated him easily in the election.

Once I was elected I became actively involved in efforts to reform New York State politics by uncovering official corruption. Sitting behind me in the Assembly, in fact, was the former governor, then assemblyman, William Sulzer, who had been forced out of the governor's office on trumped-up impeachment proceedings initiated by the bosses.

A compulsive tobacco chewer, Sulzer would spit out a stream of tobacco juice over my shoulder, aimed at a spittoon located on the floor next to where I sat. Every day I would see this awful mixture of tobacco fly over my right shoulder, but I must say, much to my relief, he never missed. We became very good friends. He was honest, able, and helpful to me in many ways.

I also became very friendly with Franklin Roosevelt, who was serving in the New York State Senate and who, in those days, was a fine Jeffersonian Democrat. We worked closely together, as two progressives, fighting political corruption and the power of the bosses and their political machines.

In 1914, Franklin Roosevelt came to me and told me he wanted me to succeed him in the New York State Senate, as he was resigning his seat to become assistant secretary of the Navy. He said that I would be elected easily, since I already had the support of the Progressives and most Republicans, and he promised me that he would provide the Democratic support, saying in a letter, "if you decide to run I shall violate every rule I have made and come up and stump the district for you."

Unfortunately, I had to decline his offer. I had already agreed to run for the New York State Assembly and had received the endorsement of the local Democratic, Republican, and Progressive parties. I also lacked the money necessary to campaign in all of Dutchess County and I was afraid that the Democratic and Republican party bosses might have the power to override Franklin Roosevelt's endorsement.

Still, I certainly appreciated Roosevelt's offer of support —so much so that I encouraged my wife to vote for him when he ran for president in 1932—and Roosevelt and I remained good friends throughout the 1920s. When I was elected to my first term to Congress in 1920, I received a letter from Roosevelt congratulating me on my victory, which read in part:

> In view of the fact that you and I are still Progressives I feel that I can very properly congratulate you on your election as my Representative in Washington during the coming two years.
>
> I hope we shall have a chance to talk things over some day soon. You will have a wonderful opportunity to be of great service in Washington in keeping the old-line Reactionaries of every kind from going to such extremes as some of them are even now proposing.

I won reelection to the Assembly relatively easily and continued my fight against government corruption. I also fought against a bill that would have allowed insurance companies to bypass the state's compensation commission in settling claims involving injured workmen. Had this bill been allowed to pass, workers would have been at the mercy of employers (who were backed by some of the largest insurance firms) and been denied the legal protection of the state. Joining me in my fight was Theodore Roosevelt, who wrote me a letter that I had introduced into the minutes of the Assembly:

> My Dear Mr. Fish:
>
> In response to your request I have to say that of course I entirely agree with you and feel that it is a great misfortune, a great backward step, to have the Workmen's Compensation Act twisted out of its proper purpose, which is to be literally a compensation act for workmen, and turned into a bill in the interest of casualty companies. I think there is scant room for argument in the matter. The case can be put in a nutshell. Do the people of the state of New York want a compensation act in the interest of the workingmen? If so, it is

the duty of those in power at Albany to defeat this proposed amendment to the already existing act. If the design is to pass a bill in the interest of the casualty companies, the proposed amendment meets that purpose.

/s/ Theodore Roosevelt

After I read this letter, the speaker of the Assembly, Thaddeus Sweet, paled and could hardly speak. The following year, Sweet tried to silence me by imposing a gag order on me after I criticized a corrupt district attorney who had wrongfully prosecuted Thomas Osborne, the warden of Sing-Sing prison and an honest and able administrator. Osborne was apparently being punished for not working as a tool of the bosses. On the floor of the Assembly I accused the district attorney of being either "dishonest or incompetent." As soon as I said this, Sweet rushed through a motion—without calling for a negative vote—to prevent me from continuing my speech. I protested vehemently at this shameful and un-American tactic, and a number of Democrats and Republicans joined together to prevent my being gagged. I was allowed to continue my speech, and I continued to uncover the shady dealings of the bosses for the rest of my tenure in the Assembly.

In the course of doing this, I found statements on file in the state comptroller's office that proved that many people had been appointed to and paid for jobs they never performed—they had not even been in Albany when they were supposed to be working there. These people, who came from the same districts as the Republican leaders who had appointed them, were part of a "no-show" job scheme that cost taxpayers vast sums of money.

I went to the floor of the Assembly, was recognized, and demanded that if a bill I had drafted to prohibit these no-show jobs was not adopted by the Rules Committee and passed by the Assembly within a week or ten days, I would present the signed statements to the district attorney for his immediate action. As a result, my bill was reported out of the Rules Committee and passed in ten days. The problem of no-show jobs, however, persists to this day.

When I wasn't in Albany, I would frequently visit Theodore Roosevelt at his office in New York City. I was important to Roosevelt for two reasons: I was the only Progressive member left in the New York State legislature and I knew Charles Evans Hughes's son. Roosevelt was a strong supporter of Charles Evans Hughes, the Republican candidate for president in 1916, in his campaign against Woodrow Wilson, and he used me as an intermediary to pass on his advice to Hughes (through Hughes's son). Wilson had earned Roosevelt's ire by vetoing a congressional bill that would have made Roosevelt a major general and put him in command of an army division.

I remember in one message Roosevelt urged Hughes to be outspoken about upholding the rights of German-Americans—despite the emotions aroused by the war in Europe—as guaranteed to them, and to all Americans, under the Constitution. He also strongly advised Hughes to meet with Governor Hiram Johnson of California, a Progressive and close friend of Roosevelt's. Unfortunately, William Crocker—railroad executive, wealthy banker, extreme conservative, and member of the Republican National Committee—did not want Hughes to meet with Johnson. Thus, when Hughes visited Long Beach, California, Crocker prevented the meeting—even though both men, unknown to each other, were staying at the same hotel—making it appear as though Johnson did not want to endorse Hughes for president.

"If I had known," Hughes lamented, "that Johnson was in that hotel, I would have seen him if I had been obliged to kick the door down." But that would not have been necessary, for Johnson later wrote that Hughes's trip to California "had been used by Crocker . . . not for the benefit of Hughes, but for [Crocker's] petty ambitions, and that he might again control California's government. . . ."

Hughes was, of course, defeated by Wilson in a close race (so close that at midnight on election day, the *New York Times* pronounced Hughes the winner). If Hughes and Johnson had met in California, it is likely that Hughes would have easily carried the state and become president, with consequences that would have drastically altered future events.

After the election, I remained close to Theodore Roosevelt. In 1917, when I was appointed chairman of a committee to welcome foreign dignitaries to New York City, I invited Roosevelt and Samuel Gompers, the president of the American Federation of Labor, to meet a delegation from the Kerensky government of Russia. Gompers used the occasion to defend the actions of a group of St. Louis union members who had resorted to racial violence during a strike, savagely attacking black strike breakers and their families. More than six thousand blacks had been driven from their homes and more than two hundred blacks had been killed before order was restored.

When it was Roosevelt's turn to speak, he strongly denounced Gompers for defending the mass murder of blacks. The former president said he would never stand on any platform and listen to anyone defend the murder of American citizens, whether they be black or white. He then walked over to where Gompers was seated and shook his fingers in Gompers's face. Labor members, most of whom were seated in the galleries, thought he had struck Gompers and rushed down to the stage. In the meantime, the audience was giving Roosevelt a standing (and cheering) ovation; but the excitement and the chance of violence was so great that I called in the police and had them escort Theodore Roosevelt to safety.

Roosevelt's action was a testimony to his courage, and I was deeply impressed by his open defiance of the AFL leader, particularly given that Roosevelt was considering running again for the presidency in 1920. But I do not want unjustly to belittle Samuel Gompers, who was one of the most intelligent leaders in the history of the American labor movement and a profound believer in freedom, democracy, and the Constitution. He was also a strong opponent of socialism. Having studied it and known many of its proponents, he told the socialists: "Economically, you are UNSOUND. Socially, you are WRONG. Industrially, you are an IMPOSSIBILITY."

As for myself, domestic politics were beginning to fade and my military career was about to begin.

Chapter Four

The Fighting 369th

I had served for two years in the national guard, training at Plattsburg, New York, while I was an assemblyman in the New York State legislature. My commanding officers were impressed by my performance and recommended that I be promoted to captain. An examination was required to achieve the promotion, but I had studied the drill regulations extensively and knew I could pass the exam. That I had graduated from Harvard with honors, been captain of the football team and a success in business, and had political experience as a New York State assemblyman, all stood me in good stead.

On the day of the examination, I was met by a major I did not know who himself had not been made captain until he was well over fifty years old. He asked me a number of questions that had nothing to do with military training and declared me too young for a captaincy.

I did not know then that my great-grandfather Nicholas Fish had been the youngest major ever commissioned in the army, aged eighteen years and three months. If I had known, I would have invoked his example. As it was, I merely told the major that I thought my age, experience, and background were sufficient to make me a qualified candidate. But the major would not even allow me to take the exam, and told me that if I did take it, he would ask me questions about cooking that I would be sure to fail. I protested that whatever my knowledge of cooking, I knew the drill instructions as well as he did. But the major persisted in his refusal.

I went back to New York City and met with Colonel William Hayward of the national guard, who was in the process of organizing an all-black regiment. He asked me if I wanted to join the regiment as a captain. I accepted his offer on the spot and became one of the first officers of what was later designated the 369th U.S. Infantry Regiment, the famed Harlem Hellfighters.

At President Woodrow Wilson's request, Congress declared war against Germany on April 2, 1917, in order, in Wilson's words, to make "the world safe for freedom and democracy." During the summer of 1917, with about two thousand men, we began training at Camp Whitman in New York. In October 1917, we were ordered to Camp Wadsworth in Spartanburg, South Carolina, for further military training before embarking for France.

Realizing that the presence of so many black troops in the predominantly white and segregated town of Spartanburg could cause trouble, I telegrammed Franklin Roosevelt, then assistant secretary of the Navy, telling him of my fears and requesting that he do what he could to have us sent directly to France. "My brother officers believe with me," I told him, "that sending northern volunteer Negro troops south would cause [a] recurrence of race troubles. This battalion could render immediate valuable service in France . . . where there is present need to relieve French troops."

Despite my appeal to Roosevelt, our orders remained unchanged, and we went to Spartanburg for twelve tension-filled days. It was made obvious that we were not welcome in the town. Soldiers were assaulted, forced off the sidewalk, and subjected to other racial harassments.

I quickly arranged a conference with the top town officials and told them that if any of the town's citizens sought by force to interfere with the rights of the black troops under my command, I would demand that swift legal action be taken against the perpetrators. This quieted things down temporarily, but it was a nervous quiet.

The War Department belatedly decided that it would be unwise to have our regiment remain in the South. On October 24, much to my relief, we were ordered back to Camp Whitman in New York. But trouble followed us. Stationed next to us at Camp Whitman was an Alabama regiment that did not care for our presence. Again, there were insults and assaults. But not once, I am pleased to say, did any of my soldiers lose to any of the Alabamians.

Early one afternoon, I learned that the Alabamians intended to attack us during the night. For our defense, I had to borrow ammunition from another New York regiment, as we had none. After arming our soldiers, I and my fellow officers told them that if they were attacked, they were to fight back; if they were fired on, they were to fire back.

Around midnight, a bugle was mistakenly sounded, calling the black troops to arms. I quickly strapped on my service revolver and went out into the darkness toward the Alabama regiment and ran into three Alabama officers. I told them that the black troops were armed and would fight back if attacked. It would be a massacre, I said, on both sides. I added that bloodshed between our troops was entirely unnecessary. Black or white, we were all Americans who had been called upon to fight a common enemy overseas; the war was in the trenches in France, not between the barracks at Camp Whitman. All three of these officers agreed and told me they would return to their regiment and do everything they could to prevent trouble—which they did, successfully. And I was left standing with my revolver cocked in the firing position, unsure how to release the hammer without discharging a round.

Though the incident passed peacefully enough, the New York newspapers blew the story out of proportion and said that I had challenged the Alabama officers to a fist fight, which was completely untrue.

We returned to New York a few days before Thanksgiving 1917, and boarded a troopship, the USS *Pocahantas*, for transit to France, but after leaving the pier, the ship developed engine trouble and had to turn back. We left again a few days later, but this time a fire forced us back. On December 13, 1917, off we went again—only to collide with another ship just off the coast. Though our transport's bow was ripped open, the men repaired the damage underway—*anything* rather than face the embarrassment of saying another good-bye to families and friends!

We had no destroyer escort to protect us from German submarines, and later I wrote to Franklin Roosevelt about this, hoping that he could use his influence as assistant secretary of the Navy to take corrective measures:

> I am writing the following facts to you as a friend who has confidence in your discreetness and as a friend who believes in your good judgement and ability to remedy a condition which in the near future will endanger the lives of thousands of American soldiers. . . .
>
> It was a great surprise to all of us to find out that our convoy was not protected by destroyers. I have no desire to criticize anyone and only hope to remedy the condition before it results in a disaster. . . .

We landed at Brest, France, on December 26—right side up! It was bitterly cold, with snow and ice covering the ground. We boarded unheated railroad cars and were taken to St. Nazaire. In St. Nazaire, most of the regiment was detailed to perform stevedore duties—making preparations for other American troops on their way to France. We had been trained to fight as soldiers, not to work as laborers, and all of us were anxious to get to the front lines. But the American military command was reluctant to integrate the armed forces by assigning black troops to white regiments. (As a congressman during World War II, I played an active role in trying to integrate the armed forces. This will be discussed in a later chapter.) Finally, however, General Pershing decided to place us under the control of the French army, as there were no other black troops to make up a division.

We were sent to Chalons, where we turned in our American military equipment and were issued French rifles, helmets, belts, and canteens that had no water but, much to the delight of the men, were filled with French wine. After a month or so we were judged ready to fight. We were assigned to the French Fourth Army under the command of the famous one-armed French General Gouraud, with whom I became quite friendly, thanks to my fluency in French.

It was a five-mile hike from our headquarters near Chalons to the frontline trenches. As a captain, I was given a horse to ride, which was the French custom. Halfway to our position, we neared a French artillery battery, which suddenly came under German attack. It sounded like a gale at sea. Several shells exploded on the battery wounding a number of French soldiers and some of mine as well.

That night we took over an advanced position, including a small defensive post. As we settled in, I called for stretcher-bearers to evacuate one of my men who had been wounded. As I watched him being loaded on the stretcher, a German shell landed right on top of him—killing him and three of the four stretcher-bearers. The fourth miraculously survived, stunned and shell-shocked.

The next morning we were ordered to move five miles west to help French troops resist an expected German assault. We filed into our new positions in the trenches, which had rows of barbed wire extended in front. When we weren't standing in the trenches, we slept in our dugouts, which were fifty feet deep.

Soon after our arrival on the front, a squad of French soldiers was ordered to capture some Germans (called "Boche" by the French) whose lines were about one hundred yards away. During the night, a lieutenant and his men tried to cut through the German wires, but they were discovered and the lieutenant was shot in the head, near his eye. Still, he managed to guide his men back to their own lines, apparently more concerned for their safety than for his own wound. As they dropped back into the trenches, the German artillery opened up. One shell landed on a bagful of grenades strapped to a French soldier. The resulting explosion killed six men.

In a letter to my father shortly after my arrival at the front, I told him of a "most unfortunate accident" involving three of my men. A French soldier, wearing a rather large, bulky coat, accidently upset a box of grenades sitting on the top of the stairs to a dugout where three of my men were sleeping. The grenades exploded and severely wounded the sleeping soldiers. I went down into the dugout accompanied by a French lieutenant to see what I could do. The lieutenant was overcome by the sight and fainted. As a result, I had to carry all three wounded soldiers fifty feet to the surface. Amazingly, despite the seriousness of their head and body wounds, all three of them survived.

Besides its combat record, the 369th was noted for its outstanding band. Its first director was the composer and band leader Jim Europe, founder of the first black musicians' union in America and bandmaster for the famous dance team of Vernon and Irene Castle. Europe was a first lieutenant in my company and I ate with him every evening. Later he was succeeded as director by his able assistant Noble Sissle. The band also included Bert Williams, a veteran performer of the Ziegfeld Follies, who had been a captain in the California National Guard until the 369th was formed. Our band won a series of competitions with other bands, which were nowhere near as good as ours. A very wealthy man, whose name I have forgotten, provided $10,000 to hire musicians from Puerto Rico to play instruments that members of our unit could not play, thus making our band one of the best in France.

In July 1918, the Germans launched an all-out offensive—the battle of Champagne-Marne—against our lines. Just before the battle began, I wrote what I thought would be my last letter to my father:

Dear Father:

I have not received any mail from America for over two weeks, and I am afraid that the mail delivery has gone to pieces again. I am writing you a few lines to say that I am assigned with my company to two French companies to defend an important position (hill) against the expected German offensive.

My company will be in the first position to resist the tremendous concentration against us and I do not believe there is any chance of any of us surviving
the first push. I am proud to be trusted with such a post of honor and have the
greatest confidence in my own men to do their duty to the end. The rest of our
regiment is dug in far to the rear except for L and M companies; the latter is
holding a village in our rear. My company is expected to protect the right flank
of the position and to counterattack at sight of the first Boche. In war some
units have to be sacrificed for the safety of the rest and this part has fallen to us
and will be executed gladly as our contribution to final victory. How fond I am
of you, and to thank you for all your care and devotion—words utterly fail me. I
want you in case I am killed to be brave and remember that one could not wish
a better way to die than for a righteous cause and one's country.

Love to Tanta, Grace, Rossy,

Your affectionate son,
\s\ Hamilton

When the attack did come my company was ready, holding its position
despite the ferocity of the fighting. Company K—my company—lost three
dead, and had six wounded and four poison-gas casualties. I survived
unscathed, though my horse was killed during an artillery attack, my
helmet was hit by shrapnel, and I had a few other close scrapes.

The German offensive had been a failure. General Gouraud remarked
soon after the battle that it was "a hard blow to the enemy. It is a beautiful
day for France." We began to sense that the tide of victory was turning in
our direction.

In this optimistic mood, I was sent to the staff school at Langres. But
things did not stay quiet long; the Germans were unwilling to admit defeat.
In late September, while I was at staff school, the Germans attacked at
Meuse-Argonne. I rushed back to my company, just in time for the
fighting, which raged incessantly for the next forty-eight hours in a horrify-
ing exchange of machine gun and artillery fire. When it was all over,
30 percent of my regiment had suffered casualties. For my part in the battle
I was awarded the Silver Star. The citation read in part:

. . . Constantly exposed to enemy machine gun and artillery fire, his un-
daunted courage and utter disregard for his own safety inspired the men of
the regiment, encouraging them to determined attacks upon strong enemy
forces. Under heavy enemy fire he assisted in rescuing many wounded men
and also directed and assisted in the laborious task of carrying rations over
shell-swept areas to the exhausted troops.

The Meuse-Argonne battle was the single most important battle of
World War I. Had the Germans succeeded, they would have had an open
path into Paris and to the North Sea. But we stopped them. It was now
only a matter of time before Germany was compelled to surrender. At
11:00 A.M. on November 11, 1918, an armistice was declared, ending
World War I. "It seems almost a dream," I wrote my father that day, "in
spite of the fact that peace has been discounted for the past two weeks. I am
glad the killing of human beings is over and hope that it will be a lost art in
the future." The record that we, the men of the 369th, compiled on the
field of battle was an outstanding one. We spent 191 days in the frontline
trenches, longer than any other American regiment. We were the first
Allied regiment to reach the Rhine River. We never lost an inch of ground.
And we never had a man captured by the enemy.

The war was over and we had survived, but not without casualties. I later
learned that Father Paul of Graymoor in Garrison, a Catholic home for
troubled men, visited my father every Sunday afternoon during the entire
time I was in France. Together, the priest and my father prayed for my
safety, and I always believed that their prayers were instrumental in my
survival.

I will always remember the brave black men who served with me in the
trenches of France: Frederick Williams; Melville Miller; Captain Bert
Williams, who left the vaudeville stage to help recruit the black volunteers
and served the entire time at the front; and men such as Henry Johnson and
Needham Roberts, who were attacked by 24 Germans on patrol and, in
spite of multiple wounds, fought fiercely against their attackers and lived to
tell the tale.

Nor will I forget the bravery of my loyal Sergeants, Clinton J. Peterson,
Herman Brown, and William Layton, who carried out their duty to the
men under heavy shelling at great risk to themselves. At the end of World
War I, I told my men, "You have fought and died for freedom and democracy. Now, you should go back home to the United States and continue to
fight for your own freedom and democracy."

I will close this chapter by noting that I was not the only Fish to serve
during World War I. My sister Janet went to Paris to visit relatives and
ended up serving as a nurse near the front lines. After the war, she went on
to a distinguished career as superintendent of nurses at a hospital in
Washington, D.C. Both she and I were later inducted into the French
Legion of Honor for our wartime service.

Chapter Five

A Congressman for Civil Rights

Two years after the Armistice, I was elected to Congress, representing the 26th Congressional District in New York. But I represented more than my own district. Because of my service in the 369th regiment, I was regarded by many black Americans as their representative, regardless of where they lived. I received letters from all over the country from black Americans requesting my assistance on a variety of issues—and I helped them whenever I could. If black Americans considered me their special representative in Congress, I must say that I also felt as though I had a special obligation to them—particularly after having watched them fight and die for freedom and democracy in the muddy trenches of France.

My sense of obligation to American blacks also stemmed from my family history. My great-grandfather, Colonel Nicholas Fish, was an active participant in manumission societies. In 1799, he played a prominent role in having the New York State legislature enact a law abolishing slavery. My grandfather, Hamilton Fish, as Grant's secretary of state, promulgated the ratification of the Fifteenth Amendment, which gave black Americans the right to vote.

For most of my first ten years in Congress, until Oscar DePriest was elected, there was no black representative in Congress. This sort of thing caused me to lead the charge on many bills for black Americans. During my first term in Congress I collaborated with the National Association for the Advancement of Colored People (NAACP) and a number of progressive Republicans to introduce antilynching legislation and a Battle Monuments Bill to commemorate the service of gallant black American soldiers.

I remember how Southern Democrats taunted me as I walked on the floor of the House just before I made an address in favor of the anti-lynching bill, chanting racial slurs and hate-inspired invectives. Along with other congressmen, I dedicated my efforts to "end the rule of the rope and faggot." In 1922, I spoke before the House, explaining why I believed it of the utmost importance to enact an antilynching bill:

> I cannot remain silent on this question. I would be untrue to those colored men of this country who paid the supreme sacrifice, especially to men of my command who gave up their lives to make the world safe for freedom and democracy, if I failed to advocate passage of the antilynching bill. Let me tell you something that perhaps members of the House do not fully appreciate, and that is that the colored man who went into the war had in his heart the feeling that he was not only fighting to make the world safe for democracy but also to make this country safe for his own race. I have sworn to support the Constitution of the United States, and on that account, if for no other reason, it would be my sacred duty as a member of the House of Representatives to vote for a drastic antilynching bill to protect the lives of American citizens everywhere in the United States.

I also suggested that Southern states, where lynching blacks was rampant, mount "machine guns in all county jails for use against mobs who attempt to substitute their desires for the orderly process of the law."

But antilynching legislation alone was not enough to ameliorate the dismal economic conditions of American blacks. Another battle was joined when I called for the creation of a national commission to study the "economic and political status" of blacks and to make specific recommendations "for the betterment of their condition and assure them equal protection and equal opportunity under the law." A similar battle took place in Congress when I introduced a bill in 1922 to provide for battle monuments honoring black soldiers who had fought in France. The bill eventually passed by a large majority. The following exchange gives a taste of that particular debate in the House:

THE CHAIRMAN: The gentleman from New York [Mr. Fish] is recognized.
MR. FISH: Mr. Chairman, this bill (H.R. 0004) authorizes the expendi-

ture of $30,000 to erect a monument to commemorate the gallant services of four colored regiments of the provisional Ninety-third Division of the American Expeditionary Forces, and I am glad to see that no Republican in the House voted against the consideration of this bill today. [Applause.]

MR. O'CONNELL of New York: Will the gentleman yield?

MR. FISH: Yes: I yield.

MR. O'CONNELL of New York: I would also like the gentleman to say that there were some Democrats who voted with him on this proposition.

MR. FISH: I will be glad to say that some of the Democrats voted in that way, but a great many more who should have voted for its consideration did not so vote.

MR. GREEN of Florida: And I am glad to say some of them did not vote for it, sir.

MR. FISH: Mr. Chairman, these colored soldiers, I will say to my friends on the Democratic side of the House, were good enough to be accepted as volunteers in time of war; they were good enough to be drafted; they were good enough to be killed for their country; but they are not good enough to permit the consideration of a bill to commemorate their gallant services. [Applause.]

The four regiments included in the bill are the Three hundred and sixty-ninth, formerly the Fifteenth New York National Guard—and I will say to my Democratic friends that they had white officers, and of these sixty white officers 15 of them were killed on the field of battle. The Three hundred and seventieth was a National Guard regiment from Chicago; the Three hundred and seventy-first a drafted regiment from the South; the Three hundred and seventy-second composed of a separate battalion from Ohio, another from the District of Columbia, and separate companies from Massachusetts, Connecticut, and Maryland. The casualties of these four regiments was 40 percent of their effectives. I have letters in my pocket from officers who served in the regiment drafted from the South, a white officers' association, and they are for this bill, and I am proud of it. [Applause.]

MR. CONNALLY of Texas: Will the gentleman yield?

MR. FISH: I will.

MR. CONNALLY of Texas: Will the gentleman explain why General Pershing, chairman of the battle commission, is against it, and Senator Reed on the commission is against it, and why the gentleman from Maryland [Mr. Hill] is opposed to it?

MR. FISH: I do not think the gentleman from Maryland [Mr. Hill] is opposed to the bill; he is on the floor of the House and can speak for himself. As far as the other gentlemen are concerned, I will answer the question. The Battle Monuments Commission made a rule that no unit under a division should be considered. Therefore, these regiments could not be included under that regulation for a battle monument. But the bill was amended in committee to obviate some of the objections of Senator Reed. In order that the appropriation would not be taken out of the battle monuments fund a special authorization of $30,000 was provided for in this bill. Both amendments were made in committee, and I think that answers the statement of the gentleman who wanted to know why we reported the bill. This is the second time in two years, after careful consideration, that this bill has been reported. [Applause.] The Battle Monuments Commission is a creature of Congress, and it is not only right but just that we instruct them to provide a separate monument for the provisional Ninety-third Division.

The four regiments that make up this division served with the French Army. They were understrength, having about 2,500 men in a regiment. Three of the four regiments had their flags decorated with the French *croix de guerre*. Very few other American regiments had their flags decorated with the French war cross. There was no dispute by the opponents in the committee as to the heroism, gallantry, and courage of the Negro fighting soldiers of the provisional Ninety-third Division. [Applause.] The facts were admitted by witnesses before the committee; even the opposition admitted that these four regiments had conducted themselves gallantly on the battlefields of France, and one of these regiments claims that it served in the line longer than any other American regiment.

MR. COOPER of Wisconsin: Will the gentleman yield?

MR. FISH: I will.

MR. COOPER of Wisconsin: I think the gentleman has omitted an important fact as stated to me by a Member sitting by my side. He expressed surprise when I told him the distinguished gentleman now addressing the House was an officer of one of those regiments. [Applause.]

MR. FISH: My friends, I would be derelict to the memory of those colored soldiers in my own regiment and the white officers who were killed in that regiment if I did not do everything in my power to see that they got proper recognition. [Applause.]

There were 400,000 Negro soldiers in our Army. There are 12,000,000 colored people in the country, and everyone is interested in seeing that recognition is given to the soldiers of the colored race who made the supreme sacrifice. [Applause.] There were 457 killed and 3,468 wounded in these four regiments out of a battle strength of approximately 10,000 soldiers. With the exception of the First and Second Divisions, there were not many American divisions which had a higher percentage of killed and wounded. All we ask here is to do away with this unjust discrimination against the heroism of Negro soldiers and erect this monument in France, which will be for all time an inspiration to patriotism, loyalty, and heroism for all the colored people of America. [Applause.]

During the New Deal years, I continued to work with the NAACP on behalf of civil rights legislation—including the perennial antilynching bill. I am sorry to say that President Franklin Roosevelt and his supposedly enlightened clique never lifted a finger to help me pass the badly needed civil rights legislation that I was continually supporting on the floor of the House. In 1937, in a speech I delivered at the Lincoln Congregational Temple in Washington, D.C., I noted my frustration with FDR's administration when I said: "It would be more beneficial to the country, if the president stopped passing moral judgments and attempting to police other nations, and instead sought to do justice in our own country, by urging the enactment of the Antilynching Bill."

In 1940, I was still fighting for antilynching legislation, without the support of the president, when I made the following remarks in the House:

> Every time a colored man or woman is lynched or burned at the stake in America it means that the Emancipation Proclamation has been suspended and that their civil and equal rights have been destroyed under the law and the Constitution. . . .
>
> The primary and paramount duty of Congress is to legislate to safeguard the security and lives of the American people and that is the reason for the existence of our government. I have taken an oath of office to support and defend the Constitution, and believe I am defending it when I am trying to protect human lives in America, whether they are white or whether they are colored. I want to commend the Members who have joined in the general attack and condemnation of this outrageous, bestial, and barbaric practice of lynching. It is the worst crime in America. It is even worse than kidnapping, because it is not only murder, it is an attack upon the courts and upon our institutions and upon our very form of government.

But while President Franklin Roosevelt told the American people that they had to fight a world war to protect democracy in Europe, he refused to support my efforts to extend the blessings of democracy to American blacks. Sadly, American blacks were learning what the people of Eastern Europe were to learn later: Roosevelt's lofty promises about freedom and democracy were empty. He never had any intention of fulfilling those promises, because his interest was not in defending principles, but in political aggrandizement; and when it served his cause to say one thing and do another, that is precisely what he did. Unfortunately, many people were disillusioned by his hypocrisy, and I regret that I couldn't do more to stop him from trampling on his promises.

Chapter Six

Founding the American Legion

The American Legion was created at a conference held in Paris on March 15, 1919, by representatives of the American Expeditionary Forces. I could not attend the conference because at that time I was stationed with the Army of Occupation in Germany.

I was, however, one of more than one thousand veteran delegates who attended the St. Louis Caucus on May 10, 1919—Lt. Col. Theodore Roosevelt, Jr., presiding—where the American Legion Preamble and Constitution were written and approved. There I was appointed to the Committee on the Constitution and made chairman of a subcommittee to write the Preamble. I was also authorized to appoint the other two members of the subcommittee. I appointed Colonel John Greenway, a Yale athlete who had served in the Roosevelt Rough Riders before his service in the First World War, and who was one of the foremost mining engineers in Arizona. (His statue stands in the U.S. Capitol building—one of two representing the state of Arizona.) My other appointment was Judge George N. Davis, who, like me, was a stalwart admirer of Theodore Roosevelt. All three of us contributed important ideas to the Preamble, and when it was approved by the Committee on the Constitution, it went to the delegates of the convention who gave it their unanimous assent. Not a word of the Preamble has been altered since, except for the word "war," which has become plural. The Preamble reads as follows:

37

PREAMBLE TO THE CONSTITUTION

For God and Country we associate ourselves together for the following purposes:

To uphold and defend the Constitution of the United States of America; to maintain law and order; to foster and perpetuate one hundred percent Americanism; to preserve the memories and incidents of our associations in the Great Wars; to inculcate a sense of individual obligation to the community, state and nation; to combat the autocracy of both the classes and the masses; to make right the master of might; to promote peace and good will on earth; to safeguard and transmit to posterity the principles of justice, freedom and democracy; to consecrate and sanctify our comradeship by our devotion to mutual helpfulness.

The Preamble is not only virtually the charter of the American Legion and its more than 1,800 posts, it is the life-blood that has infused all Legionnaires with a definite purpose and unity. It has also won for the Legion the respect and admiration of men like President Truman and General Pershing, who publicly commended the Preamble as an important statement of American ideals.

The men who founded the American Legion were imbued with enthusiasm and a determined spirit to build a powerful, nonpartisan, patriotic veterans organization, not only to uphold the principles for which they fought, but to ensure hospitalization and rehabilitation for their disabled comrades. The Preamble was written for them. This is what it means:

"For God and Country"—This signifies the Legion's devotion to the ethical principles handed down to us by the world's great religions and to the belief that if there is any country worth living in, worth defending, worth fighting for, and worth dying for, that country is the United States of America.

"To uphold and defend the Constitution"—The Constitution is the greatest charter of human liberty devised by the mind of man; it is the "civil bible of America," to use Al Smith's phrase, that protects the rights of all Americans; and it is our best defense against the tyrannies—fascism, nazism, and communism—that still terrorize man.

"To maintain law and order"—This is more necessary today than ever before and hardly needs further explication.

"To foster and perpetuate one hundred percent Americanism"— Patriotism should not be ridiculed and Americans should not be divided against themselves on the basis of race, religion, or the country of their ancestors.

"To preserve the memories and incidents of our associations in the Great Wars"—The American Legion is an organization of veterans with a duty to remember the deeds of their comrades.

"To inculcate a sense of individual responsibility to the community, state and nation"—The American Legion understands that no man is an island and that we all benefit when we work to make our neighborhoods, our states, and our country better places in which to live.

"To combat the autocracy of both the classes and the masses"—We appeal to the American people to resist demagogues of the Left and Right who would throw out the Constitution and subject us to tyrannical government.

"To make right the master of might"—We encourage all Americans to perform their civic duties according to the law and the dictates of conscience. Abraham Lincoln said: "Neither let us be slandered from our duty by false accusations against us, nor be frightened from it by menaces of destruction of our government, nor to ourselves. Let us have faith that right makes might, and in that faith let us to the end dare to do our duty as we understand it." These words of Lincoln helped inspire this aspect of the American Legion's Preamble.

"To promote peace and good will on earth"—In our nuclear age, this is not only sound advice from a veteran's organization, but necessary to preserve American lives and the principles for which America stands.

"To safeguard and transmit to posterity the principles of justice, freedom and democracy"—The American Legion understands the vital importance of perpetuating America's strengths and values from generation to generation so that our shining beacon to the world is not dimmed.

"To consecrate and sanctify our comradeship by our devotion to mutual helpfulness"—One of the main objectives of the American Legion is to look after the aid and care of our sick and disabled comrades.

The Preamble of the American Legion, written twenty-one years before our entry into the Second World War, contains five of the most important words—God, Country, Constitution, Freedom, and Peace—that should unite all Americans, regardless of party. They are the words to which I have devoted my life; and I am proud of my long-standing association and deep involvement with the American Legion, as well as with the Veterans of Foreign Wars, over these many years.

Chapter Seven

The Fish Committee

On May 1, 1923, I gathered with representatives of the Veterans of Foreign Wars and its Auxiliary on the north side of Union Square in New York City for the first annual celebration of "Loyalty Day," a day freedom-loving Americans had determined to reclaim from the communists. The communists were in the habit of marking May Day with riotous displays of hatred for America. That year, we matched their riots with peaceful ceremonies proclaiming our belief in freedom and democracy.

The first Loyalty Day was chilly in New York. Bessie Hanken, a member of the VFW Auxiliary and later its national president, was waiting to address our assembly in her white Auxiliary uniform, which was too light for the weather, so I offered my overcoat. No sooner had she put it on than gunshots rang out in our direction. We scrambled for cover until the danger passed. Though no one was hurt, I later found three bullet holes in the sleeve of my coat.

The next year Bessie Hanken organized a Loyalty Day ceremony on Boston Common and was met by a counterdemonstration of communists who burned American flags and ripped Auxiliary members' uniforms.

I mention these incidents to show that communism in those days was no idle threat but a very real menace to peace. In 1928, the Soviet government concluded the Sixth World Congress of the international communist movement by reaffirming its intention of spreading violent revolution around the globe. In the United States, the communists resurfaced with an all-out campaign to infiltrate the labor movement. Their goal was to spread

40

labor unrest and pit one class of people against another. In Gastonia, North Carolina, they succeeded in sparking bloody dissension among the textile workers. Then, in the early months of 1930, the communists, led by William Z. Foster, organized massive protests in many American cities. The intent of these protests was not peaceful—the right to conduct a peaceful demonstration is every American's constitutional right—but to goad the police into violent action that could be turned into a propaganda victory.

On March 5, 1930, I introduced House Resolution 180 calling for a congressional committee to investigate communist activities in the United States. Because the topic is so controversial, I include here what the resolution actually said:

> Resolved, That the Speaker of the House of Representatives is authorized and directed to appoint a committee of five Members of the House of Representatives to investigate Communist propaganda in the United States and particularly in our educational institutions; the activities and membership of the Communist Party of the United States; and all affiliated organizations and groups thereof; the ramification of the Communist International in the United States; the Amtorg Trading Corporation; the *Daily Worker*; and all entities, groups, or individuals who are alleged to advise, teach, or advocate the overthrow by force or violence of the Government of the United States, or attempt to undermine our republican form of government by inciting riots, sabotage, or revolutionary disorders.
>
> The Committee shall report to the House the results of its investigation, including such recommendations for legislation as it deems advisable.
>
> For such purposes the committee, or any subcommittee thereof, is authorized to sit and act at such times and places in the District of Columbia or elsewhere, whether or not the House is in session, to hold such hearings, to employ such experts, and such clerical, stenographic, and other assistants, to require the attendance of such witnesses and the production of such books, papers, and documents, to take such testimony, to have such printing and binding done, and to make such expenditures as it deems necessary.

The purpose of my committee was to investigate communist propaganda, not to delve into the activities of socialists or other left-wing groups. We were not interested in suppressing the freedom of speech of Americans who respected the law, the Constitution, and the flag—the very symbol of the United States as an entity. We were, however, interested in investigating the activities of the communists. Their stated, official intent was to overthrow our constitutional government through violence, which made them a special—and worrisome—group.

During the almost seven months that my committee conducted hearings, we heard testimony from more than 250 witnesses whose testimony concerning communist activities was chilling. The communists who testified before the committee freely admitted that they hated the American Republic, its Constitution, and all forms of religion. William Z. Foster—twice the Communist party candidate for president of the United States—said that the communists meant to tear apart the fabric of American civilization. The following is an exchange between Mr. Foster and myself on the subject of the aims and loyalties of American communists:

MR. FISH (Chairman): Would you mind stating to the Committee the aims and principles of the Communist party?

MR. FOSTER: The aims and principles of the Communist party, briefly stated, are to organize the workers to defend their interests under the capitalist system and to eventually abolish the capitalist system and to establish a workers' and farmers' government.

MR. FISH: Now, can you tell us more definitely if the principles of the Communist party, as advocated in this country or anywhere else, are the same?

MR. FOSTER: Yes.

MR. FISH: Does your party believe in the promotion of class hatred?

MR. FOSTER: This is a peculiar question. What do you mean by "class hatred"?

MR. FISH: I mean stirring up and exciting class antagonism and hatred of the working class against the other classes, so called.

MR. FOSTER: Our party believes in developing the class consciousness of the workers, to educate the workers to an understanding of their class interests, and to organize them to defend the class interest which, inevitably, brings them into conflict with the capitalist class in its whole system of ideology.

MR. FISH: Do the communists in this country advocate world revolution?

MR. FOSTER: Yes; the communists in this country realize that America is connected up with the whole world system, and that the capitalist system displays the same characteristics everywhere—everywhere it makes for the misery and exploitation of the workers—and it must be abolished, not only on an American scale but on a world scale.

MR. FISH: So that they do advocate world revolution; and do they advocate revolution in this country?

MR. FOSTER: I have stated that the communists advocate the abolition of the capitalist system in this country and every other country; that this must develop out of the sharpening of the class struggle and the struggle of the workers for bread and butter.

MR. FISH: Now, are the communists in this country opposed to our republican form of government?

MR. FOSTER: The capitalist democracy—most assuredly. We stand for a workers' and farmers' government; a government of producers, not a government of exploiters. The American capitalist government is built and controlled in the interests of those who own the industries, and we say that the government must be built and controlled by those who work in the industries and who produce.

MR. FISH: They are opposed to our republican form of government?

MR. FOSTER: Most assuredly.

MR. FISH: That is, what you advocate is a change of our republican form of government and the substituting of the Soviet form of government?

MR. FOSTER: I have stated that a number of times.

MR. FISH: Now, if I understand you, the workers in this country look upon the Soviet Union as their country. Is that right?

MR. FOSTER: The more advanced workers do.

MR. FISH: Look upon the Soviet Union as their country?

MR. FOSTER: Yes.

MR. FISH: They look upon the Soviet flag as their flag?

MR. FOSTER: The workers of this country and the workers of every country have only one flag and that is the Red flag. That is the flag of the proletarian revolution; it was also, incidentally, the flag of the American Revolution in its earlier stages. The Red flag has been the flag of revolution for many years before the Russian revolution.

MR. FISH: Well, the workers of this country consider, then, the Soviet government to be their country. Do they consider the Red flag to be their flag?

MR. FOSTER: I have answered that quite clearly.

MR. FISH: Do you owe allegiance to the American flag; does the Communist party owe allegiance to the American flag?

MR. FOSTER: The workers, the revolutionary workers, in all the capitalist countries are an oppressed class who are held in subjection by their respective capitalist governments and their attitude toward these governments is the abolition of these governments and the establishment of soviet governments.

MR. FISH: Well, they do not claim any allegiance, then, to the American flag in this country.

MR. FOSTER: That is, you mean the support of capitalism in America? No.

MR. FISH: I mean, if they had to choose between the Red flag and the

American flag, I take it from you that they would choose the Red flag; is that correct?

MR. FOSTER: I have stated my answer.

MR. FISH: I do not want to force you to answer it if it embarrasses you, Mr. Foster.

MR. FOSTER: It does not embarrass me at all. I stated very clearly the Red flag is the flag of the revolutionary class, and we are part of the revolutionary class.

MR. FISH: I understood that.

MR. FOSTER: And all capitalist flags are flags of the capitalist class, and we owe no allegiance to them.

MR. FISH: Well, that answers my question.

I also asked Mr. Foster to explain the Communist party's views on religion:

MR. FISH: Does your party advocate the abolition and destruction of religious beliefs?

MR. FOSTER: Our party considers religion to be the opium of the people, as Karl Marx has stated, and we carry on propaganda for the liquidation of these prejudices amongst the workers.

MR. FISH: To be a member of the Communist party, do you have to be an atheist?

MR. FOSTER: In order to be, there is no formal requirement to this effect. Many workers join the Communist party who still have religious scruples, or religious ideas; but a worker who will join the Communist party, who understands the elementary principles of the Communist party, must necessarily be in the process of liquidating his religious beliefs, and, if he still has any lingerings when he joins the party, he will soon get rid of them. But religion, that is, atheism, is not laid down as a formal requirement for membership in the Communist party.

MR. FISH: Have you been to Russia?

MR. FOSTER: Yes, eight or nine times.

MR. FISH: You are familiar, then, with the workings of the Communist party in Russia?

MR. FOSTER: Reasonably.

MR. FISH: Well, can members of the Communist party in Russia be married in the church and maintain religious beliefs of that nature, and practice them?

MR. FOSTER: My opinion is that a member of the Communist party of the Soviet Union who would be married in a church would not be of any value to the Communist party.

MR. FISH: Could he maintain his membership in the party?

MR. FOSTER: He would not.

MR. FISH: He would be put out of the party?

MR. FOSTER: Eventually, if not for that specific act.

MR. FISH: Would it not be the same in this country?

MR. FOSTER: As I stated before, workers who would be so imbued with religious superstitions that they would be married in a church would be of no value to the Communist party.

MR. FISH: And the same thing would happen to them in this country that happens to them in Russia?

MR. FOSTER: Of course.

Americans owe a debt of gratitude to the American Federation of Labor. If it had not been for its strong opposition to communist activities in this country, the United States would have suffered a crisis of major proportions. Beginning with Samuel Gompers, its founding president, the AFL was in the vanguard of anticommunism. In 1923, Gompers emphasized that while American labor had "sympathy and concern [for] the effort of Russian workers and peasants to establish their freedom . . . the agents of the Soviet regime . . . have rendered it impossible for the American Federation of Labor to maintain a friendly policy toward the Russian government. These Moscow world plotters plan to employ such industrial unions as the instruments of the overthrow of the American government."

In 1930, the leadership of the AFL passed into the hands of two able patriots, William Green and Matthew Woll. Both men waged a tough battle against the communists who had taken over AFL unions in the garment, needle, textile, and mining trades. I'm happy to say that the information unearthed by my committee helped Green and Woll initiate the removal of those communists. Both Green and Woll testified before my committee, underlining the dangerous uses the communists hoped to make of the labor movement. Woll went so far as to say that as far as the AFL was concerned, "at no time since the fall of the Kerensky government in Russia have we been free from the communist incubus and the communist menace. At every hour of every day since that time some part of our labor movement has been engaged in battle with communism. It is no secret that the American Federation of Labor is the first object of attack by the communist movement. Consequently, the American Federation of Labor is the first line of defense."

In December 1930, Roger Baldwin, director of the American Civil Liberties Union, testified before my committee. The ACLU had been acting as a strong public defender of the communists and their activities, arguing that it was protecting the communists' legitimate civil rights. But as I noted in my committee's final report:

> The American Civil Liberties Union is closely affiliated with the communist movement in the United States, and fully 90 percent of its efforts are on behalf of communists who have come into conflict with the law. It claims to stand for free speech, free press, and free assembly; but it is quite apparent that the main function of the ACLU is to attempt to protect the communists in their advocacy of force and violence to overthrow the government. . . .
>
> Roger Baldwin, its guiding spirit, makes no attempt to hide his friendship for the communists and their principles. He was formerly a member of the IWW and served a term in prison as a draft dodger during the war.

I also pointed out that Baldwin had recently issued a statement saying that "in the next session of Congress our job is to organize the opposition to the recommendations of the congressional committee investigating communism." Baldwin and I had the following exchange during his testimony before my committee:

> MR. FISH: Does your organization uphold the right of a citizen or alien—it does not make any difference which—to advocate murder?
>
> MR. BALDWIN: Yes.
>
> MR. FISH: Or assassination?
>
> MR. BALDWIN: Yes.
>
> MR. FISH: Does your organization uphold the right of an American citizen to advocate force and violence for the overthrow of the Government?
>
> MR. BALDWIN: Certainly; insofar as mere advocacy is concerned.
>
> MR. FISH: Does it uphold the right of an alien in this country to urge the overthrow and advocate the overthrow of the Government by force and violence?
>
> MR. BALDWIN: Precisely on the same basis as any citizen.
>
> MR. FISH: You do uphold the right of an alien to advocate the overthrow of the Government by force and violence?
>
> MR. BALDWIN: Sure; certainly. It is the healthiest kind of thing for a country, of course, to have free speech—unlimited.

I noted in the final report of my committee that during "the trial of the communists in Gastonia, not for freedom of speech, of the press, or assembly, but for a conspiracy to kill the chief of police, of which the seven defendants were convicted, the ACLU provided bail for five of the defendants, amounting to $28,500. All of the defendants convicted jumped their bail and are reported to be in Russia."

I added that in 1928 a committee of the New York State legislature had concluded that the "American Civil Liberties Union, in the last analysis, is a supporter of all subversive movements; its propaganda is detrimental to the interests of the State. It attempts not only to protect crime but to encourage attacks upon our institutions in every form."

I wrapped up the committee's report by saying that the "principles of free speech, free press, and free assembly are worthy of an organization that stands for our republican form of government, guaranteed by the Constitution, and for the ideals of Washington, Jefferson, and Lincoln, instead of an organization whose main work is to uphold the communists in spreading revolutionary propaganda and inciting revolutionary activities to undermine our American institutions and overthrow our Government."

On January 17, 1931, my committee issued its 66-page report, covering all phases of communist activity in America. On page three, the following advice was submitted: "The Committee is convinced that the surest and most effective way of combatting communism in the United States is to give the fullest publicity to the fundamental principles and aims of the communists, which are the same throughout the world, as they are not likely to prove acceptable to any considerable number of American citizens, unless camouflaged by extraneous issues." I hold the same conviction today.

The report also listed the five chief objectives of the Communist party, which were the promotion of atheism and the eradication of religion; the destruction of democracy, free enterprise, and private property; the stirring up of strikes, riots, sabotage, bloodshed, and civil war through revolutionary propaganda; the abuse of American civil liberties and the infiltration of the media (with the ultimate goal of eliminating American civil liberties and a free press); and the agitation for world revolution that would usher in the universal dictatorship of the proletariat.

My opposition to communism more than once brought me into conflict with Franklin Roosevelt. Within months after he became president in 1933, Roosevelt, without the consent of Congress, reversed the official United States policy of not recognizing bolshevik Russia—a policy that had been affirmed by Presidents Wilson, Harding, Coolidge, and Hoover—in the grossly mistaken and naive belief that recognition would open a floodgate of trade for international business interests. In this, of course, he was proved wrong (trade actually declined between the two nations). But more than that, it was the first clear indication of the arrogance that would come to typify Roosevelt's administration. Previous presidents had stood on the sound principle enunciated by President Coolidge—that he did not "propose to barter away for the privilege of trade any of the cherished rights of humanity." The official American position of not recognizing Soviet Russia was given its most eloquent voice by former Secretary of State Elihu Root: "The recognition of one government is not a mere courtesy. It is an act having a definite and specific meaning and it involves an acceptance by the recognizing government of the principles, purposes, and avowed intentions of the recognized government as being in conformity with the rules which govern the conduct of civilized nations toward each other."

Roosevelt's capricious decision gave moral approval to a nation whose behavior should have denied it a place in the family of civilized nations.

Not only was the Soviet Union responsible for disseminating revolutionary propaganda calling for the overthrow of the United States and all "capitalist" nations, it was also employing forced labor at home and systematically murdering Russian peasants whose small farms Stalin wanted collectivized. This was no secret. Reports about Stalin's genocidal policies had reached the United States by the late 1920s. In addition, my own committee's report had certainly raised the public's awareness of the dangerous intentions of the communists. But Roosevelt did not care. He did not care that literally millions of Russian peasants were being killed by Stalin's henchmen (historian Robert Conquest estimates that 14 million Soviet peasants had been killed by 1937). Nor did he care about the overt threats the communists had made against the well-being of his own country.

Former Democratic Congressman Martin Dies wrote me a letter in the early 1960s that sheds important light on why Roosevelt behaved as he did. "As I have reported many times," Dies wrote, "the President told me that he had several good friends who were communists, and that he did not regard communism as a danger to the United States. He said that he thought that Russia would be our greatest ally and that while he did not believe in communism, the Soviet government was an improvement over the Czarist government." I have the letter today.

One way in which the Soviet government certainly was not an improvement over the Czarist government was in its persecution of religion. This rejection of religion, I believe, has been the greatest weakness of communism and is the chief reason for its recent retreat in Eastern Europe. People want freedom, democracy, and religion; and there are far more people in the world who believe in God than there are communists. In Poland, the Catholics appear to have triumphed over the communists; and I tend to believe that one of the influences on Gorbachev's efforts to reform the Soviet Union is the fact that his mother and grandmother were believers. People who believe that some things are sacred are the only ones willing to recognize the rights of others. It is my own sense of the sacred that brings me to the subject of my next chapter.

Chapter Eight

The Tomb of the Unknown Soldier

The Unknown American Soldier of World War I is known only to God. The marble tomb that is his final resting place has, over the years, become an immortal shrine, representing American ideals of valor, service, duty, and patriotism. It is symbolic of the spirit of freedom, democracy, and unity that are the cornerstones of our Republic in peace and in war.

No one knows whether the Unknown Soldier was white, black, or brown; whether he was Protestant, Catholic, Jewish, or an adherent of some other faith; whether he was a Republican, Democrat, or Independent. What is known is that he unselfishly gave his life for his country, fighting "to make the world safe for democracy."

On December 21, 1920, I introduced a Joint Resolution (H.R. 426) to bring the Unknown Soldier home from Europe and place his remains in what has become the Tomb of the Unknown Soldier at Arlington National Cemetery. The Joint Resolution was given speedy approval by Congress and was signed by President Woodrow Wilson on the morning of March 4, 1921. It was one of his last official acts and the last piece of congressional legislation he signed.

There are several reasons why I introduced the legislation to create the Tomb of the Unknown Soldier. For one, I knew of the burial of the French Unknown Soldier in his sacred shrine under the Arc de Triomphe on November 11, 1920. (Years later, on two different occasions, I participated

50

in the symbolic relighting of the flame at that French Tomb shrine.) I also, of course, had first-hand knowledge of the brave sacrifices made by American forces during the First World War, and I wanted America, as a beacon of freedom and democracy, to have her own memorial to honor the Unknown Soldier.

Another reason is the close relationship I enjoyed with the many veterans of my congressional district. They and their families had played an important role in helping me overcome my opponents and win election as their congressman. I was, and remain, extremely grateful to them.

This and my active membership in the American Legion and the Veterans of Foreign Wars influenced my decision to introduce the resolution. Both organizations, along with the Disabled American Veterans and Gold Star Mothers—women who had lost husbands or sons in the war—provided a great deal of support for my resolution. I had also received wholehearted support from General John Thomas Taylor, then national legislative representative for the American Legion. With his assistance, hearings on my resolution were held before the House Committee on Military Affairs. The main witnesses who testified were General John J. Pershing, commander-in-chief of the American Expeditionary Forces; Major General John G. LeJeune, representing the Marine Corps; and Major General P. C. Harris, adjutant general of the Army. The efforts of all these fine people and organizations enabled me to win congressional approval for the resolution.

The ceremonies were originally planned for Memorial Day, May 30, 1921, but were eventually postponed until Armistice Day, November 11. The task of finding a suitable soldier took longer than anticipated. It was essential that the soldier be an American and unknown beyond all possibility of future identification. To guarantee these objectives, eight bodies were exhumed from unmarked plots in the cemeteries of Aisne-Marne, Meuse-Argonne, Somme, and St. Mihiel, located respectively at Belleau, Romagne, Bony, and Thiacourt, near where American troops had been engaged in major battles. Proof that the bodies were those of Americans was ascertained by inspection of clothing, equipment, and places of original burial. Gun shot wounds to the body were the cause of death for each of the eight soldiers. Four bodies were finally selected and transferred with utmost secrecy to Chalons-sur-Marne, in the heart of the French battle area. It was here that General Gouraud, the able and courageous one-armed Frenchman, had his Fourth French Army Headquarters in 1918.

The four bodies, under strict escort, arrived by different routes at approximately the same time—three o'clock on the afternoon of Sunday,

October 23, at Chalons. They were placed side by side in the Hotel de Ville (City Hall), where they were guarded by a detail of American soldiers. American army officers, upon receipt of the four bodies, destroyed all records relating to them, making it impossible to identify the service to which they had belonged and the cemetery from which they had come. The four identical plain white coffins were then placed in different shipping cases from those in which they had arrived.

At ten o'clock on Monday morning, October 24, 1921, as a French military band played "Aux Champ," Sergeant Edward F. Younger, surrounded by a phalanx of high-ranking American and French army officers and news reporters, prepared to select the fallen hero. The much decorated and twice wounded sergeant, a veteran of four major engagements, solemnly circled twice around the caskets. Then he stopped and placed a spray of white roses on the third casket from the left. He stood at one end of the Unknown Soldier's coffin and the French General Duport stood at the other end. Both men saluted. The Unknown Soldier had been selected.

The casket with the white roses was immediately taken to another room, where the body of the Unknown Soldier was transferred to another coffin in the presence of four American officers. The coffin bore the inscription: "An Unknown American who gave his life in the World War." It was then placed in the main room of the City Hall, guarded by five American noncommissioned officers. The three remaining coffins with the unidentified heroes were brought to Romagne for internment in the Meuse-Argonne Cemetery.

A special train took the casket, guarded day and night, to Paris, where it remained overnight. The following morning, the train continued to Havre, where Monsieur Maginot, minister of Pensions, presented the casket with the Croix de Chevalier of the Legion of Honor—the first decoration bestowed on the Unknown Soldier. The coffin was then carried on board the *Olympia*, Admiral Dewey's flagship at Manila Bay, by six sailors and two marines.

The American public has been accustomed to the term "Unknown Soldier." Actually, it should have been "Unknown American" to include more clearly marines and sailors. This problem was corrected during the selection of World War II's Unknown, when fallen Americans from each military branch were included in the selection process.

On November 9 naval guns thundered along the Potomac river, announcing the arrival of the "Unknown" to American shores. After the *Olympia* reached dock, the casket was placed on a black-draped gun caisson drawn by six black horses. Led by a regiment of cavalry, the solemn procession slowly threaded its way to the Capitol, as thousands of American citizens lining the streets of the nation's capital watched in silence. Here the Unknown Soldier's casket was placed beneath the rotunda on the catafalque in state, where the martyred presidents—Lincoln, Garfield, McKinley, and, later, Kennedy—were honored.

November 11, 1921, was the third anniversary of the ending of World War I, but the first to be proclaimed a national holiday in the United States. It was a gray, cool day. At 8:30 that morning cannons from nearby Fort Myer thundered across the rolling hills of Arlington, breaking the morning silence. This also marked the beginning of the Unknown Soldier's final journey to his resting place. The shrouded casket was placed on a horse-drawn gun carriage, flanked by an honor guard of eight Congressional Medal of Honor recipients. They were followed by President Harding; his cabinet; justices of the Supreme Court; senators; representatives; the diplomatic corps; ranking army, navy, and Marine Corps officers; veterans organizations; war mothers; more Congressional Medal of Honor recipients; wounded veterans from nearby government hospitals; and a vast assemblage of Americans.

Starting at the Capitol, the cortege slowly inched its way through the streets, past the White House, and across the Potomac to Arlington Cemetery. The guns at Fort Myer fired every minute from eight-thirty until the end of the ceremony that afternoon.

Memorial services were held in the Amphitheatre before one thousand invited guests and fifty thousand spectators. Following the national anthem, Chief Chaplain of the Army John P. Axton delivered the invocation. A trumpeter blew attention for two minutes silence in honor of the unknown hero. One hundred million Americans listening to their radios bowed their heads in silence and prayer.

Then we sang "America," with tears streaming down our faces. As the last notes faded across Arlington's hallowed graves, President Harding moved to the front of the tomb and delivered a touching oration. "We are met here today to pay the impersonal tribute. The name of him whose body lies before us took flight with his imperishable soul. We know not whence he came, but only that his death marks him with the everlasting glory of an American dying for his country."

The president, his voice choked with sadness, reminded the audience of the heavy price mothers have borne in sacrificing their sons for the preservation of freedom and democracy. "Hundreds of mothers are wondering today, finding a touch of solace in the possibility that the nation bows in grief over the one she bore to live and die, if need be, for the republic." But "as a typical soldier of this representative democracy," the Unknown Soldier "fought and died, believing in the indisputable justice of his country's cause. On the threshold of eternity, many a soldier wondered how his ebbing would color the stream of human life, flowing on after his sacrifice. I revere that citizen whose confidence in the righteousness of his country inspired belief that its triumph is the victory of humanity."

"There must be," he urged, "the commanding voice of a conscious civilization against armed warfare." The president concluded by asking the nation to join in the Lord's Prayer. Following the prayer, a quartet from the Metropolitan Opera— Rosa Ponselle, Jeanne Gordon, Morgan Kingston, and William Gustafon—sang "The Supreme Sacrifice."

President Harding then placed the Medal of Honor and the Distinguished Service Medal, the highest American decorations for valor, on the casket. This had been authorized by an Act of Congress, introduced by my very close friend, the late Representative Royal Johnson of South Dakota, a wounded war veteran and an able lawyer and legislator. Marshal Foch, representing France, presented the *Medaille Militaire* and the *Croix de Guerre* with palm; Admiral Beatty of Great Britain bestowed the Victoria Cross (which had never before been given to a non-British subject); General Diaz bestowed the Italian Gold Medal for Bravery; General Jacques, the Belgian *Croix de Guerre*; and Prince Lobumerski, the Polish *Virtute Militaire*. After Miss Rosa Ponselle concluded her solo, "I Know that My Redeemer Liveth," the audience, accompanied by the Marine Band, sang "Nearer My God to Thee."

The audience in the Amphitheatre then walked a few hundred feet toward the grave that gave upon a spectacular view of Washington and the thousands gathered to watch the service. Bishop Brent spoke a few words in the committal ceremony as the casket was lowered, and rifle salutes rang out while artillery salvos boomed from Fort Myer.

In the name of all of America's World War I veterans, I placed the first wreath on the tomb, dedicating it with the following words: "On behalf of the ex-servicemen of the Republic, I reverently place this wreath on the tomb of our unknown comrade in arms who paid the supreme sacrifice that we might live at peace with all the world."

Beneath the inscription "HERE RESTS IN HONORED GLORY AN AMERICAN SOLDIER KNOWN BUT TO GOD," the Unknown Soldier had returned home.

Chapter Nine

The New Deal and the Old Court

I turn now to an issue of the most vital and far-reaching importance, affecting the very rock and foundation stone of our representative and constitutional form of government. It was the greatest single issue raised during the decades between the World Wars, perhaps the greatest single issue raised since the Civil War. It was an issue that transcended party politics—a great American issue between liberals and conservatives on the one hand, and radicals, communists, and socialists on the other. It was a fight between those of us who had faith in our Constitution and wanted to see it preserved, and those radical forces who had no faith in our Constitution and wanted to see it undermined.

I speak of FDR's attempt to pack the Supreme Court of the United States with New Dealers to bring the judicial branch of our federal government under the control of the chief executive.

Let me first remind readers that I was Roosevelt's friend and ally for twenty years. We were both progressives at the start of our careers. He was a fine Jeffersonian Democrat, and I was a Bull Moose Republican. But while in Washington as assistant secretary of the Navy during the First World War, he succumbed to the lust for power, a change I was unaware of until after he was elected president. As late as 1933, we were still exchanging friendly letters. A month before his first inauguration, I sent him a

"Dear Franklin" letter asking his assistance in speeding the issuance of the stamp to commemorate the 150th anniversary of George Washington's proclamation of peace with the British. The proclamation was made from Newburgh, New York, which was in my district, and the stamp depicted Washington's headquarters there. Roosevelt's response was one of the last kind words he had for me:

March 18, 1933

My Dear Ham

I am happy to tell you that the commemorative stamp about which you wrote me last month has been ordered and that it is a very beautiful one.

Sincerely yours,
Franklin D. Roosevelt

Soon after he took office and began accumulating power, our relationship soured. Before long, I had become one of his sharpest critics and an ardent foe of the New Deal, which I opposed because of its socialist nature and because it assumed too much power for the chief executive at the expense of Congress and the courts. Roosevelt, I believed, was starting us down the road to socialism and dictatorship.

In his campaign of 1932, Roosevelt promised the people a "new deal," but he never explained what the "new deal" was. Once in office, he experimented with a variety of possible economic remedies devised by a group of young know-it-alls known as the "brain trust." These experiments came down to a proliferation of executive agencies that spent the country's money and told it how to do business. They were the alphabet agencies: the CCC, the CWA, the TVA, the WPA, the PWA, the AAA, the FERA, the HOLC, and, of course, the notorious NRA (National Recovery Administration), to name just a few. To fund this massive expansion of federal executive power, the supine, heavily Democratic Congress voted the president $4.8 billion to spend as he liked. In doing so, as I told a radio audience in 1937, Congress had "abjectly . . . delegated away most of its constitutional powers to the president, including control of the purse strings, leaving the Congress with no more legislative power than Ghandi has clothing."

FDR was one of the most skillful politicians in American history. He knew more about winning over public opinion and broadcasting propaganda than any one man who ever sat in the White House. He could persuade Congress to give him billions of dollars to spend as he wished.

And he could persuade the nation to accept his New Deal on nothing but his word that it was in the nation's interest. But he could not persuade nine old men on the Supreme Court that his New Deal was constitutional.

In 1935, a unanimous Supreme Court delivered its famous *Schechter* decision condemning the NRA's attempts to regulate wages and prices as an "unconstitutional delegation of legislative power" to unelected executive agencies. Two other Supreme Court decisions, announced at the same time, also ruled against the New Deal. It was clear that much of FDR's program was in plain violation of the Constitution. According to Frank Freidel's flattering biography of FDR, *A Rendezvous With Destiny*, published in 1990, Justice Louis Brandeis, himself a progressive, summoned two members of the brain trust to his chambers after the *Schechter* decision and read them the riot act. "You have heard three decisions," he said. "They change everything. The Court is unanimous . . . . The President has been living in a fool's paradise."

But FDR was not one to let the law stop him. His solution was to try to pack the Court with six additional justices, all friends of the New Deal and possibly members of the brain trust. Had this happened, the country would have had men who created the New Deal sitting in judgment on its constitutionality. By increasing the number of justices from 9 to 15, FDR would have had enough votes on the Court to dominate most rulings, though not enough to reverse a previously unanimous ruling.

As bad as this was for our Constitution and representative government, what rankled many opponents of the proposal, including many members of his own party, was FDR's deceitful way of presenting the proposal to the Congress and the people. Instead of being open about the matter, he argued that the present Court was too old and too overworked. Six more justices were needed to speed things up and help the Court function more efficiently. This was too much. Even the admiring Freidel admitted it in his aforementioned biography:

> One of the unhappier aspects of the proposal was its deviousness. No sophisticated person took Roosevelt seriously when he insisted afterward that what he had wanted was to speed the business of the court through providing additional aid to superannuated justices. That smacked of the trickery of demagogues.

As ranking Republican member of both the House Committees on Rules and on Foreign Affairs, I was very powerful in the House at the time, so I led the fight against the Court-packing. I hammered hard the need to respect the Constitution, arguing that much of what FDR was trying to do could be accomplished by constitutional means. I would not have opposed a constitutional amendment to limit the ages of the justices of the Supreme Court to 70, though I would have preferred 75. And I actually favored a constitutional amendment to enable Congress to pass minimum wage laws in order to abolish the evils and abuses of the sweatshops and other industries where men, women, and children were exploited by human vultures, and called upon Republican members of Congress to propose such an amendment.

I even favored an amendment to the Constitution granting Congress the power to enact legislation by a two-thirds vote in case of any 5-to-4 adverse decision of the Supreme Court. This seemed reasonable given the fact that Congress had the power to override presidential vetoes by a two-thirds vote. I saw nothing radical in giving Congress this power, if the people approved. In fact, I believed it would strengthen the confidence and respect of the people in the Court.

But the president's propagandists argued that the amendment ratification process would take too much time. In fact, history has proved that the people respond quickly to proposed amendments if they believe they are in their best interests. The Twelfth Amendment was adopted in nine months; the Thirteenth in less than a year; the Fifteenth, Seventeenth, and Eighteenth in a little less than a year; the Nineteenth in fourteen months; the Twentieth in eleven months; and the Twenty-first in less than a year. If the president had sent a proposed amendment to the Democrat-controlled Congress the day the NRA was declared unconstitutional, that amendment could easily have been ratified by the people, if they had wanted it ratified, in less time than FDR spent trying to pack the Court.

The truth was that FDR did not trust the American people, nor did he care what the Constitution said, as long as he got his way. Freidel quotes him telling an aide not long after his second inaugural:

When the Chief Justice read me the oath and came to the words "support and defend the Constitution of the United States," I felt like saying: "Yes, but it's the Constitution as I understand it, flexible enough to meet any new problem of democracy—not the kind of Constitution your Court has raised up as a barrier to progress and democracy.

Of course, the Constitution never was a barrier to progress and democracy, but it was a barrier to power-hungry men like FDR, as it was meant to be.

By no stretch of the imagination did the president receive any mandate from the people to circumvent the Constitution, change our very structure of government, or stack the Supreme Court of the United States. I challenge anyone to show me one single campaign speech made by the president in which he even mentioned the Constitution or the Supreme Court. He avoided both like the plague. What right had he to assume that the election gave him a mandate from the people to pack the Court as he liked and make it subservient to its new master in the White House?

In the end, FDR lost the fight in Congress for the additional justices, but he got the kind of Court he wanted without them. When Justice Willis Van Devanter retired in 1937, Roosevelt appointed Senator Hugo L. Black, a New Dealer, to fill the vacancy. Later vacancies permitted him to appoint brain-truster Felix Frankfurter, William O. Douglas, and Frank Murphy. Nothing revealed to the American people FDR's true colors better than his attempt at Court-packing. It was a bad sign of things to come. Though he remained popular, he had lost a lot of the respect of many decent Americans. Here is Freidel's assessment:

The price was high. Politically, Roosevelt had suffered a staggering setback from a Congress top-heavy with Democrats. He had expended a large part of his political capital on a failed enterprise. . . . What he doubtless intended to be political showmanship, drama to enlist the interest of the electorate, appeared to his opponents and even a considerable part of the public to be a dangerous deviousness, smacking of dictatorial ways.

Chapter Ten

Prelude to Another World War

I served as the ranking Republican member of the Committee on Foreign Affairs in the House of Representatives throughout the years leading up to the Second World War. During those years I tried to halt our step by step involvement in yet another of the eternal wars of Europe.

There is, thank God, no blood on my conscience or on my hands, but I believe that a great deal of blood lies on those of Franklin Roosevelt. His deceitful policies cost this country a million casualties and three hundred billion dollars, and saw thirteen million Americans conscripted into an unnecessary war machine.

Given that between 80 and 90 percent of the American public classed itself as noninterventionist, I held some hope during those days that the people, through their elected representatives, would be able to offset the interventionist policies of the president and his cabinet. In this hope, I was to be disappointed.

At the time the president started his campaign to create war hysteria, the United States had never been safer from attack or invasion by any foreign power. We had, for example, the most powerful navy in our history, equal for the first time to that of Great Britain. Congress had also authorized appropriations that would make the American navy 50 percent greater than the Japanese navy and three times the size of the German navy. The issue confronting the United States was not one of national defense, but of foreign policy; and Roosevelt's foreign policy was sold to the American people through the propagation of the baseless fear that Germany, Italy, and Japan were planning to invade Latin America and make war on the United States.

On January 6, 1939, in a radio address over the National Broadcasting Company's network, I made the following plea:

> President Roosevelt's sensational attacks on the forms of government in other nations and the tirades of members of his cabinet can only lead to disastrous consequences and war. As much as American citizens abhor racial and religious persecution and ruthless militarism, it is none of our business what form of government may exist in Soviet Russia, Fascist Italy, Imperial Japan, or Nazi Germany, any more than it is their business what form of government exists in our own country. We have our own problems to solve in America without becoming involved in the rotten mess in Europe or in the eternal wars of both Europe and Asia. The inflammatory and provocative message of the President to the Congress and the world has unnecessarily alarmed the American people and created, together with the barrage of propaganda emanating from high New Deal officials, a war hysteria dangerous to the peace of America and the world. The only logical conclusion to such speeches is another war fought overseas by American soldiers.

President Roosevelt said: "Once I prophesied that this generation of Americans had a rendezvous with destiny. That prophecy comes true." What was this rendezvous with destiny? Was the ultimate dirty trick in his New Deal bag to employ the twelve million Americans that remained unemployed because of the government's bungling of the economy? To establish a united front with the totalitarian Soviet Union to whom the small countries of Eastern Europe would be turned over? To open a long, costly war on two fronts—on the Rhine and in the far Pacific—scrapping our traditional foreign policy of neutrality, nonintervention, and peace? It was my own sense of where Roosevelt's prophecies were leading us that compelled me to say in my speech of January 6, 1939:

> President Roosevelt said to us in Congress that "We learned from the past what not to do." Now, the President proposes to make the tragic mistakes that will inevitably force us into war throughout the world. He wants to repeal the Neutrality Law aimed to keep us out of foreign conflicts . . . and wants Congress to turn over to him its war-making powers such as determining the aggressor nation.

The proposals of the interventionists were frequently loaded with seduc-
tive phrases about enforcing peace through "economic sanctions," "collective security," and other "measures short of war." These words captured the
imagination of many Americans who did not realize that these were the
stepping stones of Roosevelt's internationalism—the ultimate destination
of which was full-scale war, the likes of which the world had never seen.
There are two ways of getting the United States into war. One is by Act of
Congress and the other is by antagonizing other countries into declaring
war against us. Congress, reflecting public opinion, was overwhelmingly
against going to war with Germany or Japan prior to Pearl Harbor. The
German government ignored Roosevelt's provocations (which included the
repeal of the Arms Embargo, the emasculation of the Neutrality Act,
the sale of American arms to the British without the consent of Congress,
the transfer of fifty destroyers to the British in exchange for naval bases
without the consent of Congress, enormous foreign loans, the Lend-Lease
Act, the repair of belligerent warships, the deployment of American troops
to Greenland and Iceland without the consent of Congress, the construction of ports of debarkation and barracks for American troops in the
United Kingdom, and much else besides) and pursued a policy of avoiding
conflict with the United States. The Germans did not pursue this policy
because they loved us, but because they feared the power of our potential
war efforts.

President Roosevelt had promised not to send American boys "into any
foreign war," but I was far from being the only one who saw through his
lies. In a national radio broadcast, John L. Lewis, president of the Congress
of Industrial Organizations (CIO), blasted Roosevelt, accusing him of
having an "overwhelming, abnormal, and selfish craving for increased
power." Lewis went on:

> While protesting that "he hates war and will work for peace," the President
> has shown by his acts that war was his motivation and his objective. . . . War
> has always been the device of the politically despairing and intellectually
> sterile statesman. It provides employment in the gun factories and begets
> enormous profits for those already rich. It kills off the vigorous males, who if
> permitted to live might question the financial exploitation of the race.

The *Saturday Evening Post*, which had the largest ciculation of any
American magazine at the time, editorialized against Roosevelt's foreign
policy in its issue of May 20, 1939. It noted that:

For a year and a half the President of the United States has been talking war. He began it with the "quarantine speech" in Chicago in October 1937, saying there was no escape for us through mere "isolation or neutrality" and that the "peace-loving nations must make a concerted effort" to quarantine and stop aggression. . . .

Continuously thereafter the Roosevelt Administration seized every opportunity to implant hatred of foreign nations where more than enough was seeding itself and to propagate the thought that if Great Britain and France were attacked we should have to take part to save democracy in the world because American destiny, too, would be involved.

Utterances of this purport, some of them very offensive to Nations with which we were then at peace, came from responsible officers of the Roosevelt Administration and especially from members of the cabinet. . . .

That the change in our foreign policy, so far as the executive will of the government has been able to change it, is such that only two years ago the unobsessed American mind would have rejected it with horror. . . .

That so far as the executive will of government has been able to commit us, we are committed not to be neutral if war comes in Europe, which means that we may be fighting again on European soil on the side of Great Britain, France and Russia under the slogan "Save Democracy" but really in defense of the division of spoils that was made under the Versailles Treaty that we did not sign, and that for all this the President of the United States is responsible.

The *Saturday Evening Post* made another telling critique of Roosevelt's policies when it observed, on October 12, 1940, that Roosevelt's "Government has secretly collaborated with the British Government by thought and act in a manner which, even if it had not been intended to involve the United States in the European war, could have no other effect or meaning. For each act of intervention the public mind has been prepared by propaganda."

In an editorial entitled "The Dictator Process in America," the *St. Louis Dispatch* of September 3, 1940, again exposed Roosevelt's illegitimate strivings for personal power and war. It described Roosevelt's transfer of fifty destroyers to Britain in exchange for base rights as "an act of war" that made Roosevelt "America's first dictator." Roosevelt, the paper noted,

is not asking Congress, the elected representatives of the people, to ratify the deal. The authority which the President quotes for his fatal and secret deal is an opinion from the Attorney General. Whatever the legal trickery this yes-man may conjure up, the fact is that the transfer of the destroyers is not only in violation of American law, but is also in violation of the Hague Covenant of 1907, solemnly ratified by the United States Senate in 1908. It is an outright act of war.

In a bellicose speech delivered on September 11, 1941, over a nation-wide hookup and rebroadcast in eighteen languages, Roosevelt confirmed the fears of his noninterventionist critics when he announced what was essentially an undeclared war on Germany. Roosevelt said, in part:

If submarines or raiders attack in distant waters, they can attack equally well within the sight of our own shores. Their very presence in any waters which America deems vital to its defense constitutes an attack. In the waters which we deem necessary for our defense, American naval vessels and planes will no longer wait until Axis submarines lurking under the water or Axis raiders on the surface of the sea, strike their deadly blow first. Upon our naval and air patrol now operating in large number over a vast expanse of the Atlantic Ocean, falls the duty of maintaining the American policy of free-dom of the seas. Now, that means, very simply and clearly, that our patrolling vessels and planes will protect all merchant ships—not only American ships but ships of any flag engaged in commerce in our defensive waters. They will protect them from submarines; they will protect them from surface raiders.

In other words, Roosevelt had enunciated a shoot on sight order that extended over "a vast expanse of the Atlantic Ocean." Any German reprisals would have meant war; and make no mistake—a war with Germany before June 22, 1941, when Germany attacked Soviet Russia, would have exacted a horrendous price from this country, even more than that which we eventually did pay. During one of my reelection campaigns, the actress Helen Hayes accused me of delaying our entry into the war by six months. It is an accusation I fully accept and of which I am truly proud, for it undoubtedly saved millions of American lives. Imagine fighting the Nazi war machine without the Soviet Union holding down the German Eastern front. Think, indeed, of fighting Nazi Germany while it was allied to Soviet Russia (as well as fascist Italy and imperial Japan). The results would have been ruinous.

Wendell Wilkie and I disagreed on many things, but the position he took in his speech accepting the Republican nomination for president in 1940 was very much my own. "I cannot," Wilkie said, "follow the President in his conduct of foreign affairs in this critical time. There have been occa-sions when many of us have wondered if he is deliberately inciting us to war." He went on:

I know what war can do to demoralize civil liberties at home and I believe it to be the first duty of a President to try to maintain peace. But Mr. Roosevelt has not done this. He has dabbled in inflammatory statements and manufactured panics. Of course, we in America like to speak our minds freely, but this does not mean that at a critical period in history our President should cause bitterness and confusion for the sake of a little political oratory. The President's attacks on foreign powers have been useless and dangerous. He has courted war for which the country is hopelessly unprepared—and which it emphatically does not want. He has secretly meddled in the affairs of Europe and he has even unscrupulously encouraged other countries to hope for more help than we were able to give.

I emphasize once again that these noninterventionist sentiments were widely held among the American people. The American Legion was staunchly opposed to involving the country in another war in Europe and did not withdraw its opposition to Lend-Lease until the summer of 1941, after much politicking to that end by FDR. Many members in Congress and many editorial writers of many newspapers and magazines were also against interventionism. One of America's most famous journalists, H. L. Mencken, was a forthright critic of Roosevelt's foreign policy. On October 1, 1939, he said that Roosevelt had no "right to pretend neutrality when he is in fact bitterly partisan . . . to talk loftily against war when he is notoriously planning to promote it." The following week he once again excoriated America's drift towards war. The English, he said,

are in the war for a simple reason and a single reason; to wit, their desire to prevent the rise of a powerful rival in Europe, offering an inevitable challenge to their general supervision of the world. That is why they fought the last time, and that is why they go through the motions of being in war today. . . .
. . . England is a country exactly like all the rest, no worse, no better. Its one aim and purpose is to promote its own interest; it has no other whatsoever. It was willing and eager, only six weeks ago, to embrace Comrade Stalin as a brother, and it is trying to buy him back even now, just as it is trying to buy Mussolini, Franco and the Turks. So long as the Japs kept their paws off China it was their ally and buddy. . . . To admire such a great and successful nation is one thing, and quite reasonable; to fall for its pecksniffery, pay its bills, and tote its slops is assuredly something else again.

But, of course, Roosevelt did not phrase his foreign policy in Mencken's language. Instead, he spoke of the Four Freedoms and the Atlantic Charter.

Chapter Eleven

The Four Freedoms and
The Atlantic Charter

I personally admired Winston Churchill. He was one of the greatest political orators of modern times, and his indomitable courage is known throughout the world. But what I liked best about him was his all-consuming love of Britain. His life was devoted to using all his strength of heart and mind to preserving the British Empire first and always.

Franklin Roosevelt presented himself to the American people in different terms—not as a defender of a nation and its possessions, but as a defender of certain universal principles. Roosevelt enunciated his belief in "four essential freedoms" in an address to Congress on January 6, 1941:

> In the future days, which we seek to make secure, we look forward to a world founded upon four essential human freedoms.
>
> The first is freedom of speech and expression—everywhere in the world.
>
> The second is freedom of every person to worship God in his own way—everywhere in the world.
>
> The third is freedom from want—which translated into world terms, means economic understandings which will secure to every nation a healthy, peaceful life for its inhabitants—everywhere in the world.
>
> The fourth is freedom from fear—which translated into world terms, means worldwide reduction in armaments to such a point and in such a

thorough fashion that no nation will be in a position to commit an act of aggression against any neighbor—anywhere in the world.

Roosevelt pronounced further principles to which he was wedded following his secret meeting with Winston Churchill "somewhere in the Atlantic" in August 1941. Roosevelt issued a two-part report of the meeting. The second part of the report formed the heart of the Atlantic Charter, the major points of which are as follows:

. . . The President of the United States of America and the Prime Minister, Mr. Churchill . . . deem it right to make known certain common principles in the national policies of their respective countries on which they based their hopes for a better future for the world.

. . . [T]hey desire to see no territorial changes that do not accord with the freely expressed wishes of the peoples concerned.

. . . [T]hey respect the right of all people to choose the form of government under which they will live; and they wish to see sovereign rights and self-government restored to those who have been forcibly deprived of them.

. . . [T]hey desire to bring about the fullest collaboration between all nations in the economic field with the object of securing, for all, improved labor standards, economic advancement, and social security.

. . . [A]fter the final destruction of the Nazi tyranny, they hope to see established a peace which will afford to all nations the means of dwelling in safety within their own boundaries, and which will afford assurance that all men in all the lands may live out their lives in freedom from fear and want. . . .

The noble principles of the Four Freedoms and the Atlantic Charter were, in practice, ignored. The Four Freedoms represented nothing more than what Roosevelt had learned serving under President Wilson as assistant secretary of the Navy—which was how to talk the American people into war. The Four Freedoms were a propaganda ploy that Roosevelt neglected to mention again once Nazi Germany attacked Soviet Russia.

As for the Atlantic Charter, it received the official endorsement of not only the United States and Great Britain, but of the Soviet Union and two dozen other nations. Still, the very fact that it was endorsed by Stalin's Soviet Union shows that it, too, was only a propaganda ploy.

Churchill understood this from the start. He knew that the Charter was well received in America, but, to him, "the fact alone of the United States still technically a neutral power joining with a belligerent power in making such a declaration was astonishing." And, for the British Empire, obviously, it was also quite encouraging.

Once the United States entered the war, the importance of the Atlantic Charter rapidly diminished. On March 10, 1943, during a congressional foreign policy debate, I introduced a "joint resolution endorsing the principles of the Atlantic Charter." I pointed out that the Charter had become a mere "scrap of paper" because of President Roosevelt's strange silence about it. "I believe in the principles enunciated in the Atlantic Charter," I added, "and would like to see them endorsed by Congress so that all foreign nations will know that Congress has acted favorably upon them. I am for international cooperation, and for that reason I am introducing the entire Atlantic Charter as written for consideration and approval by Congress."

Almost a year later, on March 28, 1944, I asked Elmer Davis, head of the administration's Office of War Information, "if the Atlantic Charter was still alive." Mr. Davis replied that "he did not know whether it was still alive or not." This led me to conclude, in remarks I made in the House of Representatives that same day, that the Atlantic Charter "has either been buried and is actually dead or is hidden somewhere."

I also noted the tragic effects of this burial:

> [T]he Atlantic Charter stated in so many words that small, independent nations should be protected against aggression, and should be allowed to determine their own form of government, and they should not lose any of their territory. . . . We find, however, . . . that agreements have been entered into that Poland is to sacrifice part of her territory. Of all countries, Poland. War was declared in 1939 on the basis that Poland was to be protected in its territorial integrity and national independence. That was the official reason given for going to war against Germany, the aggressor nation. Under the Atlantic Charter, Poland, the Baltic States, and the Balkans were all to be protected in their sovereignty and their independence against aggression. Now we find . . . that these small, sovereign, and independent nations are to be sacrificed.

Mr. Howard J. McMurray, the speaker pro tempore, countered that the Atlantic Charter did not state "there will be no territorial changes," although he did concede that the Charter prohibited "territorial changes that do not accord with the freely expressed wishes of the people concerned."

"That is," I interjected, "exactly what I said. It was a declaration of policy made by the president of the United States and Mr. Churchill . . . in August of 1941. Since then the Soviet Government has ratified it, but since ratifying it, the Soviet Government is demanding a part of Poland

and apparently is to have the Baltic nations and probably some of the Balkans as well."

For the British, of course, the Second World War had never been about defending democracy or enforcing the Atlantic Charter. Great Britain was merely following her traditional foreign policy role of maintaining the balance of power in Europe. As Winston Churchill said, "It can be stated very simply: Britain's policy has always been to support the second strongest power on the Continent." That power was now France.

But Great Britain, like the United States, would have been better off had war been averted. The man who saw this most clearly was the Liberal David Lloyd George, Great Britain's prime minister from 1916 to 1922, and the man to whom credit for the Allied victory in the First World War should be given.

Lloyd George first came to prominence as an opponent of the Boer War. Feelings ran so high over his opposition, that he was denounced as a traitor. In one instance, a riot broke out at a meeting in Birmingham. One man was killed, several were injured, and Lloyd George had to be smuggled out of the hall in a policeman's uniform.

In the years leading up to the Second World War, Lloyd George was again a spokesman for peace. After the Soviet Union and Nazi Germany divided Poland, Lloyd George urged Prime Minister Neville Chamberlain to consider Hitler's latest peace offer "while there is yet a chance to avoid the slaughter—when the real war starts, it will be too late." The peace offer was rejected, and the pro-war party of Winston Churchill and Anthony Eden rose to ascendancy.

After the fall of France, Belgium, and Holland in the summer of 1940, Lloyd George again urged consideration of Germany's peace terms. When Hitler's offer was rejected, Lloyd George said, "The die is cast." Lloyd George foresaw that in modern wars even the victor goes down with the vanquished in bankruptcy, blood, and tears, and that in this case, communism, not the British Empire, would be the chief beneficiary. Under the guidance of Franklin Roosevelt, the foreign policy of the United States served that same disastrous end.

Chapter Twelve

Intervention through Deception

In 1940 Franklin Roosevelt announced that he was seeking reelection for an unprecedented third term as president of the United States. The decision was controversial, and even within his own party some feared that in his lust for power, Roosevelt was turning the presidency into a position fit for a dictator. Still, no Democrat dared oppose his nomination.

As the Democratic nominee, FDR was pledged to support the Democratic party platform that included the following statement:

> We will not participate in foreign wars, and we will not send our army, naval, or air forces to fight in foreign lands outside of the Americas, except in case of attack. . . . The direction and aim of our foreign policy has been, and will continue to be, the security and defense of our land and the maintenance of its peace.

Roosevelt reaffirmed his devotion to this plank of the Democratic platform frequently during the campaign. Typical of his rhetoric is this passage from a speech he gave in Brooklyn on November 1, 1940:

> I am fighting to keep this nation prosperous and at peace. I am fighting to keep our people out of foreign wars, and to keep foreign conceptions of government out of our own United States . . . and I will not stop fighting!

70

The true depth of Roosevelt's betrayal of the Democratic platform and his own public statements in his march to intervene in the affairs of Europe was brilliantly exposed in this passage by historian Charles Beard in his book *President Roosevelt and the Coming of the War, 1941:*

> If the processes of popular election had any meaning or validity, the antiwar covenants with the American people, freely entered into by the Democratic party and President Roosevelt, were specific commitments to be fulfilled after their victory at the polls in November. Those covenants were explicit mandates for the Democratic Senators and Representatives, who had indubitable control of Congress, in the enactment of legislation relative to all issues of peace and war. Those covenants were no mere incidents or practical jokes of the campaign. They were, in fact, major promises of the campaign . . . and were binding in honor and good conscience after the election. In short, unless deceiving people in matters of life and death is to be regarded as a proper feature of democratic politics and popular decisions at the polls are to be treated as chimeras, President Roosevelt's peace pledges of 1940 were imperatives for him in 1941; and only by spurning the peace pledges of their party could Democratic Senators and Representatives dominant in Congress enact into law measures calculated to take the United States into war.

The Republican party, however, once again shot itself in the foot by passing over an excellent candidate in Robert Taft and giving the nomination instead to Wendell Wilkie, a former socialist-leaning Democrat who was then a Wall Street lawyer. He was the favorite of the Republican bankers, internationalists, and interventionists, but he did not have much popular support. Mrs. Nicholas Longworth, Theodore Roosevelt's politically minded daughter, quipped that pro-Wilkie sentiment sprang from the grass roots overnight—the grass roots of America's country clubs and banking houses.

When the Republican convention opened in Philadelphia, Wilkie was still a dark horse candidate. He trailed Taft by 84 votes on the first ballot. But by the fifth ballot, Wilkie's supporters had flooded the convention with pro-Wilkie telegrams and twisted enough arms to give him the nomination. By abandoning Taft, the Republicans refused to offer the American people a principled alternative to foreign interventionism and the New Deal (three million more Americans were unemployed in 1940 than when Roosevelt first took office). The Republican nomination of Wilkie left the American people with a choice between Tweedledum and Tweedledee.

They almost had a choice with me. During the Illinois Republican presidential primary, the secretary of state of Illinois telephoned me and said that he had a petition signed by 25,000 Republicans wanting me to run for president. "What do you want me to do with it?" he asked.

"Throw it in the wastepaper basket," I said. "I don't even have enough money to get out there."

That night, while dining in New York City, I met the wife of a Chicago millionaire who said she would give me $20,000 if I would call the secretary of state of Illinois and accept the petition. I said I would.

At that time, Thomas Dewey was also seeking the Republican nomination, and I felt I could handle his challenge easily. If I had won the Illinois primary I would have given my delegates to Senator Taft. With them he would have won the nomination, and I would have become his vice presidential running mate. Given the antiwar mood of the American people and my renown as one of the chief noninterventionists in Congress, I have no doubt that we could have defeated Roosevelt, and perhaps averted World War II. As it was, the secretary of state had already discarded the petition and it was too late for me to refile and become a candidate.

Recognizing the danger posed to him by the electorate's antiwar sentiment, Roosevelt courted it and thus denied it to Wilkie, who appeared as shifty on the issue as Roosevelt. Roosevelt solemnly assured the American people that there was "no secret treaty, no secret obligation, no secret understanding in any shape or form, direct or indirect, with any government" to involve the United States in a foreign war. On the eve of the election he reiterated his promise: "I have said this before, but I shall say it again and again and again: Your boys are not going to be sent into any foreign wars."

Only a few months earlier, Roosevelt had ordered a secret military mission to London, headed by Major Generals D. C. Emmons and George V. Strong, ostensibly to study British air defenses against the German Luftwaffe. In a War Department memorandum dated August 5, 1940, Emmons was ordered to "proceed without delay to London, England, and report upon arrival to the American Ambassador, as temporary military attaché." The memorandum told Emmons that "Every effort will be made to maintain secrecy of this trip both in this country and in England. Publicity of any character will be avoided."

But the British press was hot on Emmons' tail, and the administration was worried that his mission would be exposed. In fact, the British reporters came very close to revealing that Roosevelt had ordered Emmons and Strong to make recommendations for American military bases in Great Britain in preparation for American military intervention. Earlier that year, in January 1940, Roosevelt had sent Emmons to Portugal to study the feasibility of establishing an air base there.

But that was not all Roosevelt had done to prepare for war. Robert Sherwood, Roosevelt's chief speechwriter, confessed (*Roosevelt and Hopkins*) that Roosevelt had already in 1940 drawn up plans that called for "the occupation by U.S. Forces of Greenland, Iceland, the Azores and Martinique." On September 10, 1940, the Navy Department presented a plan for American military forces to supplement "the British forces" in eight British military possessions. Over 3,200 American soldiers and five hundred sailors were to be stationed in Bermuda as part of this scheme. On October 1, 1940, Roosevelt wrote a memorandum to Secretary of War Henry Stimson and Secretary of State Cordell Hull saying: "I approve the enclosed draft of lease for property in Bermuda. . . ."

The day after FDR's speech in Boston declaring that the United States had no secret obligations, treaties, or plans to become involved in a foreign war, the administration gave its approval, in a secret document, to a proposal calling for the expenditure of $130,000 "for preliminary planning surveys and administrative purposes in connection with the development of eight Army bases in British possessions." One hundred thousand dollars of that money was to come out of the "President's Emergency Fund."

Ten days earlier, on September 20, 1940, Stimson had approved a $25 million transfer of funds from the President's Emergency Fund "for further operations." In another secret memo, dated September 24, the money was dedicated "for the construction of Army facilities for permanent garrisons at eight bases in British possessions in the Western Hemisphere." On October 7, 1940, Frank Knox, secretary of the Navy, wrote a confidential memo to Cordell Hull that it was the "President's desire to proceed with the development of these bases immediately."

Less than a year later, on June 22, 1941, the administration ordered the First Marine Brigade to Argentina to await transport to Iceland. On July 7, Roosevelt announced that despite the disapproval and resentment of many Icelanders, he had ordered American forces to occupy Iceland for "the same reasons," he claimed, "substantial forces of the United States" had been "sent to the bases acquired last year from Great Britain."

Apparently emboldened by his successful military occupation of Iceland,

Roosevelt in September ordered a military mission to Iran "to assist the British in expanding transport facilities." On October 9, 1941, Roosevelt went so far as to tell Lord Halifax that he had instructed "Stimson and Marshall to make a study of the possibility of sending an AEF to West Africa." Secretary of the Navy Frank Knox told Halifax that the administration had expressed strong interest in sending 150,000 American troops to Morocco.

Clearly then, Roosevelt, despite repeated denials that he was orchestrating a prowar foreign policy, was knowingly repudiating his party's platform and ignoring the will of the American people. And he had been doing this for some time, as witness the fact that even before Great Britain declared war on Germany, Roosevelt had assured Churchill that the United States would join the Allies, and through his ambassador to France, William Bullitt, encouraged the French to take a strong stance against Hitler. In 1939 Bullitt, moreover, had told the Polish ambassador to Washington, Jerzy Potocki, "It is the decided opinion of the president that France and Britain must put an end to any sort of compromise with the totalitarian countries. They must not let themselves in for any discussions aiming at any kind of territorial changes. They have the moral assurance that the United States will leave the policy of isolation and be prepared to intervene actively on the side of Britain and France in case of war."

Robert Sherwood condoned this policy of deceiving the American people. "The inescapable fact," Sherwood said, "is that this is what Roosevelt was compelled to say in order to maintain any influence over public opinion and over Congressional action." Congress did see through Roosevelt's plotting, and it held firm for a while. In June 1939, the Roosevelt administration attempted to scrap the United States' arms embargo. But Congress voted the measure down by forty-one votes, even though the Democrats had a hundred-seat majority in the House. Congress, of course, took this action because most members realized that repeal was the first step towards war, the administration's arguments notwithstanding.

Undeterred, the administration redoubled its propaganda efforts in favor of repeal, and when war broke out in Europe, Congress was more receptive. In October, Congress allowed the administration to amend the Neutrality Law to provide for a cash and carry amendment to the Arms Embargo— the virtual equivalent of its repeal.

I, however, continued to fight against the emasculation of the Neutrality Bill and addressed the House on the matter on November 2, 1939:

I am opposed to the traffic in arms, in the first place because I believe it to be an utterly immoral, un-Christian, and vicious system turning our country into a great slaughterhouse for the sake of blood money and war profits that will involve us in every war all over the world. There can be no compromise on that issue—the issue of blood money and war profits. Why should we in Congress gamble with the lives of the youth of America by repealing the arms embargo that was enacted into law to keep us out of war?

I would not gamble with the life of one single American for all the bloodstained dollars of Europe. I would not gamble with the life of one single American soldier to sell arms, poisonous gas, and flamethrowers.

I was joined in my opposition to Roosevelt's interventionism by some brave Democrats. One was Senator Burton K. Wheeler of Montana who told an audience in St. Louis that "Roosevelt is doing his agonizing best to get us into the war, and he is doing so without the approval of public opinion." Another brave Democrat was Senator David I. Walsh of Massachusetts who said in a radio address on October 18, 1940:

Americans are being terrorized into believing that this is our war and that we will be attacked if we remain neutral. No public man has dared to advocate openly or directly our entrance into the European war, because they know the American people would resent it. Their method is more subtle, better conceived, but they have an eye always on the ultimate goal. Many European nations have no choice between war and peace. We are not presented with any such alternatives. We are not protected by 20 miles of channel, but by 3,000 miles of sea.

But I remained one of Roosevelt's special targets. In a speech he gave at Madison Square Garden in New York City on October 28, 1940, he led a mocking chant against "Martin, Barton, and Fish," referring to Congressmen Joseph Martin, Bruce Barton, and me. I was not angered by this attack because I knew that it would make the three of us better known throughout the United States as staunch opponents of FDR.

Many people who listened to FDR's speech probably assumed that the three of us worked in concert against Roosevelt's foreign and domestic policies. Actually, I was very friendly with Joseph Martin, having formed a close friendship. But my relationship with Bruce Barton, while not unfriendly, was that of a colleague. We were both Republicans from New York, but we seldom collaborated on political issues. In 1940, I was asked to run for the Senate, but I declined because I knew that FDR and the

Democratic party would flood the state with money to the opposition. Congressman Bruce Barton won the Republican nomination, but, unfortunately—and predictably—he was defeated.

Just after Election Day 1940, I sent FDR a telegram saying:

> CONGRATULATIONS. PLEDGE MY SUPPORT FOR
> NATIONAL DEFENSE AND UNITY AGAINST AGGRESSOR
> NATIONS AND TO KEEP AMERICA OUT OF WAR—
>   HAMILTON FISH OF THE FIRM OF
>   MARTIN BARTON FISH

Chapter Thirteen

Lend-Lease to Russia

In January 1941, Roosevelt ignited a powder keg of political opposition when he caused the introduction of House Resolution 1776, commonly referred to as Lend-Lease. Even members of his own party found it difficult to believe that the bill, as the administration claimed, was vital to America's interests. Lend-Lease basically provided for an initial appropriation of seven billion dollars worth of arms and military equipment that the president could sell, transfer, exchange, or lease to any country whose defense he deemed vital to American security.

On January 21, 1941, I spoke on national radio and cited John Bassett Moore—the world's leading authority on international and constitutional law—who described Lend-Lease as an attempt "to transfer the war-making power from the Congress, in which the Constitution lodges it, to the Executive. It is evident that the tide of totalitarianism in government, which has swept over many other lands, has not only reached our shores but has gone far to destroy constitutional barriers, which, once broken down, are not likely to be restored." This view was echoed by the United States Chamber of Commerce and even by the *New York Herald Tribune*, the most consistently pro-British, pro-interventionist newspaper in the country.

Senator Bennett Clark, Democrat of Missouri and one of the founders of the American Legion, joined the debate against the bill:

> This is not a defense bill; it is a war bill. We pledge ourselves to assuring, guaranteeing military victory of one belligerent over another. We all know

77

that we will have to follow that up by any means that may be necessary. We all know that that is equivalent to a declaration of a state of war ourselves, and must be followed up by sending our warships, our planes, our guns, and, ultimately, the men, the boys of this country of the coming generation who are the hope and heart of the future of the United States, across the seas. Once committed, Mr. President, we cannot turn aside. . . .

Mr. President, we are facing a situation in which, if we pass this bill, we are taking certainly the next to the last step leading to our involvement in war. It may be that we are taking the last step, because under the powers given in this bill steps may be taken which will create a state of war.

Democratic Senator David Walsh argued that even among proponents of the bill, "There is now a tacit admission . . . that the bill does in fact take us down the road to war." Democratic Senator Pat McCarran of Nevada charged that if "this bill is enacted into law, Mr. President, it is war—war under the ignominious circumstances of never having been declared by the Congress of the United States."

But all to no avail. More pressure was exerted on Democratic members of the House to vote for this measure than I had seen at any time in my twenty years experience in Congress. And it worked. The Lend-Lease bill was enacted on March 11, 1941. The American economy was thus firmly linked to the Allies' war effort, and American security interests became inextricably intertwined with those of the Allies.

By the end of the war, Lend-Lease had cost the United States more than fifty billion dollars, none of which was ever repaid. Ohio Senator Robert Taft, one of my closest friends, quipped half in jest, "Lending war equipment is a good deal like lending chewing gum. You don't want it back." And the lending would get worse.

On June 22, 1941, Germany launched a massive invasion of the Soviet Union, breaking the nonaggression pact that both countries had signed in August 1939. For noninterventionists, this new war on Germany's Eastern front was merely another reason to stay out of the conflict. Noninterventionists, for their part, believed that those two noxious systems—national socialism and communism—should be allowed to destroy each other on the battlefield.

Surprisingly, news of the invasion was greeted with unrestrained glee by American communists, socialists, and leftists, as well as some interventionists. Their anger that Soviet Russia had been stabbed in the back was minor compared to their joy that the United States might provide military assistance to the Soviet Union under the Lend-Lease bill and eventually accept Communist Russia as an ally and friend of democracy. President Roosevelt endorsed their views and immediately set to work to alter Lend-Lease to include the Soviet Union.

On June 30, 1941, I spoke over the radio warning that "there is one thing worse [than nazism] and that is the bloody hand of communism." I also bemoaned the fact that the interventionists proposed "to turn the Lend-Lease bill into a Lenin-Lease bill and send our money and defense articles to Soviet Russia in the name of the four freedoms. What a travesty! Oh, Democracy, what crimes are committed in thy name!"

The ever feisty Harry Truman (then a senator) denounced both dictators and said: "If Russia were winning, help should be given to Germany and if Germany were winning, help should be given to Russia."

Senator Robert M. La Follette was exactly right when he stated: "The American people will be told to forget the purges in Russia by the OGPU [the Soviet secret police], the confiscation of property, persecution of religion, the invasion of Finland, and the vulture role Stalin played by seizing half of prostrate Poland, all of Latvia, Estonia, and Lithuania."

And Senator Robert Taft expressed the feelings of many when he spoke these words: "In the name of democracy we are to make a communist alliance with the most ruthless dictator in the world. Could there be a greater travesty on the false propaganda fed to the American people that this is a great moral issue between ideologies? If Hitler wins it is a victory for fascism. If Stalin wins it is a victory for communism. From the point of view of ideology there is no choice."

Roosevelt tried to put a good face on it by painting a glowing picture of Stalin's Russia. In a press conference on September 30, 1941, Roosevelt had the following exchange with the press:

> ROOSEVELT: As I think I suggested to you a week or two ago, some of you might find it useful to read Article 124 of the Constitution of Russia.
> QUESTION: What does it say, Mr. President?
> ROOSEVELT: Well, I haven't learned it by heart sufficiently to quote—I might be off a little bit, but anyway: Freedom of conscience. . . .
> QUESTION: Would you say. . . .
> ROOSEVELT: Freedom of religion. Freedom equally to use propaganda against religion, which is essentially what is the rule in this country; only, we don't put it quite the same way. For instance, you might go out tommorrow— to the corner of Pennsylvania Avenue, down below the Press Club—and

stand on a soap box and preach Christianity and nobody would stop you. And then, if it got into your head, perhaps the next day preach against religion of all kinds, and nobody will stop you.

This was blatantly untrue, and every informed person—and we would have to count Roosevelt as one—knew it was untrue. Virtually all religious denominations in the country branded FDR's remarks as utterly misleading and false. I remarked on Roosevelt's fatuousness by suggesting that he "invite our comrade and ally—palsy-walsy Joe Stalin—to Washington so that he might be baptized in the swimming pool of the White House. It could be a fine, big ceremony, with all the members of Congress there to see that it was done properly. And then afterward I suggest that all of us join the Stalin Sunday School."

Roosevelt then tried to cover one deception—Soviet religious freedom—by engaging in another. On October 2, Secretary of State Cordell Hull was instructed to send a telegram to Averell Harriman, Roosevelt's roving ambassador who was in Moscow coordinating the Lend-Lease program. The telegram said:

> In view of the outstanding importance of this question [of religious freedom in the Soviet Union] from the standpoint of public opinion in this country the President earnestly hopes that from the highest authorities of the Russian government you may be able to secure some statement that can be sent to this country's press which would be confirmatory of and responsive to, the statement contained in [the remarks of the September 30 press conference]. . . .
>
> Please make every effort to see that the Soviet authorities make some statement of this kind at the earliest moment possible. [Raymond Dawson, *The Decision to Aid Russia, 1941*]

So confident was Roosevelt that Stalin would support him on this issue that he claimed, on October 2, 1941, that "complete freedom of religion is on its way" in the Soviet Union. Harriman, despite his best efforts, had to notify the White House on October 4 that he had a "feeling that the Russians will give lip service to meet the President's wishes and make a few gestures, but they are not prepared yet to allow freedom of religion. . . ."

Roosevelt's propaganda campaign failed to convince the American people, but he did exert sufficient pressure on Congress to get its approval for one billion dollars in military aid under the Lend-Lease bill. By the end of the war, the Soviets had received eleven billion dollars of American aid.

This money was supposed to be repaid five years after the war, but we never received a single dime.

Roosevelt adhered to the naive belief that, if given a chance, the Soviet Union would willingly embrace democratic values—as though the Soviets had no values of their own. Philosopher Sidney Hook wrote in his autobiography *Out of Step* that "Roosevelt was profoundly ignorant about the nature of communism, not only as an ideological system but as a functioning totalitarian society. He was probably influenced by his wife, Eleanor, who could never distinguish between the rhetoric and reality of communism. . . ." Franklin Roosevelt's hubristic self-deception about the nature of communism and Eleanor Roosevelt's blithe ignorance of its reality were to place horrific shackles on the people of Eastern Europe, which those people are only now beginning to escape.

Chapter Fourteen

Last Efforts for Peace: Meeting with von Ribbentrop

Let me backtrack for a moment to describe how I endeavored not only to keep the United States out of the Second World War, but to prevent the war from erupting in Europe in the first place. Two weeks before the outbreak of the war, on August 16, 1939, I arrived in London as chairman of the congressional group of the Interparliamentary Union at the Oslo Conference. The American delegation in Oslo was composed of twenty-four members of the House of Representatives, equally divided between the two parties, and four U.S. senators.

For a number of years, Senator Alban W. Barkley, later vice president of the United States, had been elected chairman of the American delegation to the Interparliamentary Union by members of the House and Senate. But in early 1939, there was a good deal of war talk and fear that President Roosevelt would involve us in another European war, and since a majority of congressmen, both Republican and Democratic, were in favor of staying out of war unless attacked, they decided to back another candidate for chairman of the delegation.

As ranking Republican member of the House Foreign Affairs Committee, my anti-war views were well known in Congress and throughout the nation. Thus a number of my friends in Congress asked me if I would be interested in serving as chairman of the American delegation. I agreed, and to my surprise I was elected by a two-to-one margin.

After Congress adjourned at the end of July 1939, I went to Ireland where I met with Prime Minister Eamon De Valera in Dublin. A tall, intelligent, kindly, and outspoken public official, he stated without reservation that if war broke out and England were involved, Ireland would remain neutral but would sell food and other products to England.

From Dublin I flew to London to keep an appointment with Lord Halifax, the British foreign secretary and later ambassador to Washington. He was very tall, charming, and able—a cultured gentleman and statesman. Lord Halifax agreed with me that another European war would be ruinous and that every step should be taken to avoid it. He added that the Nazi government had offered to limit its army to 300,000 men in France if France would agree to do the same and deplored the French refusal to agree.

(While I was in London, I received an urgent call from an old friend of mine, attorney Fanny Holtzman, who was in Berlin, asking my help with Jewish refugees. The full story will be told in a later chapter.)

From London, I proceeded to Paris where I met the French foreign minister, Georges Bonnet. A talented and experienced diplomat, he was inclined to a defeatist attitude—war was inevitable and would, in fact, break out in a few weeks. Obviously, he did not want France to become involved in another war with Germany, but from reports I received, he was being pressured into it by certain powerful public figures both in the United States and Britain.

During my stay in Paris, I received a telephone call from a German friend of mine, Mr. Sallett, in Berlin, asking if I would like to meet the German foreign minister, Joachim von Ribbentrop. I told him I would be glad to stop off on my way to Norway for the convention.

It was thus that, two weeks before the outbreak of World War II, I had an exclusive and unique interview with Joachim von Ribbentrop at his mountain villa near Salzburg, Austria. I came, at his invitation, in my official capacity as chairman of the American delegation of the Interparliamentary Union in Oslo, Norway.

The United States at that time had no ambassador to Germany. I believed then, and still believe, that this was a serious blunder on the part of the Roosevelt administration. Our chargé d'affaires in Berlin, Mr. Alexander Kirk, although an able and trained diplomat, was unable to see Hitler or

von Ribbentrop and might as well have been in Timbuktu. Had we maintained an American ambassador in Berlin, we might have been in a position
to exert our influence for peace and prevent the costly war that gave half of
Europe to the communists. When our ambassador was recalled from Berlin
the year before, the United States was left without influence or leadership in
the pre-war crisis.

Unable to see von Ribbentrop right away, I spent four delightful hours
wandering around Salzburg, one of the most picturesque cities in Europe
with its ancient castle perched up above the town. The inhabitants, men
and women, still wore the old peasant costumes, the women in bright red
and blue and the men in leather shorts with green or black Alpine hats.

At 3:30 P.M. an automobile arrived at the hotel for me. It took me over
some country roads and hills for about seven miles to von Ribbentrop's villa
overlooking an exquisite mountain lake called Fuschel. His villa had
formerly been a hunting lodge of the archbishop of Salzburg.

Ribbentrop met me in a most cordial manner as I entered his country
residence. I was impressed by his youthful appearance, which belied his
forty-five years. He was also good-looking and was a gracious and charming host.

He told me he had worked for six years in the United States and Canada
on the railroads and in the contracting business in the Middle West, if
memory serves. At any rate, his English was excellent and he was never at a
loss for the right word or expression. I had been in politics for over twenty
years, but I had never spoken with anyone in a more informal and open
manner. We sat at a tea table on the porch of his villa overlooking the lake,
the huge mountains surrounded by clouds in the distance.

Now I listened as von Ribbentrop gave the German view. He told me
that Hitler regarded Britain's guarantee of Poland's borders as a hostile act
of encirclement. The Germans believed the borders that had been established at the Versailles peace conference after the First World War were
unjust. He went on to explain that he and Mr. Jozef Beck, the Polish
foreign minister, had practically agreed to transfer Danzig (Gdansk) to
Germany and to create a Polish corridor to the sea. The British, however,
had encouraged the Poles not to negotiate, and Mr. Beck had become
powerless in the hands of what von Ribbentrop called "the Polish military
clique" who were preparing for war with the backing of England and
France. German patience had come to an end, he added, and unless
Danzig were restored and the rights of Germans living in Poland safe-
guarded, war would break out within two weeks.

He presented me with a great deal of data about the maltreatment of Germans in Poland, much of which I considered sheer propaganda. He assured me, however, that war with Poland would be popular, as the Germans believed they had liberated Poland from the bolsheviks and had been rewarded by having their own territory stripped from them and given to the Poles.

I remember clearly his saying that "the mechanized German army can crush and overwhelm Poland in two weeks." I laughed at that and said, "You mean two months, don't you?" To which he replied, "No, in two weeks. We are familiar with every road in Poland from the last war and know Poland as well as the Poles, and the muddy roads of Poland do not frighten us."

Herr von Ribbentrop then related how he had flown at least twenty times to London with friendly proposals and goodwill messages from Hitler (von Ribbentrop had been the German ambassador to London for a number of years). The Germans, he noted, had offered to limit their navy to one-third the size of the British fleet, an offer that the British had accepted. According to von Ribbentrop, Hitler believed that cooperation between England and Germany was essential for the maintenance of peace; to that end, Hitler had "offered to place fifteen German army divisions and the entire fleet at the disposal of the British government to support her empire in case of war anywhere in the world." At this time, I did not believe him, but years later it was substantiated. Not until the British inaugurated their program of encirclement, he continued, and guaranteed the status quo in Danzig did Hitler turn from friendship to bitter enmity— so much so that Hitler "would stop at nothing to destroy the British Empire, even to the last German soldier."

As regards the French, von Ribbentrop told me that he had written the French foreign minister to tell him that the Germans had no quarrel with the French, but if the French insisted on attacking, they would lose a million men. The responsibility for peace belonged to France.

It was not my mission to quarrel with von Ribbentrop, though I reminded him that I too had been an officer in the last war and his contention that the German army had not been defeated was wrong. German soldiers and replacements in 1918 were either young boys or old men. Germany was exhausted in manpower and resources, I said, and could not have lasted another six months regardless of the revolution at home. He did not press the issue further.

During our conversation, which lasted more than an hour and a half, we

drank tea and ate cookies and preserves. He invited me to go to the opera
with Hitler that evening and assured me that if I did, he would arrange for
his plane to get me to Oslo by 9:00 the next morning. I declined. He
escorted me to the motor car that took me to the airfield, and that was the
last I ever saw of him. Ten days later he signed the pact with Stalin for a
German-Russian alliance—one week after the Interparliamentary Union
failed to adopt my resolution for a moratorium of thirty days in order to
settle the Danzig issue by arbitration.

Though I would have been torn to shreds by the American press, radio,
and every communist and FDR crony available had I accepted von Ribbentrop's offer to meet Hitler, in retrospect I am ashamed I did not do so. I
would have urged him not to attack Poland, but to use every means within
the law to recover the city of Danzig and a land corridor to the Baltic Sea—
thereby ending German resentment over the Versailles Treaty.

But, on my departure for Oslo, I still had not given up my hope for
peace.

Col. Nicholas Fish, great-grandfather of Hamilton Fish, born in 1758 to ardent Tories and supporters of George III. Nicholas himself served with Alexander Hamilton as an officer in the American Revolution.

Hamilton Fish's birthplace and childhood home in Garrison, New York.

Stuyvesant Place, home of Hamilton Fish's grandparents, Col. Nicholas Fish and his wife Elizabeth Stuyvesant, the grand-daughter of Peter Stuyvesant, the last Dutch governor of Niew Amsterdam (later New York City). (Photo courtesy of New York Historical Society)

New York City residence of Hamilton Fish I, (1851–1893), grandfather of Hamilton Fish and secretary of state to President Ulysses S. Grant. (Photo courtesy of *1893 King's Handbook*, New York Historical Society)

BOTTOM LEFT: Julia Kean Fish, grandmother of Hamilton Fish; Fish's older sister was named after her. (Photo courtesy of New York Historical Society)

BELOW: Hamilton Fish I, grandfather of Hamilton Fish, New York State governor, U.S. senator, and secretary of state to President Ulysses S. Grant. He turned down an offer to be chief justice of the Supreme Court. (Photo courtesy of New York Historical Society)

Hamilton Fish II, father of Hamilton Fish, elected New York State assemblyman at age 24 and a leading candidate in 1896 for the governorship of New York State. (Photo courtesy of the Fish Collection, Alice Curtis Desmond and Hamilton Fish Library, Garrison, New York)

Emily Mann Fish, mother of Hamilton Fish. (Photo courtesy of the Fish Collection, Alice Curtis Desmond and Hamilton Fish Library, Garrison, New York)

Janet Fish, Hamilton Fish's sister, served in the Red Cross during World War I. Brother and sister were both inducted into the French Legion of Honor. (Photo courtesy of the Fish Collection, Alice Curtis Desmond and Hamilton Fish Library, Garrison, New York)

Hamilton Fish from infancy to the age of 12.

Hamilton Fish, age 12, with his sisters, (L-R) Rosalind Fish (who later married John W. Cutler), Helena Fish (who later married Henry Forster), Janet Fish, and Julia Kean Fish (who later married William Lawrence Breese), in Paartenkoerchen, Bavaria. Fish persuaded his father to let him climb the Zutzpitzer, pictured in the background.

Hamilton Fish with his father and his son, Hamilton, Jr., U.S. congressman from New York's 21st District.

Congressman Fish with his first wife, Grace Chapin Fish, son Hamilton, Jr., and daughter Elizabeth Stuyvesant Fish.

Hamilton Fish on his 80th birthday in 1968 with (L-R) Russian-born Marie Blackton Fish, his second wife; U.S. Congressman-elect Hamilton Fish, Jr., his son; Julia Mackenzie Fish, his daughter-in-law; Hamilton III and Nicholas his grandsons.

Alice Curtis Desmond, Hamilton Fish's third wife.

Cheree, Hamilton Fish's devoted poodle, never strayed from her master's feet. (Photo courtesy of Marvin Edelman, Chairman, Social Studies Department, Robert E. Bell School)

Hamilton Fish listens as Lydia Ambrogio Fish, his fourth wife, sings "Happy Birthday" at his 102nd birthday party at the Dutchess Manor on December 8, 1990.

Chapter Fifteen

Failure of the Oslo Conference

The airplane that Foreign Minister von Ribbentrop had placed at my disposal was a sixteen-passenger commercial craft with two pilots and an assistant, not the famous smaller plane that had been provided for Prime Minister Chamberlain when he visited Hitler. Herr Sallett, a representative of the German foreign office, accompanied me to our first stop—Berlin.

We were the only passengers. The first hour's flight over the Bavarian Alps was very beautiful. Darkness fell as we crossed into Czechoslovakia. From Berlin, where Herr Sallett departed, the plane took me to Copenhagen, Denmark, and after a six-hour rest, we flew to Oslo, arriving precisely at nine, as promised.

When I joined up with the Interparliamentary Union Conference I was surrounded by reporters who wanted to know all about my interview with von Ribbentrop. I refused to make any statement except to say that I had flown over in one of his airplanes and that I believed—after my meetings with both French and German sources—that war would break out between August 24 and September 1.

On the basis of that statement, I was viciously attacked in the American press as being an alarmist with no knowledge of foreign affairs. When war did break out two weeks later, there were no apologies from the

arrogant editorialists and columnists who condemned me—not that I
expected any.

King Haakon of Norway welcomed the Interparliamentary Conference
by holding a reception in the spacious and beautiful ballroom of the royal
palace, where the crown prince and the royal family were also on hand to
meet the guests. An equerry of the king invited me to meet His Majesty
who was standing alone in front of a large mantlepiece in the middle of
the ballroom. He was a very tall, handsome, intelligent individual, past
middle age.

The king greeted me cordially and asked me about my interview with
von Ribbentrop, and I relayed to him what von Ribbentrop had said: if
Germany recovered Danzig, it would be the final liquidation of the Versailles Treaty; and Germany had no territorial ambitions in the West. I
added that the Germans considered their own western borders invulnera-
ble to attack, which led me to conclude that if war broke out, the Germans
would not invade France or Belgium. He questioned me further about the
timetable for war (as expressed by both the French and the German foreign
minister) and about my own plan for a thirty-day moratorium to settle the
Danzig issue.

After talking for about fifteen minutes, I reminded the king that I was in
an embarrassing position, because all the other delegates were waiting to
meet him. But he insisted on continuing our conversation and held forth on
the matters of war and peace with considerable knowledge and intelligence.
I finally received the king's permission to leave, but only, I'm sure, after
arousing the enmity of many waiting diplomats, delegates, and their wives.

At the opening of the Interparliamentary Congress, I introduced my
resolution for a thirty-day moratorium to prevent war and reach a peaceful
settlement of the Danzig issue. The resolution read as follows:

> RESOLVED, that the Interparliamentary Union, in its session at Oslo,
> urges upon the governments of Great Britain, France, Germany, and Italy,
> the immediate consideration of a moratorium on war (Danzig) for thirty days
> or more with a view to the settlement of international disputes by arbitration,
> mediation and peaceful methods, consistent with the principles for which the
> Interparliamentary Union was founded.

I urged the adoption of the resolution in the most important and
dramatic speech I ever made. After paying my respects to the Scandinavian countries and the contributions made by persons of Scandinavian
heritage to the United States, I said:

We are all members of representative and parliamentary governments from throughout the world which believe in the fundamental rights of the people to govern themselves under free institutions and in the preservation of peace as a paramount and continuous policy. I never had more faith in the final triumph and extension of democracy and the right of the people to rule than I have today, in spite of its temporary challenge by dictatorships of the Left and of the Right. The answer to all dictatorships is to make democracy work in our own countries and to put our own houses in order. Parliamentary and representative forms of government are still the hope and aspiration of the struggling masses of mankind throughout the world.

Free institutions, including free speech, free press and radio, and free assembly, together with personal liberty and economic justice, are the natural aspirations of free men and women throughout the civilized world.

I regret deeply to state that I believe that a European war is more imminent today than at any time since last September. If the Danzig and the Polish agitation continues, the slightest spark may start a world conflagration. This conference has listened to numerous interesting and able speeches from the point of view generally of the nation involved. As one who served in the French Fourth Army under General Gouraud, I hate and loathe war, and do not offer any apologies for raising my voice in behalf of peace. I refuse to admit that the door to peace is closed or to yield to the defeatist war talk that apparently covers Europe. I refuse to believe that if there is a will and sufficient determination, a way cannot be found to open the door of peace and the road to a peaceful settlement of international controversies.

Pointing then to the horrors of war, I went on to say:

We have no power as delegates to enforce peace, but we have a solemn and sacred duty to exert our moral and political influence in our own countries to preserve peace through arbitration, mediation, and conciliation. We cannot dodge or evade the peace issue. We would be shirking our duty as representatives of millions of free people throughout the world if we join in any defeatist attitude towards peace and wash our hands, like Pontius Pilate, over the crucifixion of Europe, and maybe of civilization and Christianity. I urge this conference to make a strong, united plea to the governments of the world, including the Vatican, in support of a thirty-day moratorium on political and international disputes and, in the meantime, to explore anew every avenue and possibility for a fair and peaceful settlement of the issues that are leading European nations into war, and to provide for a program of world recovery.

If we refuse to act and no armistice on war is arranged, the whole peace issue may go by default. Peacemaking machinery has broken down. The tension has been so continuous and so acute that it is not surprising if the statesmen of Europe are worn out and find themselves in an impasse or a deadlock that leads directly to war. If this conference can contribute the leadership in a democratic manner to world peace, it will deserve the grateful thanks and prayers of millions of peace-loving people throughout all of Europe and the world.

My concluding words were in French and were greeted with loud and prolonged applause: "Je dis aux membres de cette Conference Interparlementaire: A bas la guerre. Vivent la democratie et la paix."

It appeared as though my proposal had been well received by most of the delegates of the twenty-five nations represented at the conference. The head of the French delegation told me that he favored it, and I was told that Mussolini and the Italian government favored it, but, for reasons best known to themselves, the British and Norwegian delegations later opposed it. Norway, in fact, put forward the only speaker against my resolution—a speaker who charged that the United States had never done anything to help any of the European nations.

The next day at the Executive Committee meeting, composed of two members from each nation, I rose and withdrew my resolution because I believed that, to be effective, it should have British support and be unanimous. But in doing so, I asked the chairman of the Executive Committee, a former Belgian foreign minister, if it were not true that the United States, through Herbert Hoover, had given great quantities of food relief during World War I to the Belgian people. He jumped to his feet and said that no nation had ever done more, unselfishly and on such a large humanitarian scale, as the United States. I then turned to the Polish representative and asked him if he did not remember the food supplies and relief that were sent to Poland by the United States during and after World War I, and he too took occasion to praise the humanitarian efforts of our country. By that time, Mr. Hambro—the Norwegian delegate who had spoken against me—had left the committee room.

Eventually the committee adopted an innocuous and futile resolution that praised peace but provided no effective deterrent to war. My proposed moratorium would have punished Hitler—if he had ignored it—by putting him in blatant opposition to a proposal put forward by twenty-five democratic nations offering a peaceful, diplomatic resolution of the Danzig issue.

Before we could leave Norway, Germany and the Soviet Union invaded Poland, and Britain and France declared war on Germany. On the cruise home, the joke among members of our delegation was that we had so infuriated the British Foreign Office that the U-boats lurking about were there to protect us from the British!

On my return to the United States, I received numerous pathetic cablegrams from the Finnish, Hungarian, Lithuanian, Estonian, and Latvian foreign ministers, saying what a tragedy it was that my resolution had not been adopted. It might only have delayed war for a year, but it might have averted it entirely and prevented the wreck and ruin of Europe that ensued.

As soon as Hitler made his pact with Stalin on August 23, 1939, he ordered the mobilization of the German army. This act terrified the governments of Europe. The British government, led by Prime Minister Neville Chamberlain, completely reversed the position taken by its delegates at the Oslo conference the week before and urged the settlement of the Danzig issue by negotiation. The British were supported by the French, the Vatican, the king of Belgium, and even, at the last minute, by Franklin Roosevelt. But even though Hitler cancelled the mobilization orders subject to direct negotiations with Poland for the return of Danzig, the protests of the Western European powers were too little too late. Armed with its totally useless guarantees from the British government, the Polish government evaded open negotiations with the Germans.

Danzig's population, it must be remembered, was 90 percent German and it had voted overwhelmingly in a referendum to be restored to the German Reich, in accordance with the principles of self-determination. And the Germans agreed that if they were given Danzig they would sign a treaty guaranteeing the independence and integrity of Poland. Polish control of this city was not, then, an issue for which it was worth plunging the world into war. Though the ultimate blame must rest with Hitler for forcing the issue and not having the patience to wait a few days when it was evident that the pressure was mounting on Poland to negotiate, it is almost unbelievable that the Polish government could have been so completely deceived about the chances of defending itself against the finest army in Europe attacking from the west and the huge Russian army attacking from the east.

In June 1940 the *New York Daily News* editorialized on the disaster that was facing Western Europe:

> The French catastrophe is a part of one of the great tragic ironies of history, as we see it. Hitler said in *Mein Kampf* that he wanted to go east into Russia.

The Ukraine looked to him like the ideal place for Germans to colonize and build up a farming and industrial civilization.

Hitler devoted pages in the same book to kind words about the British, how he considered them the same kind of people as the Germans, what fierce fighters the British were in an emergency, and how Germany's best single bet would always be an alliance with England.

Mein Kampf contains some harsh words about France, but by building the Westwall, Hitler indicated that he didn't want a war with France—but what he still wanted last August was to go east. The allies wouldn't let him go east. They insisted that he come west. He has come west, with a vengeance.

How true! And if Hitler had not come west, Poland, which hated the communists, could either have remained neutral or fought on the side of the Germans against Soviet Russia.

The Poles had no reason to trust the power-hungry Nazi dictator Adolf Hitler, but the price they paid for their refusal to negotiate with him was ghastly. I will regret to my dying day my failure to establish the thirty-day moratorium I had proposed to settle the Danzig issue, which would have prevented the most destructive and unnecessary war in history—a war that killed millions and that brought Stalin into Eastern Europe where he enslaved millions more.

As tragic as they were, the events in Europe were not, ultimately, the cause of the United States becoming part of the calamity of the Second World War. It was the Japanese attack on Pearl Harbor that brought us into the conflict.

Chapter Sixteen

The Smoking Gun: FDR's Unconstitutional War Ultimatum

On Monday, December 8, 1941, as ranking Republican member of the Committee on Rules, I opened the debate on a resolution declaring war on the Japanese Empire. Here are my remarks:

> Mr. Speaker, it is with sorrow and deep resentment against Japan that I rise to support a declaration of war. I have consistently opposed our entrance into wars in Europe and Asia for the past three years but the unwarranted, vicious, brazen, and dastardly attack by the Japanese navy and air force while peace negotiations were pending at Washington and in defiance of the president's eleventh-hour personal appeal to the emperor, makes war inevitable and necessary.
>
> The time for debate and controversy within America has passed. The time for action has come. Interventionists and noninterventionists must cease recriminations, charges, and countercharges against each other, and present a united front behind the president and the government in the conduct of the war.
>
> There can be only one answer to the treacherous attack of the Japanese, and that is war to final victory, cost what it may in blood and treasure and

tears. This unprovoked and senseless aggression by the Japanese armed forces upon our possessions must be answered by war.

Although I have consistently fought against our intervention in foreign wars, I have repeatedly stated that if we were attacked by any foreign nation, or if the Congress of the United States declared war in the American and constitutional way, I would support the president and the administration to the bitter end.

Whom the gods destroy they first make mad. The Japanese have gone stark raving mad and have by their unprovoked attack committed military, naval, and national suicide. I shall at the proper time volunteer my services as an officer in a combat division, as I did in the last war, preferably with colored troops.

There is no sacrifice too great that I will not make in defense of America and to help annihilate these war-mad Japanese devils.

Now that we are to fight, let us go in with our heads and chins up in the American way, and let us serve notice upon the world that this is not only a war against aggression and in defense of our own territories, but a war for freedom and democracy all over the world, and that we will not stop until victory is won.

I appeal to all American citizens, particularly to members of my own party, and to noninterventionists, to put aside personal views and partisanship, and to unite behind the president, our commander-in-chief, in assuring victory to the armed forces of the United States.

Our country! In her intercourse with foreign nations may she always be right, but right or wrong, our country!

When I delivered this speech, I was proud of my remarks. Now I am ashamed of them. President Roosevelt's speech to the American people referring to an unprovoked attack on our forces at Pearl Harbor—a "day of infamy"—had roused us all to the defense of our country. But those passionate feelings have turned to ashes in the light of the hypocrisy and deceit that forced us into war. Franklin Delano Roosevelt was living proof of Lord Acton's adage, "Power tends to corrupt and absolute power corrupts absolutely." After breaking the traditional rule limiting American presidents to two terms—a rule established by George Washington himself and maintained for a century and a half by men who understood the meaning of the word *republic*—Roosevelt began to behave increasingly like a dictator. He had never shown much respect for constitutional limits on the power of government. And now, in his third term, encouraged by his growing cult of personality and his successful bullying of Congress and the Supreme Court, he sought to increase his powers by extraordinary means.

Roosevelt wanted a war with Japan. Winston Churchill made this plain in an address before the House of Commons in 1942:

> It has been the policy of the Cabinet at almost all costs to avoid embroilment with Japan until we were sure that the United States would also be engaged. . . . On the other hand, the probability since the Atlantic Conference, at which I discussed these matters with Franklin Roosevelt, [is] that the United States, even if not herself attacked, would come into the war in the Far East. . . .

Secretary of War Henry L. Stimson, Army Chief of Staff General George C. Marshall, and Navy Secretary Frank Knox were all ardent interventionists, and all wanted war with Japan. Stimson had an almost obsessive hatred of the Japanese and was only too eager to reinforce Roosevelt's prowar sympathies. Only ten years earlier, Stimson, as President Herbert Hoover's secretary of state, had to be restrained by Hoover from provoking war with Japan over Manchuria.

Fortunately for us, Stimson kept a detailed diary of his service as secretary of war, first made public in 1945. On November 9, 1941, less than a month before the infamous attack on Pearl Harbor, he wrote:

> Everything looks as if we were getting into the war pretty fast now and everybody is pretty sound about it. Coming as it does on Armistice Day Anniversary, it is a curious, almost ironic, anniversary.

Two weeks later on November 25, he added:

> This was a full day indeed. At 9:30 Knox and I met in Hull's office for our meeting of Three. Hull showed us the proposal for a three month's truce, which he was going to lay before the Japanese today or tomorrow. It adequately safeguarded our interests, I thought as we read it, but I don't think there is any chance of the Japanese accepting it, because it was so drastic.

On November 26, 1941, United States Secretary of State Cordell Hull sent the Japanese a secret ultimatum—sanctioned solely by the authority of Franklin Roosevelt—demanding the withdrawal of all Japanese troops from China and Indo-China. The ultimatum was written by none other than the notorious Harry Dexter White.

Historian Anthony Kubek has said in *How the Far East Was Lost, 1941-49* that White had a "profound and unprecedented" influence on

American foreign policy. No American public official, Kubek wrote, "exercised such arbitrary power or cast so ominous a shadow over the future of the nation as did Harry Dexter White."

White's parents had emigrated from Czarist Russia in 1885. As a trusted lieutenant of Treasury Secretary Henry Morgenthau, White was a key behind-the-scenes player in the Roosevelt administration. Six months before he wrote the war ultimatum, he drafted the Lend-Lease bill, which transferred such unprecedented war-making powers to the president.

Even in 1941, White's procommunist sympathies were known. Less than a month before Pearl Harbor, Texas Democratic Congressman Martin Dies furnished the Roosevelt administration with information pointing to White's involvement with a communist spy ring. The administration not only took no action, but Roosevelt told Dies that he had a number of friends who were communists and had no interest in removing communists from the government. In a speech delivered in San Antonio, Texas, on May 17, 1951, Dies reported:

> When I told the President what we had, he turned to me and he laughed and said, "You know, Martin, I think you see a Red under your bed every night." He said, "You know—you're unduly alarmed about Communists"; he said, "I'm not a Communist, and I'm not a Communist sympathizer, but I've got some good friends who are Communists and I think the Communists are harmless and I believe that Russia is our natural ally."

The full extent of White's treason became known only after the war. According to a 1948 FBI report, Soviet diplomat Alexander Gregory-Graff Barmine identified both Harry Dexter White and State Department official Alger Hiss as agents of Soviet Military Intelligence. Walter Krivitsky, who defected to the United States in 1937 after having been head of the Soviet Union's Red Army Intelligence unit in Western Europe, confirmed that White and Hiss had worked as Soviet agents in the 1930s.

Further stunning revelations came from Whittaker Chambers—a former communist agent—who provided the House Un-American Activities Committee with microfilmed documents that Harry Dexter White had intended for Chambers to pass on to the communists. Through these documents, the Soviets knew of Roosevelt's hostility to Japan. Among other things, they learned that Roosevelt had considered a boycott on Japanese trade as early as 1938.

Chambers testified that he first became aware of White's intelligence activities in 1935. According to Chambers, the Soviets had instructed White to facilitate the appointment of communists in positions of authority in New Deal agencies and to provide the Soviets with secret government documents. Chambers insisted that White had done as he was told.

Another former communist, Elizabeth Bentley, corroborated Chambers' testimony. White, she said, had been deeply involved in the Silvermaster spy ring that had passed secret documents to the Soviets. He had, in fact, appointed at least nine members of the ring to posts in the Treasury Department. In 1953, J. Edgar Hoover, director of the Federal Bureau of Investigation, stated that "all information furnished by Miss Bentley, which was susceptible to check, has proven to be accurate."

FBI surveillance of White during 1945 established that White met frequently with Nathan Silvermaster and other communist agents. Silvermaster, the alleged head of the spy ring (see Earl Latham, *The Communist Controversies in Washington*; David Rees, *Harry Dexter White*; Allen Weinstein, *Perjury*) was also of Russian extraction and a close friend of White's, but he was much more reckless in exhibiting his belief in communism. In 1934, Silvermaster and his wife gave refuge to Earl Browder, former chairman of the American Communist party, who was then fleeing from California longshoremen outraged at Browder's attempts to communize their union. Despite Silvermaster's communist affiliations, he was appointed to a prominent position in the Department of Agriculture in 1935. In 1944, White appointed him chief of the Division of Economic Analysis in the Treasury Department.

The FBI also learned that during the entire time White was Morgenthau's top assistant, he passed classified Treasury Department documents to Silvermaster and William Ludwig Ullman, who sent copies to Jacob Golos, a known Soviet agent. After Golos died in 1943, the documents were delivered to Anatole Borisovich Gromov, the first secretary of the Soviet Embassy in Washington.

Much more recently, on August 30, 1988, historian Tony Troncone conducted an interview with former Attorney General Herbert Brownell. Troncone asked Brownell if, in his opinion, there was sufficient evidence to convict White of passing documents over to the Soviets. Brownell answered: "Yes, I was absolutely stunned by it."

At the time, there were other important allegations against White, but of greatest concern to the FBI was President Truman's intention to appoint

White to head the International Monetary Fund. The FBI feared, and rightly so, that White would use the considerable powers of the position to advance the economic interests of the Soviet Union. High-level sources in the Canadian government told the FBI that incriminating evidence had been discovered linking White to a Russian spy ring in Canada. Igor Gouzenko, a Russian agent who defected to Canadian authorities in October 1946, provided additional evidence of White's activities.

In November 1945, the FBI compiled a detailed twenty-eight page report on White, which J. Edgar Hoover forwarded to President Truman, warning that White was a grave security risk. On December 4, Hoover delivered another report—seventy-one pages long—providing additional documentation on White's involvement with the Silvermaster spy ring.

Truman chose to ignore Hoover's reports and on January 23, 1946, appointed White to head the International Monetary Fund. Though White's official duties as head of the IMF were beyond the purview of congressional committees investigating communist subversion, the FBI continued to uncover evidence of White's communist activities. In 1947, Hoover provided President Truman with a report on White so compelling that Truman finally had to dismiss White from the IMF. Even Roosevelt's closest advisor, Henry Morgenthau, who had stubbornly defended White, admitted to the FBI in 1952 after he had examined some of the FBI's evidence that there was "no question but that White was working for the Russians" (FBI documents obtained under Freedom of Information Act).

Back then, in the spring of 1941, White wrote the first draft of the Japanese secret war ultimatum and submitted it to Morgenthau on June 6, with a note saying, "It is a preliminary and incomplete draft which I can . . . modify if you think that the general idea therein can be of any use to you."

The proposals in White's draft were harsh and unyielding. They demanded that Japan withdraw its military forces from China, Thailand, and Vietnam, and abandon its economic independence in international trade. The revised November ultimatum was ever harsher. In addition to the earlier demands, Japan was ordered to remove its troops from Manchuria, which would have been tantamount to allowing the Soviet Union, long covetous of the area's rich resources, to take over. It also required Japan to break its September 1940 pact with Germany and Italy. It would, that is, have amounted to national suicide for the Japanese.

White's interest at that time in forcing a war between the United States and Japan is perfectly clear—it would plunge Soviet Russia's main competitor for influence in the East into an immensely costly war with the powerful United States.

Then, on June 22, 1941, Germany invaded its former partner-in-crime, the Soviet Union. Now, the Russians needed the Americans in the war to help defeat Germany. Since Germany had refrained from provoking the United States into war, White must have realized that the only way the United States could come to the aid of the Soviet Union was to bring the nation into the war in Europe through the back door; that is, by forcing Japan into attacking the United States. During the next several months, he worked diligently toward that end.

There is no doubt, in any case, that the inflammatory war ultimatum was intended to provoke Japan into attacking the U.S. Both FDR and Stimson referred to it as "the war ultimatum," which stated "a point beyond which we would fight." On November 25, 1941, Roosevelt called a meeting of his "War Cabinet" to discuss the deterioration of U.S. relations with Japan. Stimson wrote in his diary that day:

> Then at 12:00 o'clock we went to the White House, where we were until nearly half past one. At the meeting were Hull, Knox, Marshall, Stark and myself. There the President . . . brought up entirely the relations with the Japanese. He brought up the event that we were likely to be attacked perhaps next Monday . . . and the question was what we should do. The question was how we should maneuver them into the position of firing the first shot without allowing too much danger to ourselves.

President Roosevelt insisted that Secretary of State Hull hand the harsh White-Morgenthau ultimatum to the Japanese ambassador Nomura the next day, November 26. The ultimatum—the immediate withdrawal of all Japanese army, air, naval, and even police forces from China, Vietnam and North Korea, and Japan's break with its September 1940 pact with Germany and Italy—was an insult that left the Japanese, a proud people, with no alternative but to fight.

After reading the White-Morgenthau proposals, the Japanese diplomats, Admiral Nomura and Saburo Kurusu, were stunned; they had expected to negotiate a *modus vivendi* with the United States in the Far East. Secretary of State Hull, under strong pressure from Roosevelt, declined to engage in further negotiations. Kurusu replied that Hull's statement was "tantamount to meaning the end."

The Japanese militarists had no love for the United States, but they realized its tremendous potential strength and wanted to avoid a ruinous war if peace with honor could be maintained. This was the position too of our ambassador in Tokyo, Joseph Grew, but he was unable to convince Roosevelt to join the prime minister of Japan in a peace conference. Instead, Roosevelt spent the months leading up to Pearl Harbor stalling for time so that our army and navy could strengthen their defenses in the Philippines and elsewhere. The Japanese finally set a deadline. That day was November 29, and Roosevelt knew of it because we had cracked the Japanese codes.

On November 28, two days after the presentation of the drastic war ultimatum, Stimson discussed with FDR what measures might be taken against Japan. "I told him," Stimson wrote in his diary,

> there was an important coalition of facts and that I thought he ought to read it before his appointment which he had made for us at 12.00 o'clock, when the so-called War Cabinet was to meet him—Hull, Knox, myself with Stark and Marshall. He branched into an analysis of the situation himself as he sat there on his bed, saying there were three alternatives and only three that he could see before us. I told him I could see only two. His alternatives were— first, to do nothing; second, to make something in the nature of an ulti- matum again, stating a point beyond which we would fight; third, to fight at once. I told him my only two were the last two, because I did not think anyone would do nothing in this situation, and he agreed with me. I said of the other two my choice was the latter one.

Two days later, on November 30, Stimson met with Knox to discuss further measures that they could take against Japan:

> Later in the evening Knox came over and we talked over the situation and made a draft for the finale of whatever message is used. This was in the shape of a virtual ultimatum to Japan that we cannot permit her to take any further steps of aggression against any of the countries in the southwest Pacific including China.

In his diary, Stimson revealed an incredible sense of relief, tinged with smugness, when he discovered that the Japanese had finally been provoked into war with the United States:

> Today is the day that the Japanese are going to bring their answer to Hull, and everything in MAGIC [our codebreaker] indicated they had been keeping the

time back until now in order to accomplish something hanging in the air. . . . Hull is very certain that the Japs are planning some deviltry and we are all wondering where the blow will strike. . . . [T]he president called me on the telephone and in a rather excited voice to ask me, "Have you heard the news? . . . They have attacked Hawaii." Well, that was excitement indeed. We three all thought that we must fight if the British fought. But now the Japs have solved the whole thing by attacking us directly in Hawaii. When the news first came that Japan had attacked us, my first feeling was of relief that the indecision was over and that a crisis had come in a way which would unite all our people. This continued to be my dominant feeling in spite of the news of catastrophes which quickly developed. . . . I advocated the view that we should ask for a declaration of war against Germany also.

FDR's unconstitutional ultimatum was deliberately withheld from Congress until after Pearl Harbor—until, that is, Congress had no choice but to rally round the president. Not until 1945, when Stimson's diary was made public, would the American people learn how they had been deceived by their own president into joining in a war they didn't want. Not until then would they learn that Roosevelt and his coterie had deliberately repudiated their solemn oaths of office, had, in fact, committed treason against their own country.

In 1945, during the Yalta Conference, Roosevelt admitted to Churchill that if it had not been for the Japanese attack at Pearl Harbor "he would have had great difficulty in getting the American people into war." Churchill, of course, had been tremendously pleased by the Japanese attack: "Now at this very moment I knew the United States was in the war, up to the neck and in to the death. So we had won after all!"

A final note: On December 15, 1941, one week after the Japanese attack on Pearl Harbor, Treasury Secretary Henry Morgenthau issued the following order:

> On and after this date, Mr. Harry Dexter White, Assistant to the Secretary, will assume full responsibility for all matters with which the Treasury Department has to deal having a bearing on foreign relations. Mr. White will act as a liaison between the Treasury Department and the State Department, will serve in the capacity of advisor to the Secretary on all Treasury foreign affair matters, and will assume responsibility for the management and operation of the Stabilization Fund without change in existing procedures. Mr. White will report directly to the Secretary.

We were to hear more of Harry Dexter White.

Chapter Seventeen

The Morgenthau Plan

In September 1944, at the second Quebec Conference, Henry Morgenthau, secretary of the Treasury, unveiled his plan for controlling—destroying would be a better way of describing it—postwar Germany. Morgenthau, whose name became attached to this monstrous plan, was the son of a wealthy Dutchess County (New York) landholder. Like his father, Henry Morgenthau looked the part of a country squire, self-assured and exuding the confidence that came with his social, educational, and economic background. Judging from his appearance, one would have thought him incapable of inflicting harm or punishment on any human being. But looks proved deceptive.

President Roosevelt's instructions to Morgenthau left no doubt as to FDR's desires for the future of Germany. In early September, Roosevelt told Morgenthau, "Germany should be allowed no aircraft of any kind, not even a glider . . . nobody should be allowed to wear a uniform, and there would be no marching, and that would do more to teach the Germans than anything else that they had been defeated."

With the approval and backing of FDR, Morgenthau proposed to carry the destruction of Germany many steps further, turning Germany into an agrarian state by eliminating all industry in the Ruhr and Saar basins. Just prior to the conference, Morgenthau told aides that "the only thing . . . I will have any part of, is the complete shut-down of the Ruhr. . . . Just strip it. I don't care what happens to the population. . . . I would take every mine, every mill and factory and wreck it. . . . Steel, coal, everything. Just close it down. . . . I am for destroying first and we will worry about the population second. . . . Why the hell should I worry about what happens to their people?" The Germans, said Morgenthau, should be reduced to a "subsistence level of food . . . soup kitchens would be ample to sustain life."

The Morgenthau Plan was vindictiveness run amok. To have punished all the German people for the crimes committed by a handful of their leaders would have been a gross miscarriage of justice. I personally believe that the majority of the German people never knew anything about Hitler's secret extermination of the Jews. Even if they had, there was little they could have done to have stopped it in time of war. Even my friend Bernard Baruch, who was Jewish, came to realize that if the drastic provisions of the Morgenthau Plan were carried out, the very existence of Germany would have been placed in jeopardy. He understood that an economically revitalized Germany was necessary to stop the march of communism, not just in Germany but throughout Europe.

Despite the strong objections made against the plan by Secretary of State Cordell Hull and Secretary of War Henry Stimson, Roosevelt gave it his wholehearted endorsement. Hull stated that the plan angered him "as much as anything that I had happen during my career as secretary," adding that it was an act of "blind vengeance . . . it failed to see that in striking at Germany it was striking at Europe." Not surprisingly, the secretary of state was not invited to attend the Quebec Conference. As for Secretary of War Stimson, he was in "violent disagreement" with Roosevelt when he learned that the president had agreed to Morgenthau's plan for the destruction of Germany. (Quotes from Forrestal Papers, Mudd Library, Princeton, New Jersey)

On August 25, 1944, Roosevelt, Morgenthau, Stimson, and Secretary of the Navy James Forrestal met to discuss plans for postwar Germany. Forrestal, a close friend of Roosevelt's, wrote a detailed account of the meeting in his diary. He noted that Roosevelt wanted the Germans "stripped clean." Stimson, however, protested, arguing that Germany was an industrialized nation and efforts made to dismantle Germany's industry would in effect destroy it. Later, Stimson angrily charged that he had "yet to meet a man who is not horrified at the 'Carthaginian' attitude of the Treasury." The administration, Stimson argued, was laying the "seeds for another war in the next generation" (Forrestal Papers, Mudd Library, Princeton, New Jersey).

On September 14, 1944, Morgenthau presented his plan at a state dinner in Quebec, Canada. Attending the dinner were Morgenthau,

Franklin Roosevelt, and Winston Churchill. The main points of the plan called for the removal from Germany of all industrial machinery, the permanent closing of all mines, cession of the Saar and Rhineland industrial areas to France, and most damaging of all, cession of East Prussia to Poland. It would also withhold economic aid, food, clothing, and other relief supplies to the German people.

The real author of the Morgenthau Plan was Harry Dexter White, assistant secretary of the Treasury. The communists, needless to say, had a special interest in crippling Germany—the Soviets' chief competitor for influence in Eastern and Central Europe. Not only was White "in charge of all foreign affairs as they affected the Treasury Department," Eugene Davidson notes in his excellent and well-documented book *The Death and Life of Germany*, "he was Morgenthau's alternate on the Economic Defense Board, and in charge of economic policy for Germany." Davidson continues:

> The Morgenthau plan itself bears a strong resemblance to the proposal of the Soviet economist Eugene Varga, published in Russia in 1943 under the title "War and the Working Class," which foresaw the dismantling of industrial plants and equipment for reparations, and denial of all economic aid to Germany, including food, clothing, and means for the repair of devastation. In addition, the Varga plan included the confiscation of all German property held abroad.

No wonder Churchill was aghast as he listened to Morgenthau dispassionately explain his proposed plan. "I am all for disarming Germany," Churchill interjected, "but we ought not prevent her living decently. There are bonds between the working classes of all countries, and the English people will not stand the policy you are advocating" (*Triumph and Tragedy*).

Churchill's opposition to the plan failed to budge Roosevelt and Morgenthau, who remained adamantly committed to it. And they held an economic trump card. On September 15, Roosevelt informed the British that he would not agree to further economic assistance unless Great Britain agreed to the plan. Still dependent on Lend-Lease aid and desperate for even greater American economic assistance, Great Britain was in no position to pressure Roosevelt to abandon the Morgenthau Plan, and Churchill reluctantly acquiesced and gave his approval to the plan.

I myself bitterly opposed the Morgenthau Plan, because of its inhumanity and because it would have played into the hands of Joseph Stalin. Among other predictable evil consequences, the plan would likely have resulted in enormous unemployment and potential recruits for the Communist party.

Former Kansas governor Alf Landon was another who denounced the Morgenthau Plan in no uncertain terms. "We must reverse our policies in Germany," he warned, "and abandon the evil Morgenthau plan, whose principles are the enemy of God, of decency, of mercy, and of common sense, if we are to build a durable peace."

On March 24, 1924, I introduced a resolution, "Providing Relief for Starving German Women and Children," in a speech before Congress (Congressional Record, 1924), which passed the House by a vote of 240 to 97. If anyone had good reason to hate the Germans it was I. I had fought them in the trenches of France, and I had experienced the horrors that war produces. But when the war ended, I welcomed the end of human carnage. It was a time to end the senseless killing; it was a time to promote peace. "This bill will do more than the League of Nations has done in five years," I said on the floor of the House, "to promote peace and good will in the world. It is sound policy, high policy, American policy. We recognize our obligation to help others." I went on:

> It will not only save the 2,000,000 children who are starving as we stand here discussing this bill but it will promote peace and good will and friendly relations with Germany. What is needed in the world today is the triumph of the gospel of good will over hatred and revenge. There can be no peace in the world until there is a desire for peace based upon reconciliation, cooperation, and justice. This is an investment in humanity and civilization, and its dividends will be good will and peace.

Having never served in combat during World War I, neither Morgenthau nor White could understand any of this. Their understanding of war was a detached one—that of a bureaucrat many miles removed from the scene of death on the field of battle who reads the sanitized accounts of warfare but can never feel or experience the agony of fighting on a foreign battlefield.

I felt no differently during the Second World War, and in 1943 I introduced two bills for European food relief. One of them, approved the following year, provided large-scale relief to France, Belgium, the Netherlands, Norway, Poland, Greece, Yugoslavia, Czechoslovakia, and other nations that had been invaded and occupied. The relief saved millions of lives, particularly the lives of many children, and gave people hope who might otherwise have succumbed to the siren song of communism.

The fate of the Morgenthau Plan was decided after Roosevelt's death by his successor Harry Truman. Heeding the advice of Henry Stimson and former president Herbert Hoover, who to his lasting credit remained a deeply committed humanitarian, Truman shelved the plan on May 18, 1945. Truman, who had never lacked for common sense, like most Americans, had been opposed to the plan from the beginning but, unfortunately, had not been part of Roosevelt's inner circle of advisors. But once he became president, he acted forcefully and courageously to restore Europe as a strong economic partner of the United States and a bulwark against the spread of communism.

Chapter Eighteen

The Crucifixion of Poland

In relating the story of the tragic murder of Poland, I must first disclose my personal ties to it. My great-grandmother, Susan Livingston, was married to Count Julian Ursyn Niemcewicz in 1800. He was one of the foremost Poles in history. Author, poet, historian, soldier, and statesman, he is credited with writing the famous Polish Constitution of 1791 that brought freedom and democracy to the brave people of that troubled land. He adopted his wife's only son, Peter Kean (from whom I am descended), by her former marriage to John Kean, whose death had left her a widow. John Kean's great-grandson, incidently, is Thomas Kean, who was elected governor of New Jersey in 1982. Whether my great-grandmother's marriage to Julian Niemcewicz makes me Polish by adoption is an academic question, but Niemcewicz claimed that his adoption of her son was for all time.

Another reason for my warm feelings towards Poland was my late second wife, Marie, who, although of Russian origin, had a Polish grandmother of the famous Chartoryski family and a Polish great-grandmother, Countess Pokorski of Galicia, once a part of South Poland.

On January 15, 1940, I introduced a joint resolution to provide $10 million "for the relief of the distressed and starving women and children of Poland." I pointed out that one-third of the population of Poland was "literally starving, without proper food or clothing, and in view of the fact that there seems to be no immediate prospects of improvement of these conditions among the Polish people who have always been friends of the

United States, we should contribute of our surplus foodstuffs in the United States."

I was heartened to receive support for my efforts on behalf of Poland from Herbert Hoover. On February 11, 1940, former President Hoover sent me part of a speech he had delivered the day before outlining the difficulties of Polish relief:

> We are faced today with a gigantic task of alleviating the sufferings of the people of Poland. There are destruction and suffering in Poland that I could not adequately portray even if I wished to do so. Millions of people must have food; they must have clothing; they must have shelter. Whatever can be done by public charity must be done. But before the next harvest, imports of food from abroad on a large scale must be found. It may cost as much as $20 million. Charity can be of great aid, but starvation can be prevented only by the cooperation of governments.
>
> With views to securing this cooperation I joined last fall in organizing the Commission for Relief in Poland. Its primary purpose was to serve the people of German-occupied Poland. It has the presidency of Mr. McCormick and the direction of Richard Pate, both of whom so ably administered the relief of Poland in 1919.
>
> This problem must be understood by you to whom it is so vital. In order for it to succeed the following conditions must be met:
>
> First: Supplies to German-occupied Poland must pass the British blockade. The British must be guaranteed that these supplies are going to the Polish people and not to their enemy.
>
> Second: Any supplies must be transported over German territory and the German authorities must cooperate to give the necessary guarantees.

Hoover worked tirelessly on behalf of Polish relief. Somehow he was able to persuade the German government to permit the relief supplies through. But tragically, all of our efforts to feed the starving Poles were blocked by Winston Churchill who refused to allow relief ships through the British blockade of European ports.

As disheartening as this was, we continued to do what we could. In March 1943, I introduced House Resolution 221 to provide food relief for Poland. The resolution passed on April 17, but realizing that even more support was needed, I appealed to the American people over national radio on April 26 to help feed the poor people of Poland.

I maintained my efforts to aid the suffering peoples of Europe throughout the war. The following year, I spoke to the American people in a radio address in an appeal to help feed the children in the occupied nations, including Poland, who were suffering horribly under the calamity of war and Nazi tyranny. I called upon the humanitarian impulses and moral responsibilities of the American people to help these innocent victims who were being abused by the twin terrors of starvation and disease. To those Americans who feared that feeding starving children in Europe would somehow help the Nazis, I quoted Dr. Howard E. Kershner, the director of the American Friends Service Committee:

> Hitler wages biological war. He seeks to destroy whole peoples and we play into his hands by doing nothing to save them. Those who survive will be subnormal in mind and body, unable to compete with the Germans in the reconstruction of Europe. The people who established the principles of free speech, free press, free religion, trial by jury, and all the institutions of free men are dying while the Nazis are still getting enough to eat. What will the future be if the people who believe in human freedom are not here when the war is over?
>
> It is not a choice between sending food to the children or sending more bombs, for the food would go in neutral ships that cannot be hired for the war effort, and would not cost the American people a dollar. No food needed for ourselves or our allies would be sent from this country. It could be brought from South America and South Africa. Half of what we waste here would save the lives of at least 10 million children.
>
> Impressive testimony was given by spokesmen for the occupied countries showing that the children are dying. In some areas over half of them have tuberculosis and others are threatened [by its spread]. They faint in the schoolrooms. They have stopped growing, are tragically underweight, have no breakfast, a small piece of bread for lunch, with an onion or a turnip, and vegetable soup for supper—perhaps one small portion of meat a week. Millions of children are getting no more than 700 to 900 calories of food daily, about one-third of what we give our children, and not enough to sustain life over a long period of time. I have seen these children with starvation bloated stomachs. I have seen their blue lips and bloodless faces, their rickety legs and hollow chests. Their sad little eyes accuse us of murder. I have heard the tubercular cough mingled with the cry for bread, and I can never forget it.

This was the tragic cost of war. This was why Roosevelt should have done everything in his power to encourage a diplomatically negotiated peace rather than to plunge the United States into worldwide conflagration, the only outcome of which could be untold human misery.

The Congress of the United States, I pointed out, had done its part to help bring succor to these helpless children:

In the Senate, the Gillette-Taft Bill was adopted [by unanimous vote], calling upon the State Department to use its influence to persuade the British government to relax the blockade against food ships. The House of Representatives, also by a unanimous vote, passed House Resolution 221, introduced by me, which was practically the same as the Senate Resolution, except that it specifically included France as one of the occupied countries to which relief was to be sent along with Belgium, Holland, Norway, Poland, and other occupied nations.

The time for action has come. Every week that passes endangers the lives of untold thousands. I am giving the Macedonian cry for help to American men and women, and am asking them to write to Secretary of State Cordell Hull, at Washington, and request him to use his influence with the British government to carry out the purposes of my Resolution to provide immediate relief to the starving women and children in the occupied nations of Europe.

I am asking you to communicate with Secretary Hull because American public opinion is the greatest and most powerful moral force and influence in the world today. I am convinced that if American citizens make known their views and sentiments in favor of feeding the children in the stricken and hungry nations that have been invaded by the Nazi armies, that the British government will relax the blockade and cooperate to save millions of helpless children from mass starvation within the next ten months.

I am proud to be the author of the Resolution, and doubly honored in having it reported and passed in my name, which is an unusual honor for a member of the minority Party in Congress. It goes to show that there is not the slightest degree of partisanship in it.

Now let me give you the facts and show you the motives that have impelled Congress and thousands of churchmen and leaders in all walks of life to demand that these helpless and innocent children who are facing death from disease and starvation be afforded immediate relief.

. . . The Resolution, without firm action by the State Department, would become a mere scrap of paper and a useless gesture.

I take it that it is the unanimous desire and purpose of the House of Representatives and the United States Senate to insist that the State Department make every possible effort to persuade the British government, our friendly ally, to relax the blockade to permit food to reach millions of destitute children who are now on the verge of starvation. Many of them have already died of starvation and dread diseases, such as rickets. Sixty-five percent of them have some form of incipient tuberculosis. Most of them will not survive another winter. . . .

. . . I know of no military reason for not permitting those occupied countries to buy food, or even for us to put up the money to buy food and let them buy it elsewhere, in Argentina, or South Africa, or wherever food may be had. We have a great moral responsibility in America. We cannot simply sit quietly and wash our hands like Pontius Pilate and let millions of innocent children die in the agony of starvation, with bloated stomachs, or die from some dread disease while we evade the issue and the moral responsibility as one of the partners in a war, with food abundant to save these unfortunate and helpless children from death or from living with twisted and distorted bodies and minds.

But one thing I want to make abundantly clear is that if one pound of this food goes to the German army, or goes to the German population, then we should stop [delivering food] immediately. . . .At least we would have made an honest effort. At least we would have carried out the desire of the American people to help these starving children. . . .

I reiterated the necessity for immediate action to prevent "the greatest tragedy of the war." But all the goodwill and humanitarian impulses of the American people and their elected members of Congress to do something to ease the suffering of Europe's children and the torment of Poland had no effect. Without the support of President Roosevelt, Polish relief efforts and the fate of a free, democratic Poland were doomed. At no time during the war did Roosevelt heed the cries of the suffering Poles or offer to lend them support. Why did he refuse to help the Poles? The most likely answer is Roosevelt's growing friendship with Stalin.

Only a year before I appealed for aid to Poland, the American-Polish National Council, composed of twenty-two organizations, appealed to President Roosevelt to uphold the Atlantic Charter pledges he had made in 1941 on behalf of national self-determination. "You know, Mr. Roosevelt, as well as we do," the Council reminded Roosevelt, "that Poland comes before the world tribunal with clean hands. Poland never broke any signed agreements with any nation. Poland has no quislings. She has a long record as a defender of Christianity, freedom, and democracy. She has no claims to somebody else's territory, but desires to regain what rightfully belongs to her. She is willing to cooperate with Russia, but not at the expense of losing her territory and liberty"—by which the Council meant Poland's eastern boundaries, which Stalin had swallowed, and which the Allies appeared content to let him keep.

The Council noted that Poland's eastern territories had not been added to the country through some ancient conquest, and certainly had never been taken "from the Grand Duchy of Moscow." These territories had . . .

> joined with the Kingdom of Poland as equal with equal, as brother with brother, and did it willingly, without any coercion, solely on the spontaneous and willful agreement, so-called "The Union of Horodolo in 1413." Since that time up to the present the eastern sections have been the "E Pluribus Unum" and an inseparable and indivisible unit and should stay thus forever. Besides this historic fact the eastern part of Poland is cooperating now with the western part of Poland in the secret-underground movement against the invading foe, as one nation.

The Council told Roosevelt that since the Russian occupation of eastern Poland, "Stalin's forces had rounded up 181,000 Polish officers and soldiers and put them in Russian prison camps. About two million Poles, including children and aged women, were deported as slaves to Russia to be tortured under inhuman conditions of enforced labor, without adequate clothing, food and shelter. Over half a million have already died."

Noting that "the United Nations are now fighting for freedom and democracy as outlined in the Atlantic Peace Charter," the Council asked Roosevelt if he would "intervene in behalf of the unfortunate Polish men and women and children who are being held as slaves by Soviet Russia."

But Roosevelt remained silent, refusing to intercede on behalf of Poland. Shortly after he received the written appeal he met with Czechoslovakia's President Edward Beneš (June 1943). Following the meeting Beneš said that FDR "was in general ready to accept the Russian standpoint, but the matter must be arranged in a manner which would give the least offense to American public opinion." Beneš also noted Roosevelt "believed that the Curzon Line represented an equitable solution to the Russian frontier problem"—the Soviet point of view.

Arthur Bliss Lane, FDR's ambassador to Poland, was so incensed by the president's callous treatment of Poland that he wrote a book entitled *I Saw Poland Betrayed*. Lane was aghast at Roosevelt's surrender—first at Teheran and then at Yalta—to Stalin's territorial demands, especially since such capitulation was in direct opposition to FDR's public pronouncements. During the 1944 presidential campaign, Roosevelt had promised Polish-Americans that "Poland must be reconstituted as a great nation. It is very important that the new Poland be one of the bulwarks of the structure upon which we hope to build a permanent peace."

Yet, Lane noted, Roosevelt conveniently failed to mention that when he gave these assurances to Polish-American voters, [FDR] did not recall that less than a year before he had, at the Teheran Conference, agreed to Stalin's plans for a Soviet-Polish frontier along the Curzon Line, which lopped off seventy thousand square miles of Polish territory, without consulting the Polish people or its constitutional government.

For the despairing Poles, the worst was yet to come. In early 1944, a physically ailing Roosevelt, along with Winston Churchill, met with Stalin at Yalta in the Crimea. "By President Roosevelt's own admission," Lane wrote, "the Yalta agreement with respect to Poland was a compromise. To put it more brutally, it was capitulation on the part of the United States and Great Britain to the views of the Soviet Union on the frontiers of Poland and on the composition of the Polish Provisional Government of National Unity." In short, FDR turned his back on the democratic Polish government-in-exile and gave his stamp of approval to Stalin's ruthless suppression of the Polish people.

Jan Ciechanowski, the author of *Defeat in Victory* and the man who succeeded Jerzy Potocki as Polish ambassador to the United States during World War II, says in his book that he

> was repeatedly told bluntly by the New Dealers of the palace guard that the appointment of Ambassador Lane to replace Biddle as American ambassador to the Polish government on September 2, 1944, was not only proof of the President's "abiding" interest in Poland but also a political move which they hoped would be reflected by the "Polish vote."

Ciechanowski writes that in spite of all these maneuvers, the Polish-American Congress, representing most voters of Polish extraction, was still doubtful about Roosevelt's intentions—until, that is, Roosevelt met with Charles Rozmarek, head of their organization, in Chicago on October 18, 1944. During that meeting, Ciechanowski reports, Roosevelt "definitely promised" Rozmarek "to take active steps to insure Poland's independence." Whereupon the main Polish-language press and the Polish-American Congress came out for Roosevelt's reelection for a fourth term.

Mikolajczyk, the great Polish peasant leader, went to Moscow in 1945 to see Stalin. He raised the question of Polish boundaries at a meeting that Averell Harriman and Prime Minister Winston Churchill attended. Ciechanowski tells the harrowing tale:

> At this point Molotov made a surprising statement. He said that he saw it was necessary to remind those present at Teheran [that] President Roosevelt

had expressed his complete agreement with the Curzon line as the Polish-Soviet frontier and regarded it as a just solution which should be satisfactory both to the Soviet Union and to Poland and that the president had merely added that, for the time being, he preferred his agreement on this point should not be made public.

Molotov . . . turned to Churchill and Harriman and challenged them to deny his statement . . . "because it appears to me," he said, "that Mr. Mikolajczyk is not aware of this fact and is still in doubt regarding the position of America on this subject."

Molotov paused dramatically . . . to see if anyone would take up his challenge, which no one did.

Look at the dates. Roosevelt had agreed, as Molotov said, to the Curzon line on December 1, 1943, but all through 1944 he was telling the Poles another story.

In the spring of 1945, Bishop Richard J. Cushing delivered an impassioned speech, "A Plea for Poland," in which he described in chilling detail the tragic results of Roosevelt's false promises to the Polish people:

> While freedom is being won and city after city is being liberated throughout the world, it is sad to note that those who first suffered the impact of the invader, and who have never given up the struggle, appear destined to be mercilessly crushed in their attempt to regain their freedom. I speak of the heroic people of Poland.
>
> Against seeming insurmountable difficulties and in the face of almost certain defeat, the Poles fought on. Almost one million of their soldiers gave their lives on every battle front of Europe. In Poland itself the losses are said to be approximately 5,700,000. Of this number, 3,500,000 are reported to have been executed, murdered, or to have died in concentration camps, in prisons, or in gas chambers. Two hundred thousand are said to be in prison camps and the remaining two million are listed as deported to forced labor in foreign lands. England's prime minister has said that Poland contributed immeasurably to save Great Britain. Our late president once called Poland the "inspiration of nations." We are hopeful that those who owe Poland a debt of gratitude will demand justice for her.
>
> Today Russia claims that she must have at least half of the country for her own security. According to prewar statistics Russia is 54 times the size of Poland, twice the size of all the rest of Europe, about three times the size of the continental United States. She has one-sixth of the land area of the globe. Poland has one-third of 1 percent of the earth with 35,000,000 people, while Russia counted 170,467,000 people. Since the war Russia has taken over much more territory and millions more in population. It is hard for me to

follow the reasoning that Russia needs a goodly part of Poland for her security. The problem came before the three great victorious powers in the Crimean [Yalta] Conference. The solution was a disappointment to all who had built their hopes on the Atlantic Charter.

The Polish people had placed their hopes of freedom and democracy upon the Atlantic Charter. Little did the Poles know that all of their hopes would be dashed by the architect of that charter, Franklin Roosevelt, who sacrificed the brave and suffering Poles for the sake of maintaining a cordial relationship with Stalin.

Chapter Nineteen

Betrayal at Yalta

In February 1945, Roosevelt, Churchill, and Stalin met at the Yalta Conference in the Crimea and agreed that Russia would enter the war against Japan. Admiral William D. Leahy, Roosevelt's personal chief of staff, advised against making concessions to bring Stalin into the war in the East. General George C. Marshall, on the other hand, did not. But he was both an ardent supporter of FDR and beholden to him for past favors—he would have supported war against Patagonia if Roosevelt had urged it. Marshall later became an appeaser of the Chinese communists, with dire and tragic consequences.

Also among the president's staff at Yalta was Edward Stettinius, recently appointed secretary of state to replace Cordell Hull, who had resigned. The most important staff member, however, was Harry Hopkins, who had little or no knowledge of foreign affairs, but who played a vital part in most of the major conferences. Hopkins and Alger Hiss sat directly behind FDR at all the Yalta meetings and kept up a continuous exchange of notes with him. Four years later, Alger Hiss was convicted of perjury for denying that he had supplied secret documents to a communist spy ring and was sent to prison. The same Alger Hiss testified before a congressional committee, "It is an accurate and not immodest statement to say that I helped formulate the Yalta agreements to some extent."

The United States ambassador to the Soviet Union, Averell Harriman, was under the misapprehension that Stalin was merely a Russian nationalist and not a treacherous mass murderer who believed in communism

(Raymond Dawson, *The Decision to Aid Russia, 1941*). Harriman later admitted before a congressional committee that he also played an important part in the decisions at Yalta. Moreover, according to Nicholas Baciu in his book *Sell-Out to Stalin*, Averell Harriman played a key role in Stalin's absorption of Eastern Europe. Since Harriman believed that Stalin was a friend of the United States and could be trusted—despite all the massive evidence to the contrary—he "demanded . . . recognition of the Russian government installed by Vishinsky in Bucharest. . . .When [Harriman] went to Bucharest in 1946, it was not to 'reconcile' and 'smooth' things, but to convince the Rumanian people to accept Russian domination."

Roosevelt's great failing was in not recognizing his own limitations. He thought he could handle "Uncle Joe" Stalin, though the dictator hoodwinked Roosevelt repeatedly—giving up nothing, taking everything. The betrayal of Poland, the Morgenthau Plan, sacrificing principle for the sake of bringing the Soviet Union into the proposed United Nations—all these decisions were made by Roosevelt to appease Stalin. Our mentally tired and physically sick president turned the Yalta Conference into the greatest communist victory since Lenin seized control of Soviet Russia from the Kerensky regime in 1917.

Prime Minister Winston Churchill and British Foreign Secretary Anthony Eden did not fare much better. Churchill was much more vigorous in his opposition to communism than Roosevelt, because he saw international communism as a force that could strangle the lifelines of the British Empire and stir up rebellion and civil war. Churchill states in his book, *Triumph and Tragedy*, that on October 21, 1942, he wrote to Anthony Eden, "It would be a measureless disaster if Russian barbarism overweighed the culture and independence of the ancient states of Europe." To prevent such a disaster, Churchill asked the Americans to join in an invasion of the Balkans, but FDR refused, apparently because Stalin opposed it.

There was little, however, that Churchill could do to stave off catastrophe at Yalta because his country was the weakest of the Big Three. Churchill's one success—won through persistent negotiation—was to obtain for France the right to participate in one of the four spheres of military control in Germany.

In his memoirs, Churchill explained his dilemma in dealing with Stalin:

The United States stood on the scene of victory, master of world fortunes, but without a true and coherent design. Britain, though still powerful, could not act decisively alone. I could at this stage only warn and plead. Thus, this . . . was a most unhappy time. I moved amid cheering crowds with an aching heart and a mind oppressed with foreboding.

Here indeed was a paradox: The moment of victory was for the victor Churchill "a most unhappy time."

The lone conqueror at the Yalta Conference was Stalin. Britain and the United States gained nothing and lost everything. The United States lost a million casualties and billions of dollars in war expenditures. Great Britain lost half its empire, endured huge casualties, and was brought to near bankruptcy. Though the Atlantic Charter stood as noble testimony to the ideals of the United States and Great Britain, both countries capitulated to Stalin and permitted the downgrading of freedom and the upgrading of totalitarian communism on a gigantic scale.

When President Roosevelt spoke in Congress with regard to the agreements reached at Yalta, he stated that no secret concessions had been made. Several weeks afterwards—with FDR dead and Harry Truman president—Truman discovered, locked away in a safe, agreements FDR had made to give two Chinese cities and Japan's Kurile islands to the Soviet Union. It was for reasons such as this, perhaps, that the Yalta agreements were never submitted to the Senate for ratification. It also points out the extent to which Roosevelt was willing to mislead the American people for the sake of maintaining his "friendship" with Stalin. Secretary of the Navy James Forrestal, in his book, *The Forrestal Diaries*, noted that Stalin "had good reasons for liking FDR because he got out of him the Yalta agreement, anything he asked for during the war, and finally, an opportunity to push communist propaganda into the United States and throughout the world." Forrestal, by the way, was a Democrat.

Forrestal was right. The communist advances were enormous. Eastern Europe had been handed over, and shortly thereafter the communists conquered China, North Korea, and North Vietnam. The advance continued: fifteen years later they would gain a beachhead in the Americas by seizing Cuba. In fact, they were active everywhere around the globe, one of their key objectives being to encircle and undermine the United States. It was not until the Reagan administration that the tide began to turn—the communist system began to collapse and its armies to retreat. But communism's troubles were in the future. In 1945, American surrender and communist subversion were continuing apace. Harry Hopkins, for example, was assailed in Congress as the Rasputin of the White House for lifting the ban on communists in the officer corps. As Walter Trohan reported in the *Washington Times Herald* on March 10, 1945: "The House Military Affairs subcommittee, investigating appointment of officers who had communist records, was informed that the change in policy originated at the door of the number-one White House intimate." Nor did he bother to hide his feelings. In fact, in his public statements, Hopkins made clear his sympathy for Stalin and the Soviet Union. Six months after the Yalta Conference, when Stalin had already utterly ignored his commitments by communizing Poland, Czechoslovakia, Hungary, and other Eastern European nations, Harry Hopkins made this incredible statement: "We know or believe Russia's interests, so far as we can anticipate them, do not afford any opportunity for a major difference with us in foreign affairs."

Three or four months after Roosevelt's death, Hopkins issued this absurdity: "The Russian people think and act just like you and I do"— conveniently ignoring the fact that the Russian people were enslaved and terrorized by a government devoted to spreading world revolution. As Congressman Dewey Short—a Republican from Missouri and former Methodist minister—noted in an address to the House on July 13, 1946:

> The communists are at war with the rest of the world. They do mean to destroy all other governments. And they will do all these things if the rest of us let them win through default.
>
> If you are in doubt, just take a look at the record. Have a look in Bulgaria, Romania, Greece, Hungary, Austria, Germany, Czechoslovakia, Poland, Finland, France, Italy, China, Korea, just to mention a few in which communist policy has come out from under cover.
>
> Take note of the accomplishments of J. Stalin at Tehran, Yalta, and Potsdam.
>
> Think over the performances of his man Gromyko before the United Nations Security Council and add to all this the gradually toughening words of Britain's Foreign Minister Bevin and our own Secretary of State Jimmy Byrnes.
>
> Just why do you suppose the sweetness and light has so quickly faded from the postwar world now that Russian communism has become increasingly powerful in world politics? No, communism is not a joke in 1946. . . .

It was also no joke to Chiang Kai-shek and the Chinese Nationalists, whose interests had also been betrayed by Roosevelt at Yalta. The evidence is overwhelming that the concessions of Chinese territory that Roosevelt made to Stalin were made secretly and without the knowledge of Chiang

Kai-shek. Roosevelt's desire to be Stalin's friend blinded him to all other considerations. In his excellent book, *Roosevelt's Road to Russia*, George M. Crocker says that the argument that Roosevelt made the concessions on the basis of military advice had always been a sham. The decisions were Roosevelt's alone.

One of the most dishonorable aspects of the agreement on China was the statement that "The heads of the three great powers had agreed that these claims of the Soviet Union shall be unquestionably fulfilled after Japan had been defeated." This meant that Roosevelt would compel Churchill to go along with him in forcing Chiang Kai-shek to acquiesce to the surrender of Manchuria, Darien, and Port Arthur. Churchill emphasized that he was in no way responsible for FDR's action in selling out the Republic of China. "It was regarded as an American affair. . . . We were not consulted but only asked to approve."

Eden, in fact, was flabbergasted when he saw the secret pact agreed on by Stalin and Roosevelt. He urged Churchill to refuse to sign, but Churchill did not dare antagonize or anger either Roosevelt or Stalin on such an issue, as "the whole position of the British Empire in the Far East might be at stake." Roosevelt was threatening to hand over Hong Kong to China. Churchill also foresaw that if Darien and Port Arthur were given to Russia, the attempt to cut Britain out of Hong Kong would be untenable.

Even the faithful Robert Sherwood condemned this agreement as "the most assailable point in the entire Yalta record, because if China had refused to agree to any of the Soviets' claims, presumably the United States and Britain would have been compelled to join in enforcing them." Sherwood sought to defend the president by adding that "Roosevelt would not have agreed to that final firm commitment had it not been that the Yalta Conference was almost at an end and he was tired and anxious to avoid further argument." FDR may have been tired, but he had been a tired man and a sick man long before he was nominated and elected for his final term as president. Nor can his physical condition in any way excuse his betrayal of an ally. If his health was so disabling, he should not have been in his powerful position in the first place.

Unfortunately, General Marshall was consistently wrong on all issues involving China. This was probably due to the advice given him by the pro-communists in the Far Eastern Division of the State Department.

I am unwilling to believe that General Marshall, a graduate of the Virginia Military Institute and a successful officer in the United States army, was pro-communist.

Marshall later insisted that Chiang Kai-shek bring communist leaders into his government and communist troops into his army. On Chiang's refusal, he stopped shipment of all arms to Chiang's army, ensuring its defeat. Marshall, who headed the mission to China, described the tragic act: "As chief of staff I armed thirty-nine anticommunist divisions. And now with a stroke of a pen, I disarmed them."

The Russians had entered the war on August 8, 1945 knowing that the Japanese were ready to surrender on terms protecting their emperor. The Japanese had asked the Soviets to act as intermediaries with the United States, but the Russians kept quiet and merely joined what they knew would be a short Asian war to plunder as much as possible. On obtaining a tremendous supply of surrendered Japanese arms, the Soviets turned them over to the Chinese communists who put them to use against the anticommunists General Marshall had decided not to support.

Later on, as secretary of defense, Marshall testified before a Senate committee on May 8, 1951, that "our purpose in Korea was to bleed the Chinese till they got tired and cried halt." These were the very same Chinese communists Marshall had asked Chiang Kai-shek to accept into his forces. Because we would not support Chiang in his fight against them, we were now fighting the Chinese communists ourselves. And our strategy? To bleed to death one of the most overpopulated countries in the world. Of all the cockeyed absurdities, this wins top honors. It was the acme of military ineptitude and sheer ignorance.

Ignorance and ineptitude seemed to be in great supply among the men of Roosevelt's administration. The historian John A. Flynn, in his book *The Roosevelt Myth,* summed up what happened at Yalta:

Stalin got everything he wanted—everything without any exception. Churchill did not, because Roosevelt in pursuit of his vain policy sided with Stalin against Churchill. Roosevelt got nothing. . . . He got, of course, the United Nations. But this had already been settled on before he went to Teheran. And what is more, this was no victory, because Stalin got the United Nations precisely on his own terms and in a form that enabled him to put his finger into every problem in the world and to completely frustrate the British and Americans in every effort to introduce order, peace and security.

At home, Roosevelt's red and pink collaborators and his closest consultants were busy pouring out Soviet propaganda. Harry Hopkins never tired of plugging for his friend Stalin. Henry Wallace, then vice president, was talking about encouraging a people's revolution in Europe to advance the cause of the common man. . . . All this had been instigated and urged by Roosevelt himself. And no one knew this better than Stalin.

On the day that President Roosevelt left for Warm Springs, embittered by Stalin's refusal to abide by the agreements made at Yalta, he asked Mr. Leo T. Crowley, administrator of foreign aid, how much Lend-Lease had been given to the Allies since the start of the war. Mr. Crowley replied, "Over 40 billion dollars worth." Roosevelt then asked, "How much did we give the Russians?" "About 11 billion." The president said, "I have yet to get any concessions from Stalin," and added, "Leo, we are getting down to the tail end of the war. I do not want you to let out any more long-term contracts on Lend-Lease. Further, I want you to cut off the Lend-Lease the moment Germany is defeated. Don't wait for any further orders. Just cut it off the day Germany surrenders" (Jim Bishop, *FDR's Last Year*. New York: William Morrow, 1974.)

Evidently the president did not tell anyone else about his decision; obviously he felt that Stalin had betrayed him in violating their agreements. These angry instructions to Mr. Crowley showed the president's determination to exact revenge, but too little and too late. Stalin had already begun to communize the captive nations. The tragic result brings to mind a passage from John Milton: "Tears, such as angels weep, burst forth. Which, if not victory, is yet revenge."

Chapter Twenty

Selling Out Europe

The story of how China was lost to the communists and Eastern Europe surrendered to Stalin is fairly well known. Less well known is that Franklin Roosevelt was prepared to give Western Europe to the Soviets as well.

On September 3, 1943, three months before the Teheran Conference, President Roosevelt met with his close friend Bishop (later Cardinal) Francis J. Spellman and outlined his plan to give Stalin control of continental Europe. President Roosevelt told Bishop Spellman that

> although it might be wishful thinking that Russian intervention might not be too harsh, it is probable that the communist regime will expand—France might eventually escape if it had a government á la Leon Blum. The Front Populaire would be so advanced that eventually the communists might accept it.

Bishop Spellman—whom I knew personally and regarded as a man of the highest integrity—took copious notes and wrote out a precise account of this conversation, which was reproduced in *The Cardinal Spellman Story* by the Reverend Robert Gannon. Bishop Spellman merely recorded what Roosevelt told him; the memorandum contains no comments of his own. The extracts that follow come under the heading "Russia." Roosevelt began by giving away the land of some of the most courageous people on earth.

Stalin would certainly receive Finland, the Baltic states, the eastern half of Poland and Bessarabia. Furthermore, the population of eastern Poland want to become Russian.

The president then proceeded to give away the rest of the world as well.

China gets the Far East; U.S. the Pacific; Britain and Russia get Europe and Africa. But as Britain has predominating colonial interests, it might be assumed that Russia will predominate in Europe. . . .

President Roosevelt went on to say:

We should not overlook the magnificent economic achievements of Russia. . . . Their finances are sound. It is natural that the European countries will have to undergo tremendous changes in order to adapt to Russia. The European people (which includes France, Belgium, Holland, Denmark and Norway, and of course our wartime enemies, Germany and Italy) will simply have to endure the Russian domination in the hope that in ten or twenty years they will be able to live well under the Russians.

In other words, more than a year and a half before the war had been won, and before any peace conferences had been held, FDR planned to give Europe to Russia as a sphere of influence, allowing it to act as a predominating force there.

The French, Belgians, Dutch, Danes, and Norwegians who had suffered the horrors of Nazi invasion and conquest, only to have FDR plan to hand them over to the Soviets, should have hanged him in effigy. His proposal was a travesty of Allied war aims, a mockery of the Atlantic Charter, and a repudiation of the sacrifices made by veterans of all the Allied powers.

Moreover, had continental Europe been dominated by the communists, British influence would have been nonexistent—the massive power of a communist Europe would have hung over Britain like the sword of Damocles.

Bishop Spellman also quotes Roosevelt as saying that "Russian production is so high that American help, except for trucks, is negligible." What an incredible and misleading statement. The truth is that the bulk of the Russian factories had been destroyed by the invading German armies. The United States loaned the Soviets eleven billion dollars, and under the terms of Lend-Lease sent them twenty thousand aircraft and close to 400,000 trucks—twice as many trucks as the Soviet Union had before the

Nazi invasion. This is not to mention the vast quantities of leather for shoes, cloth for uniforms, hundreds of miles of barbed wire and telephone lines, railroad locomotives, automobiles, food supplies on a huge scale, and equipment for setting up new industrial plants.

When Francis Spellman had this interview with Roosevelt, he had just returned from a six-month mission, as Roosevelt's personal representative, to Europe, Africa, and South America. The night before, he had dined at the White House with the president and Winston Churchill. It is difficult to believe that Churchill would have consented to these ruinous terms. If he did, it must have been in a limited and lukewarm way—while working quietly and effectively to undermine the whole project.

It is also hard to believe that this abominable plan was conceived by FDR alone. After all, among his advisors on foreign affairs were Harry Dexter White; Alger Hiss; Lauchlin Currie, his executive secretary, who was accused of being pro-communist; and Harry Hopkins, who got along with Stalin "like a house on fire" (Earl Lathan, *The Communist Controversies in Washington*; David Rees, *Harry Dexter White*; Allan Weinstein, *Perjury*).

Another factor might have been Roosevelt's strong animosity to General Charles de Gaulle. In a letter to Churchill on May 8, 1943, FDR accused de Gaulle of stirring up trouble in Algiers and said, "I do not know what to do with de Gaulle; possibly you would like to make him governor of Madagascar." Roosevelt went on to recommend the reorganizing of the French National Committee, the resistance movement de Gaulle headed. "I am sorry, but it seems to me the conduct of the bride [de Gaulle] continues to be more and more aggravating." The bridegroom, according to the president, was General Henri Giraud—Roosevelt's choice to replace de Gaulle.

In any event, FDR did not intend to let the French run their own affairs. Roosevelt wrote, "I am inclined to think when we get into France itself we will have to regard it as a military occupation run by British and American generals. . . . I think that this may be necessary for six months or even a year after we get into France." About 90 percent of the mayors and subordinate officials of French cities and departments could be used, Roosevelt suggested, "but the top line of national administration must be kept in the hands of the British and American commanders-in-chief. The old former government simply will not do."

Robert Sherwood noted in *Roosevelt and Hopkins* that FDR's charm was often marred by a large capacity for personal vindictiveness. He also had a penchant for sadism and demagoguery. As quoted in his book, *We Planned It That Way*, Frank Knox, writing two years before he accepted the appointment as secretary of the Navy under Roosevelt, said: " 'Sadistic anti-capitalism is illustrative of the methods used in the working out of the program Mr. Roosevelt 'had in mind long before he was even nominated.' It is also illustrative of the effectiveness of the New Deal's propaganda machine, once it swings into action. As already said, this is a political propaganda machine the like of which this country has never before seen." Whenever FDR was blocked in getting his way, he simply became a dictator. He recognized the Soviet Union without asking Congress for its approval, packed the Supreme Court when it rejected his unconstitutional policies, and, in an anti-capitalist fit, proposed a tax bill that would have created a top tax bracket of 98 percent and limited the amount of income a person could have. All this from a man who was elected in 1932 on a very conservative platform. But since then, Roosevelt found that he could increase his power by buying voters with government handouts. Roosevelt's political transformation from a Jeffersonian Democrat into an extreme leftist who surrounded himself with radicals, socialists, and pro-communists might have been a result of his ruthless passion for power. Even the creation of the United Nations could be viewed as a continuation of this passion, because Roosevelt intended to retire from the presidency of the United States and become president of the United Nations—president, that is, of the entire world.

Chapter Twenty-One

Speaking Out for the Jews

During my entire political career in Congress, a career that began in 1920 and ended in 1945, I was a consistent supporter of Jews, particularly their right to have a national homeland.

I introduced the Fish Palestine Resolution—House Joint Resolution 322—on June 20, 1922. It was passed by both the House and the Senate and was signed into law by President Harding on September 21, 1922, making it the permanent policy of the United States. My resolution pledged the United States to endorse the creation of a homeland in Palestine for East European Jewish refugees where they could enjoy a religious, civic, and cultural life of their own choosing, free from the oppression that they so frequently endured in Europe and elsewhere.

The return of the Jewish people to Zion has had the good wishes of our foremost American statesmen. President Wilson, in a letter dated August 31, 1918, wrote:

I welcome the opportunity to express the satisfaction I have felt in the progress of the Zionist movement in the United States and in the Allied countries. Since the Declaration of Mr. Balfour, on behalf of the British government, I welcome Great Britain's approval of the establishment in Palestine of a national home for the Jewish people, and his promise that the British government would use its best endeavors to facilitate the achievement of that object with the understanding that nothing would be done to

127

prejudice the civil and religious rights of non-Jewish people in Palestine or the rights and political status enjoyed by Jews in other countries.

President Harding also expressed his friendly interest in and for the Zionist movement when he said, on June 1, 1921: "It is impossible for one who has studied at all the services of the Hebrew people to avoid the faith that they will one day be restored to their historic national home and there enter on a new and yet greater phase of their contribution to the advancement of humanity." Again on May 11, 1922, President Harding wrote: "I am very glad to express my approval and hearty sympathy for the effort of the Palestine Foundation Fund in behalf of the restoration of Palestine as a homeland for the Jewish people."

My resolution was based partially on the Balfour Declaration, which was approved by the British cabinet in 1917. British Foreign Minister Arthur James Balfour wrote to Lord Rothschild on November 2, 1917, saying:

> I have much pleasure in conveying to you on behalf of his Majesty's government, the following declaration of sympathy with Jewish Zionist aspirations which has been submitted to, and approved by the Cabinet.
>
> His Majesty's government view with favour the establishment in Palestine of a national home for the Jewish people and will use their best endeavours to facilitate the achievement of this object, it being clearly understood that nothing shall be done which may prejudice the civil and religious rights of existing non-Jewish communities in Palestine or the rights and political status enjoyed by Jews in any other country.
>
> I should be grateful if you would bring this declaration to the knowledge of the Zionist Federation.

My resolution created a flow of hundreds of millions of dollars from organizations in the United States that helped purchase land in Palestine from 1922 to 1948 and provided homes for 400,000 Jewish refugees from Germany, Poland, Hungary, Romania, and the Soviet Union. In Palestine, these people could practice their religion and enjoy their own culture in the ancient land of their fathers given by Jehovah to Abraham and consecrated in the hearts of the Jewish people as the birthplace of their religion, traditions, and history.

When the British government started to ignore and undermine the Balfour Declaration in 1939 by limiting the number of Jewish immigrants to Palestine, I protested in Congress and sent a petition signed by fifteen of my colleagues to Secretary of State Cordell Hull. His letter in response showed that my resolution of 1922 was recognized by the State Department as the permanent policy of our country:

> I have received your letter of May 26, 1939, enclosing an extract from the Congressional Record containing the petition of fifteen members of Congress with reference to the Palestine question in the light of the British Government's statement of policy of May 17 regarding Palestine.
>
> I think you will find the treaty rights of the United States in relation to Palestine, clearly and explicitly set forth in the Department's public statement of October 14, 1938, as well as in a memorandum, copies of both of which are enclosed. The position of this Government as set forth in the statement of October 14, 1938, remains unaffected by any subsequent developments.
>
> The interest which our people have in Palestine, as reflected in that statement and as manifested and limited by the debates which took place on June 30, 1922 . . . [on the Fish Palestine Resolution] continues to be borne in mind by the Department. We have kept that interest constantly before the British Government, which is fully aware of public opinion on the matter in this country.

The issue did not end there, for in 1944 the British government issued a white paper that proposed cutting off all Jewish immigration into Palestine. On February 8, 1944, I stood on the floor of the House, "prompted by the beatings of my heart and the impulses of my mind," to condemn this betrayal of the Balfour Declaration. I reminded the House of my role in sponsoring the so-called Zionist resolution that placed Congress and the American people in favor of the establishment of a Jewish homeland in Palestine.

I then shared with the House just two of the more than one thousand telegrams I had received from my constituents asking me to protect this British white paper. Seymour S. Cohen, president of the Newburgh Jewish Community Council, recalled my sponsorship of the Lodge-Fish resolution of a quarter century ago, as

> one of the finest actions taken during your lengthy public service. Today, as never before, it is vital that the United States publicly and officially stand back of Prime Minister Churchill, who has always been a friend of world Jewry, in voiding the dastardly white paper which threatens cessation of immigration into Palestine. . . . Alleged suspensions of the white paper as reported in the press, is a subterfuge. It merely extends visa rights to several thousand immigrants, but closes the door to multi-thousands who, if denied

entry where wanted, will die the Hitlerian death. Establishment of the Jewish commonwealth, as urged in the Lodge-Fish resolution in 1922, is paramount today. . . . Palestine welcomes all the Nazi victims who can be transported, and, remember, the Mediterranean today is ours. I urge your valiant effort in this matter. . . .

I certainly gave it.

In my speech I noted that it "is eminently proper that American citizens should protest against the violation and betrayal of the Balfour Declaration by the British Government." I went on:

It must be self-evident to Jews and non-Jews alike that suspension of Jewish immigration into Palestine means that the homeland which was promised cannot be attained under the new British policy enunciated by the white paper. The establishment of a homeland in Palestine depends from the beginning to the end on permitting Jewish immigration into the ancient land of their fathers.

The action of the British in prohibiting Jewish immigration into Palestine destroys the constructive efforts of Zionists the world over to create a home-land and restore prosperity to the Holy Land. The betrayal by the British Government of the Balfour resolution will be justly and deeply resented in the United States, because, relying on the good faith of Great Britain, millions of dollars were contributed by American citizens to help reconstruct Palestine as a center of Jewish culture.

Friends of Great Britain are amazed that the British Government should deliberately attempt to nullify the Balfour Declaration and turn it into another scrap of paper. Public opinion in the United States demands that Great Britain uphold the pledges given in the Balfour Declaration and the mandate convention of 1924 to facilitate the establishment of a Jewish national home in Palestine.

I am not one of those who delights in twisting the tail of the British lion simply to hear him roar. I am still unwilling to believe that the British Government has definitely repudiated its plighted word. Great Britain has always gloried in the fact that its word was its bond, and it is not conceivable that it should default on the promises and pledges given in the Balfour Declaration and repeated in numerous peace treaties. Lord Balfour would turn over in his grave at the thought of such a betrayal of trust by the British Government. . . .

I am a convinced Zionist, and do not believe that this temporary set-back will discourage Jewish leaders from continuing their constructive efforts to build a new center of Jewish civilization in Palestine.

Jewish people in America will still carry on and make even greater sacrifices, persuaded that no British Government can long endure and maintain the support of its people if it stands for the repudiation and betrayal of the Balfour Declaration which has been sanctioned by all civilized nations. Ever since the exile of the Jewish people, 1900 years ago, from the land given to Abraham by Jehovah, their hopes and dreams have centered upon Jerusalem and Palestine.

The Jews of the United States, in common with Jews everywhere, have a deep attachment to their racial and religious ideals, and have remained devoutly loyal to the idea of rebuilding a center of Jewish civilization where their unique genius might again find unhampered expression as it did in the days of old.

Many of the most loyal Jews in this country are determined to make any sacrifice consistent with honor and their allegiance to the United States to help enable the persecuted and oppressed Jews of central and southeastern Europe find a refuge and a homeland in Palestine. In America, where 4,000,000 Jewish people now live, they have made outstanding contributions in every phase of our country's life and development. In peace and war, in science and in industry, in commerce and in art, the Jews of America occupy a foremost place in our national life. They have contributed of their blood and treasure in all our wars. Their sons lie buried on the fields of France, in Africa and Italy, in the islands of the Pacific, or in American cemeteries on the battlefields wherever our heroes have fought and died. No one can impugn their loyalty, patriotism, or devotion to our flag and to the Republic.

The Balfour Declaration proclaimed on November 2, 1917, was a war measure. The United States was at that time in the World War on the side of Great Britain, and American Jews, along with those the world over, were thrilled by the pledge of one of the world's greatest nations to facilitate the establishment of the Jewish national home in Palestine. Because of the nobility of the idea, every civilized country in the world supported the Balfour Declaration.

All lovers of fair play and respecters of sacred promises should be aligned with them in protesting against the repudiation of the Balfour Declaration by the British Government and help to make it possible for hundreds of thousands of Jews in Eastern Europe, suffering from Nazi persecution and brutality, to find a haven in that ancient biblical land and once more make it flourish with milk and honey as in the days of Solomon and David. . . .

I hope that the Zionists and their friends all over the world will not yield to this proposed breach of trust in order to cajole the Arabs by double-crossing the Jewish people in Palestine and elsewhere and selling them out for a mess of porridge.

I urge the President, the State Department, and the Congress to demand that there shall be no modification of our treaty rights in Palestine without our consent. . . .

In conclusion, I do not anticipate in 1944 that many American Jews will return to live in Jerusalem or Palestine, but they will make it possible for their coreligionists in central Europe, where they are hounded like animals and are in great distress, to enter Palestine from whence they were driven out centuries ago to endure centuries of persecution in many climes and in many foreign lands.

In my remarks of the same day before the House Committee on Foreign Affairs I had noted that "the greatest single tragedy of the war is the beastly, inhuman, and barbaric treatment of the Jews in central Europe. There are more Jews who have died in this war than in all the Allied armies through sheer persecution, hunger, and famine." And I had more kind words for Winston Churchill:

Nobody admires Winston Churchill more than I do. I know him personally. He always puts the interests of the British Empire first. I believe in that kind of philosophy. But I also admire him in view of the fact that he is for Zionism and for a homeland for the Jewish people. I see no reason why we should not help him. . . . Why should we not pass a resolution so he can get up in Parliament and say, "Here is a resolution from our greatest friends and allies in favor of keeping immigration open to the Jews"? . . . We cannot in this war repudiate what we did in the last war and serve notice on the Jews of this war that their aspirations are at an end and that they can no longer hope for anything in the way of establishing a homeland in Palestine.

I was not only a consistent supporter of the right of the Jews to have a Jewish homeland, but I actively protested the persecution of Jews in Germany and other parts of Europe. I suppose I inherited many of my feelings about Jews from my grandfather, the first Hamilton Fish.

As President Grant's secretary of state, my grandfather exerted a great deal of diplomatic pressure to end the persecution and killing of Rumanian Jews, stating:

Although as a rule, we scrupulously abstain from interfering directly or indirectly in the public affairs of foreign nations, the grievance adverted to is so enormous as to impart to it as it were a cosmopolitan character, in the redress of which all countries, government and creeds are alike interested.

On December 9, 1941, I stood on the floor of the House and after outlining the Palestine resolution I had introduced nearly twenty years before, asked that Lend-Lease money be provided to obtain equipment for a Jewish army:

MR. FISH: . . . Today the Jewish people in that Holy Land are asking for an army of their own, for a Jewish army to protect that homeland, to fight under British high command but as a separate unit and identity. Just as we have loaned money through Lend-Lease bills to the Poles and the Czechs and others, I think it is highly proper that we should furnish supplies and arms for a Jewish army in Palestine. Let them volunteer, and let us provide them with an opportunity to fight.

These Jewish people, who have more at stake in this war than any other people in the world, who have suffered more, who have been the victims of barbarous treatment in Eastern Europe, who have been outlawed and discriminated against on account of their race and religion, who have been deprived of their economic and civic rights and by inhuman and brutal persecution by the Nazis forced back in the poverty and misery of the ghetto or into concentration camps, should have the unquestioned right to fight.

Let us give them that opportunity without delay. Let us give them some of our Lend-Lease money as we have given it to the Poles, the Czechs, the Free French, and the Greeks. Let them have an army in Palestine of 50,000 or even 100,000, with American Lend-Lease money with which to obtain equipment and guns. Let them have a Jewish military unit under their own flag, under the Star of David, and manned and officered by their own people.

The gentleman from New York [Mr. Somers] has already introduced a resolution to carry this purpose into effect of providing Lend-Lease money and defense articles for a Jewish army in Palestine.

MR. SACKS: Mr. Speaker, will the gentleman yield?

MR. FISH: I yield.

MR. SACKS: I want to make an observation here to the gentleman from New York. I hope the gentleman from New York does not mean Americans of Jewish extraction. We want to take our responsibility in the American Army and fight.

MR. FISH: The gentleman is quite correct. I am glad the gentleman injected that remark, because I already discussed that with him today. The people of Jewish origin naturally will serve and are serving in our armed forces the same as all other citizens. However, the Jewish people in Palestine are in the same category as the Czechs, Poles, and others who want to defend their own country; and I know the gentleman from Pennsylvania is in accord with that proposal.

MR. SACKS: Yes. Will the gentleman yield further?

MR. FISH: I yield.

MR. SACKS: For the gentleman's information, of the million men we now have in our Army it is reported that over 100,000 are Americans of Jewish faith. This is their land.

MR. FISH: That is true and has always been so. Americans of Jewish origin fought gallantly in the last World War in our armed forces.

MR. SACKS: But those who live in Palestine want an army of their own, and so far Britain has refused to permit such an army to be raised and equipped. That is the one the gentleman is talking about.

MR. FISH: Precisely. That is what the gentleman is in favor of and what I am urging as the author of the Zionist resolution adopted by Congress in 1922.

MR. SACKS: That is right.

MR. FISH: And I think that war material should be furnished under the Lease-Lend Act to equip a Jewish army to fight in Palestine or elsewhere in the Near East.

In early 1943, I introduced in Congress a resolution denouncing Hitler for his inhuman racial policies and for killing millions of Jews in gas chambers, and calling upon all the nations of the world to protest the barbarous liquidation of the Jews. Every nation in Europe knew by that time of the brutal extermination of the European Jews, but for some unknown and unexplained reason, FDR's State Department claimed it had no knowledge of the atrocities, and it actually opposed my resolution.

In his autobiography, *A Child of the Century*, Ben Hecht wrote that "President Roosevelt's failure to raise one of his humanitarian fingers to prevent the extermination of the Jews, his many sullen statements about the Jewish situation, and his spiritual anesthesia to the greatest genocide in history" was beyond comprehension. He added, "I was informed by David Niles, FDR's chief secretary and a Jew, that Roosevelt would not make a speech or issue a statement denouncing the German extermination of the Jews."

Arthur Morse, whose book *While Six Million Died* is a shocking exposure of how FDR turned his back on the plight of millions of European Jews, says that in January 1944, President Roosevelt was shown the startling conclusions of a secret memorandum, "Acquiescence of this Government in the Murder of the Jews." The memorandum charged that the State Department had "not only failed to use the Governmental machinery at their disposal to rescue Jews from Hitler, but have gone so far as to use this Governmental machinery to prevent the rescue of these Jews." The report also accused "certain officials in our State Department, who are charged with actually carrying out this policy," of refusing "to take effective action to prevent the extermination of the Jews. . . ."

Morse's indictment of President Roosevelt and virtually all of his cabinet officials is supported by David Wyman in his book *Abandonment of the Jews*. Wyman is emphatic in stating that Roosevelt by December 1942 "was fully aware of the extermination program." Yet, as Wyman points out, Roosevelt refused to lift a finger to help the imperilled Jews. Wyman mentions that R. Borden Reams, a high-ranking State Department official, actually asked Jewish leaders to "tone down the present world-wide publicity campaign against 'mass murders.' "

Arthur Morse picks up the story:

> Representative Hamilton Fish, Jr., of New York telephoned the State Department and inquired about reports of mass murder and whether the State Department had any suggestions for thwarting the Nazis. Fish was an isolationist, but he had been moved by a letter to the *New York Times* from Pierre Van Passen. Van Passen, a journalist who had observed the Nazis at first hand, had written: "To be silent in this hour when thousands of unarmed, innocent Jewish human beings are being murdered each day, is not only a betrayal of elementary human solidarity, it is tantamount to giving the Gestapo carte blanche to continue and speed its ghastly program of extermination."
>
> Fish's call to the State Department was transferred to [R. Borden] Reams. When asked about Van Passen's statement, the man in charge of "Jewish questions" replied that the matter was under consideration and that the reports of the Nazi killings were unconfirmed.

President Roosevelt's complete refusal to make Hitler's genocidal racial policies an issue, his absolute silence while millions died, did nothing to help stop Hitler's maniacal extermination plans.

The issue, after all, was not a new one. As early as 1933, I had introduced a House Concurrent Resolution that said:

> Whereas the German Government is pursuing a relentless and ruthless policy of economic persecution and repression of Jews in Germany; and
>
> Whereas it is the avowed intention of the German Government to deprive the Jews of their civic, political, and economic rights; and
>
> Whereas the comparatively small number of Jews in Germany, not exceeding 600,000, or one percent of the German population, constitute a

peaceful, law-abiding, industrious, and defenseless element of the population: Therefore be it

Resolved by the House of Representatives (the Senate concurring), That the Congress of the United States regrets the continued persecution of the Jews in Germany and expresses sympathy for them in their hour of trial, humiliation, and economic discrimination, and requests the President of the United States to use his good offices and make friendly representation to the German Government in the interest of humanity, justice, and world peace, to respect the civic and economic rights of its citizens of Jewish origin, and to put an end to racial and religious persecution.

It has always been a matter of deep regret to me that my resolution of 1933 at the outset of the persecution was not adopted, as it might have had far-reaching influence in stopping it and, in doing so, have changed the course of history for the better. My speech in defense of my resolution was carefully, but forcefully, stated. It encapsulated for me what America's proper attitude to world Jewry should be:

Without in any way desiring to interfere with internal German institutions I appeal to a sense of justice, a spirit of tolerance and fair play not to turn back the hands of progress two centuries by disqualifying German Jews of citizenship and economic rights and driving them as outcasts into crowded and poverty-stricken ghettoes. . . .

The tragic persecution of the Jews in Germany is just another page in the long and dark history of the much-suffering Jewish people. The American Government has never given any sanction to bigotry or assistance to persecution, but, on the other hand, does guarantee to all citizens full liberty of conscience. Our traditional American policy toward our citizens of Jewish origin is best expressed in the words of George Washington to the Jewish congregation at Newport in 1790:

"May the children of the stock of Abraham who dwell in this land continue to merit and enjoy the good will of the other inhabitants, while everyone shall sit safely under his own vine and fig tree, and there shall be none to make him afraid."

I appeal for a square deal and justice for the Jewish people in Germany, as elsewhere, who are decent and honorable citizens, practicing an ancient faith in peace and tranquility and desiring merely the protection of their lives, property, and an equal opportunity to work. A continuation of the economic persecution of the Jews would be a disgrace to the cause of civilization and will be a constant source of friction and irritation in maintaining friendly relations between nations.

In a letter I wrote to Justice Wendell P. Stafford that same year, and which I had entered in the June 6, 1933, Congressional Record, I said, in part:

> No nation, or no people, particularly the American people accustomed to equal opportunities under the law, can remain silent at the cruel, brutal, and systematic policy being pursued by the German Government to turn the hands of progress back two centuries and force peaceful and law-abiding Jewish citizens to return to the poverty and disease of the ghetto.
>
> The American people are shocked and horrified that any civilized government, and I speak as a tried and true friend of the German people, could in our day and generation undertake to outrage civilization by strangling through economic weapons a whole race. Stupid and ruthless leadership turned the world against Germany twenty years ago, and God forbid that it should again come to pass. By encouraging and promoting intolerable injustices to the Jews, the German rulers are prejudicing their own demands for justice before world public opinion.
>
> The fight has just begun and must continue until human rights and Jewish rights prevail.

Soon after this letter became public, I was gratified to learn that Samuel Untermyer, president of the World Jewish Foundation and of the nonsectarian League for the Defense of Jewish Rights, said of me that "Mr. Fish is known to be one of the best friends and champions the Jews ever had in this country." I only wish that Mr. Untermyer's praise of FDR's congressman had had some effect on FDR's own actions.

Roosevelt was aware, at the very least, of the dangers facing the Jews as the result of the war. In a confidential memorandum to Secretary of State Hull, the president wrote:

> We have . . . the thought that at the termination of the European war . . . there will be a very large number of refugees. These people will be refugees because the place they live in will no longer allow them to stay; or they may be refugees whose homes and property have been utterly destroyed and have no chance to start life anew in the old setting: refugees who for reasons of conscience, Christian and Jewish, feel that they can no longer tolerate the civilization in which they have been brought up; refugees whose family ties have been destroyed and who want to start life in a wholly new environment.

I also, of course, did my best to keep the administration focused on issues concerning the Jews. On December 10, 1942, I wrote to Secretary of State Hull protesting the massacre of European Jews:

I have been shocked by the repeated statements appearing in the American press concerning the alleged slaughter of 7,000 Jews daily by the Nazis in conquered territories.

I would appreciate receiving from you any data that you may have concerning such atrocities and any suggestions you may care to make that might help put a stop to the massacre of Jews in Central and Eastern Europe.

Is there not some action that may be taken by the United States Congress and the administration that will stop these pogroms of Jews in Poland and Eastern Europe? Would it be possible to enlist the support of such neutrals as Sweden, Spain, and Turkey?

I am and always have been against the persecution of minorities here and abroad on account of race, color, or creed and shall be glad to cooperate in Congress in any constructive way to stop this wholesale murder and butchery of defenseless people.

A week later, Rabbi Herman Bick, whose friendship and advice I had long valued, wrote the following letter to me:

I read in the Congressional Record, page 9868, your speech and your letter sent to the Secretary of State in regard to the Jewish pogroms by the Nazis. God bless you. It was you who helped put through the Congress the Palestine Resolution based on the Balfour Declaration. If you recollect, the Jewish people in Middletown, NY, gave you a banquet and a Jewish Bible. I was then the rabbi and had the pleasure to preside.

I read your letter before the meeting of the Rabbinical Association of Boston. It was also becoming a colonel of a colored regiment during the First World War to speak so beautifully of the only out-going Negro Congressman. I wish we had more of your type in Congress, and the future of America would be assured.

Thanking you, I assure you these words come from the bottom of my heart.

Rabbi Bick, one of your former
constituents.

Another prominent New York State Jewish leader, Seymour S. Cohen, president of the Newburgh Jewish Community Council, wrote the following letter to the editor of the *Newburgh News*:

Of late there has been much printed about the wanton murder against Jews in Hitlerized Europe. I am particularly impressed with the public statement by my longtime friend, Congressman Hamilton Fish, that whatever can be done to curtail wholesale elimination of these defenseless people should be undertaken at once. Colonel Fish, through his long public career, has been a champion of minorities. I feel his assistance as an official in Washington will be of great importance. Two million Jews, according to documented evidence in the hands of our State Department, have been eradicated and five million more remain in the death holes of concentration camps fearing death in gas ovens or shooting. The young and the old fall dead in graves which they had dug, and there is no organized protest in the United States.

On one occasion, of which I am proud, I enlisted the help of my lawyer friend, Lawrence Berenson, in an attempt to save a Jewish refugee ship. Berenson raised about $100,000, and after I made contact with General Rafael Trujillo of the Dominican Republic, we offered the sum to the island dictator who thereupon agreed to take one of the ships. Many of the descendants of these refugees live there to this day, with no idea, I suspect, of the identity of their benefactors.

An anecdote told by others about my efforts on behalf of the Jews should perhaps be repeated here. The incident occurred in August 1939 when I was in Europe as chairman of the congressional delegation attending the Interparliamentary Union Conference. A close friend of mine whom I had known for many years, Fanny Holtzman—an excellent lawyer, by the way—asked me to assist her in obtaining visas for German Jews who wanted to leave Germany. Previously, we had worked together to help Jewish immigrants who had become bogged down in bureaucratic trouble at Ellis Island when they were trying to enter the United States.

I told her I would do anything—or sign anything—that might help more Jews escape from Hitler and his ilk and make it to the safety of America's shores. I also offered to round up whatever other congressional support I could, though I told her, frankly, that the Roosevelt administration was very unlikely to approve any legislation calling for a massive influx of Jewish refugees.

Fanny called me again the next day—I was in London—and told me that I had to come meet her in Berlin immediately because all her attempts to generate help for Jewish refugees were being defeated. The refugees, she told me, were being dismissed as "hysterical Jews."

This phrase set fire to my temper. "What are they supposed to do," I shouted, "stand by calmly and wait for Hitler to kill them? If there's anything we can do together, I'm with you."

I cancelled my luncheon plans and took the next available flight to Berlin. When I arrived I discovered that Fanny had prepared a large batch of visa applications for me to sign and had warned the American Embassy that an unnamed—but powerful—congressional leader was on his way.

Fanny told me that the embassy would need some sort of "correct procedure" to make my intervention on behalf of these Jews acceptable to the higher-ups at the State Department. Our ambassador to Germany had been recalled by FDR the year before. She then told me a joke about granting visas to allow immigrants to visit the World's Fair. To me, it was no joke, but the answer. I told her that we should arrange three-month transit visas for as many people as possible—all of whom would officially be visitors to the World's Fair in New York.

We went to the embassy and I told the staff that I wanted a large stack of three-month tourist visas for the World's Fair, that I wanted them immediately, and that Fanny had already gathered all the names and necessary papers. Then I started signing blank visa application forms, acting as a sponsor for the refugees. It was a good day's work.

I also remained active in the Jewish cause through more normal channels. On January 14, 1943, I submitted the following resolution in Congress, protesting Hitler's extermination policy:

> Whereas the grievances adverted to are so enormous as to impart to them an international character in redress of which all countries, governments and creeds are alike interested:
>
> THEREFORE BE IT RESOLVED IN THE SENATE AND HOUSE OF REPRESENTATIVES OF THE UNITED STATES OF AMERICA IN CONGRESS ASSEMBLED,
>
> That the Congress of the United States looks with abhorrence and dismay on the mass murders of helpless Jewish men, women and children by the Nazis, their continued persecution and attempts to exterminate minorities in Central Europe and territories occupied by them under the intolerable and indefensible doctrine of racism, and protests the deliberate persecution, the cruel and barbarous treatment and systematic policy of exterminating defenseless racial and religious minorities in violation of international law and the laws of humanity and God.

I shall always be glad that I introduced and spoke in favor of this vital protest resolution against Nazi racism and Hitler's extermination policy.

Under Hitler, Jews were rounded up and shipped from all over Europe to Nazi concentration camps such as Dachau and Auschwitz. There, millions of Jews were liquidated. Incidentally, there is no record of any protest by Stalin or Soviet Russia against the slaughter of Jews by the Nazis—that is understandable given Stalin's own record of genocide. What is beyond comprehension is that the White House and the State Department should have met the butchery of millions of defenseless Jewish men, women, and children—the high blood mark of man's inhumanity to man—with silence.

Chapter Twenty-Two

Vendetta

Because I was the ranking Republican member of both the Foreign Affairs Committee and the powerful Rules Committee, I was in a position to block many of Roosevelt's prowar policies and his many attempts to increase his own power beyond that given to the president by the Constitution.

It was also a source of irritation to Roosevelt that I represented the district in which he resided on his estate at Hyde Park. It was particularly galling to him that though he rarely carried the town of Hyde Park in the presidential elections, I could always count on Hyde Park to provide me with overwhelming majorities when I ran for reelection every two years. FDR took an active role in trying to unseat me from Congress. When he failed to defeat me at the ballot box, he decided to have me indicted.

The first attempt was made in the late 1930s by the Treasury Department, which tried to manufacture a tax case against me. I was told by Treasury that I owed five thousand dollars in back taxes. I insisted that I had reported my income honestly and had no desire to cheat the government of its fair share of taxes. I asked my friend, Lawrence Berenson, a distinguished lawyer who had been a substitute player on my Harvard football team, to represent me in this case. He immediately said that I was being unfairly singled out by the Treasury Department and that I owed no additional taxes. He then told me that he would represent me without compensation.

The case dragged on for several years, costing the government many thousands of dollars as it attempted to make me pay the money, which, if

I had agreed, would have besmirched my reputation. As time went by, Treasury officials kept lowering the amount they said I owed the government. At one point I could have settled the case for five hundred dollars; at another, the price fell to one hundred dollars. I told Lawrence Berenson that, as I owed nothing, I would not pay one cent. Finally, the Treasury Department admitted that it had erred—and gave me a refund of eighty dollars.

As a side note, I should add that FDR's own tax forms might have deserved closer scrutiny from the Treasury Department. Roosevelt took large deductions on his returns, claiming that his palatial estate at Hyde Park was used for farming. Roosevelt, of course, was not a farmer and knew nothing about farming—as the residents of Hyde Park knew very well. I teased the newly elected president about his claim to farming in a February 1933 "Dear Franklin" letter that contained a handwritten postscript, "As one farmer to another, if I can be of any help let me know."

The next attempt to indict me came when I went to Oslo, Norway, as head of the American delegation to the Interparliamentary Union. Of the twenty-eight members of my party, there were twenty-four congressmen and four senators, evenly divided on party lines—fourteen Democrats and fourteen Republicans. Roosevelt must have been so incensed that I had been elected to head this committee and so fearful that we might somehow persuade the heads of the European states to avoid war through peaceful negotiations, that he ordered the State Department to maintain surveillance of my activities and report my public comments to him.

In November 1939, Roosevelt wrote to my friend Bernard Baruch telling him that he, Roosevelt

> had a check-up made by various embassies on the recent visit of that world-renowned, selfless statesman, Honorable Ham Fish, to Europe this past summer. Here is an excerpt which I think will amuse you because I am quite certain that neither you nor I, who belong to the practical school of thought, would ever have commissioned Honorable Ham to represent us or speak for us.
>
> I wish this great Pooh-bah would go back to Harvard and play tackle on the football team. He is qualified for that job.

(Baruch, incidentally, asked me before I left for Oslo to help him get the heads of Great Britain, France, and Germany to agree to a colonization plan for European Jews. I agreed, of course.)

While I was in Europe I met and dined with Roosevelt's travelling ambassador William Bullitt, with whom I discussed everything freely and openly, and he agreed with all that I was doing; not once did he even intimate that I had done anything illegal. Evidently, in this he did not represent the views of the president.

On August 29, 1939, Roosevelt wrote the following memorandum to Secretary of State Hull:

> I think the time has come to make a careful check-up on Mr. Fish. His statements when he first arrived in Europe, his statements and actions at the Oslo meeting, and, finally, his statements yesterday and the day before in Berlin come pretty close to a violation of the statute forbidding any citizen from entering into relations concerning foreign affairs with a foreign nation.
>
> If a definite case could be made out against him, any one of three things can be done (a) he can be indicted under the existing law because obviously he is not acting in any official position as a Member of Congress (b) the case can be submitted to the House of Representatives itself when they reconvene (c) he can be taken to task on the basis of the information either by the Speaker or by some other colleague in the House.

Hull, however, told Roosevelt that there was no basis for taking any action against me, as I had broken no law and had acted within my official duties as chairman of the committee.

Two more attempts to have me indicted were made in 1942. On April 15, 1942, Roosevelt instructed Secretary of the Treasury Henry Morgenthau, another Hudson Valley land baron, to use a Treasury Department intelligence unit to check my income taxes over a period of several years. Again, the Treasury Department was unable to fabricate a case against me. Quite simply, I had done nothing wrong.

A month later, in a confidential memo, Roosevelt informed J. Edgar Hoover, director of the Federal Bureau of Investigation, that a Mrs. Vanderbilt Webb of Garrison, New York, who had organized a committee to fight my reelection, had "uncovered checks totaling several hundred thousands of dollars which passed through Fish's hands for subversive activities." This allegation, like all the others, was simply absurd. I had neither seen nor even heard of the "several hundred thousand dollars" I was supposed to have handled. I barely had enough money to put together for my reelection campaigns, I had to borrow money to send my children to school, and my congressional salary was only $10,000 a year. This attempt of FDR's to blacken my reputation also failed.

Roosevelt's vindictive attacks on me were in stark contrast to my own attempts to be honest and fair. I actually defended FDR on the floor of the House after I learned that he had been subjected to smear attacks from American Nazis and Bundists.

> MR. FISH: Mr. Chairman, I rise today to an unusual role in the House of Representatives and possibly in the country. I happen to represent the district from which the President of the United States comes. I have probably been foremost amongst those who have criticized his policies, and I have repeatedly pointed out the failure of those policies. But last week at a Washington's Birthday celebration the Nazi Bund . . . which aims to destroy American liberties, our free institutions, and our republican and constitutional form of government, met in Madison Square Garden in the city of New York. Their spokesman abused and villified the President of the United States. They attacked him viciously. I want to say as the Representative in Congress from his district . . . that when it comes to Nazis . . . heaping personal abuse . . . on the President of the United States, I, as a Republican, resent such slurring attacks and openly denounce them. . . . We Republicans will continue to attack the policies of President Roosevelt, we will continue to expose his unsound, radical, and dangerous policies, but we will not resort to personal abuse or mud-slinging attacks upon the President of the United States.
>
> I have introduced a bill in the House of Representatives that should have the support of both sides of the House. This bill prohibits the arming, drilling, and disciplining of all foreign groups, the Nazis, Communists, and Fascists. So I ask the Democrats and Republicans, particularly those on the committee to which the bill has been referred, to report it to the House and give us a chance to enact it into law.

The use of smear attacks is another link between Roosevelt and all those groups—national socialists, communists, and radical leftists—that worship power. In their hunger for power they will use any tool to hammer their opponents. Living at the doorstep of New York City where most of the false and vicious propaganda emanated—and being one of the few Easterners who led the fight against the New Deal, communism, and our entrance into the war—I was the main target for such smear attacks.

During the 1940 presidential campaign, one hundred thousand pictures of Nazi Bundist leader Fritz Kuhn and myself were distributed throughout my district. The text that accompanied the photo alleged that he and I were engaged in some nefarious joint conspiracy to overthrow the government. The fact of the matter is that I had only met Fritz Kuhn on one occasion and that was in the summer of 1938 when I was a delegate to

the New York State Convention in Albany, New York. At that convention I
was appointed chairman of the Committee on Military Affairs. I introduced a resolution to prohibit the arming, drilling, uniforming, and parad-
ing of Bundists and similar organizations, including the communists. A
large hearing was held on my proposal in the Assembly Chamber where I
was presiding over my committee. Fritz Kuhn appeared uninvited before
the committee, denouncing my proposal.

Despite his objections, the committee gave its full approval to my
proposal and it was adopted by the convention. During the hearings,
however, a photographer took a snapshot of Fritz Kuhn talking to me, and
thus the smear began—linking me to a man I despised and whose organization I proposed to ban.

Another picture of me that was distributed during the 1940 campaign
showed me speaking at the German Day meeting in 1938 at Madison
Square Garden. The picture showed a small Nazi emblem in back of the
speakers' platform—the implication being that I was talking to a gathering
of Bundists and Nazis. The truth was virtually the exact opposite. The
Bundists and Nazis actually boycotted the meeting because I had been
invited to speak. Among other things, they resented my having introduced
a resolution in Congress condemning Hitler for his brutal persecution of
German Jews. The one small Nazi flag at the meeting was merely the usual
German emblem at that time.

The German Day meeting of loyal Americans of German origin had
been held annually for generations on October 30th in New York City. The
German ambassador, Senator Robert Wagner, and other prominent officials had been among its past speakers. In my speech, I urged all Americans
of German origin to stand behind our government in peace and war. I also
reiterated my conviction that the United States should keep itself removed
from Old World quarrels. The picture of me and the Nazi flag was circu-
lated by the communist *Daily Worker*, which wanted to ignore the content
of my speech and disparage my Americanism in order to advance—
through despicable smears—the communist cause.

Other more reputable newspapers went in for the same kinds of smear
tactics against anyone who opposed intervention in the war in Europe. In
1943, John O'Donnell, chief of the Washington bureau of the *New York
Daily News*, won a $50,000 libel suit against the *Philadelphia Record*, which
had printed an editorial calling O'Donnell a "Naziphile" and saying he
supported "the destruction of the British Empire, suppression of labor
unions, and liquidation of the Jews." I myself was the victim of a persistent

campaign to link me with Nazis and Bundists by the newspaper *PM*, which headed every article about me with a drawing of a dead fish.

I was also smeared by columnist Drew Pearson—a muckracking journalist who was denounced and repudiated by many public officials, including President Roosevelt, President Truman, General MacArthur, and Secretary of State Hull. Pearson wrote in a column of 1939 that I owned a house in New York City which I rented to the German counsel Otto Von Kiep. Pearson claimed that I had increased the rent twice since Hitler had come to power, intimating that I was either being bribed or was profiting in some way by the Nazi regime.

The truth was that the house had been owned by my father, who had rented it to the German counsel before the Nazis came to power. After my father's death, my brother-in-law, Harry Forster, who was in the real estate business, assumed control over the house. He told me that far from raising the rent since Hitler's accession to power, the rent had actually decreased by $400 annually because of the declining rental market caused by the Depression.

I should also say something about Otto Von Kiep himself. Once Germany declared war on the United States, he returned to Germany where he had the courage to criticize Hitler's policies openly. In 1944, he joined in the conspiracy to assassinate Hitler. Its failure led to his arrest. He was then tortured to death for refusing to reveal the names of his friends who had participated in the plot. This was the man who lived on the real estate in question—a man who should have received a memorial for his heroism.

Like so many of his ilk, Pearson was motivated by sensationalism and a perverted desire to assassinate the character of those with whom he disagreed politically. He never wrote a word about the heroism of Kiep or of his tragic death at the hands of the Nazis. That was not his style.

In another case, the actress Helen Hayes was used by President Roosevelt to spread false and misleading propaganda against me. Several newspapers in New York and New Jersey reported Miss Hayes' public charge that I had not voted for the fortification of Guam. This was an appalling misrepresentation. There never was a "vote for the fortification of Guam" in Congress. Years later, the clerk of the House of Representatives wrote me a letter verifying that there never had been a vote on this issue, but rather one over the dredging of the harbor on Guam, which I favored along with most Republicans. Ironically, Roosevelt and the Democratic leaders in Congress opposed it. In short, Miss Hayes was used as a pawn, as are many people in the entertainment industry.

But there were also the good moments, those times when the decency and loyalty of people made the tumult of politics worthwhile. In this respect, I owe a debt of gratitude to my old friend, Bill Doulin, who for many years was prominent in Orange County Republican politics, and, during his long tenure as GOP county chairman, was referred to as Mr. Republican.

During the 1944 campaign, Bill was approached by a woman (whose name I do not recall) who was an aide of my opponent Bennett. She indicated that Bennett was eager to win the support of the Orange County Republicans, and she told Bill, who was then vice chairman of the county committee, that if he would "just come over to Bennett's headquarters and sit at the desk" until after the election, he could "name his price." Bill's sense of humor prompted him to tell the woman that his price was $15,000, a large sum of money in 1944.

"I thought she would be thrown out of Bennett's office," Bill told me several months later. "Instead, she called me on the phone and told me that I would get half the money now and the other half the day after the election . . . I told her that I was only kidding. . . not interested. I wouldn't betray Ham Fish for a million dollars!" Bill Doulin tells that story to this very day. Everyone in Orange County must have heard it at least twenty times.

It was no accident that, with loyal supporters like Bill Doulin, I carried Orange County by a large majority.

The stifling of legitimate political dissent was fast becoming government policy. I refused to be intimidated into silence when the Democrats enacted the 1940 Alien and Sedition Act at the request of President Roosevelt. In 1943, the Roosevelt administration brought to trial thirty-four Americans on flimsy charges concerning some kind of conspiracy with Hitler. Their real crime was in opposing Roosevelt's interventionist policies and American involvement in the war. Fortunately, most of the convictions made under the Alien and Sedition Act were later overturned by the Supreme Court.

The smears of Walter Winchell were more difficult to refute because he would never retract them and there was no Supreme Court to overrule his irresponsibility. A typical example of his type of contemptible propaganda was an item in his gossip column accusing me of having asked the piano player at a restaurant in New York to play a certain tune—naming it in German, which was held to be unpatriotic. I had, in fact, never heard of the tune and do not speak German. A first cousin of President Roosevelt, and an American, was with me. He asked to have some music played, referring to the tune by its original German name.

If that incident sounds trivial—and it is—I should add that Walter Winchell was in great glee when a resolution was railroaded through the American Legion denouncing me for allegedly misusing my franking privilege. Winchell announced that if the Legion ever rescinded that action, he would give me a quarter of an hour of his radio time and eat the Congressional Record. The Legion did rescind the resolution by unanimous vote when it was proved to be entirely fabricated, based on falsehoods, but I never received the radio time Winchell had promised me. Nor would I have wished such a misfortune on the Congressional Record as to have it eaten by Walter Winchell.

Chapter Twenty-Three

The Non-Campaigns
of 1940 and 1944

It would be a mistake to blame the American people for Roosevelt's disastrous policies, because the American people had no option—they had no political means by which to express their views. In two critical elections, 1940 and 1944, the Republican and Democratic candidates held the same foreign policy positions. The Republicans, represented by Wendell L. Willkie in 1940 and Thomas E. Dewey in 1944, went about the nation me-tooing Roosevelt's interventionist foreign policies, as well as the New Deal, urging their own election on the ground that they could do a better job.

This was an absurd platform on which to run, especially given the gravity of the issues facing the United States and the public's thin support for Roosevelt's foreign interventionism. By running a campaign that merely paralleled the Democrats', the Republicans effectively disenfranchised the electorate by denying them a real choice in the ballot booth. How foolish to say, "The incumbents have done a fine job, but they should be thrown out because we can do the same job better." What an insult to the intelligence of the American public.

By 1940, the American people were, in fact, deeply suspicious of the Roosevelt administration, which looked more and more as if it were edging the country towards war. If Wendell Willkie had stood on the issue of no war and no intervention unless we were attacked, chances are he would have been elected by an overwhelming majority. But he did not do that. Instead, he focused on trivialities, while the electorate was burning with fear about war; he avoided discussions of foreign policy as much as he could.

This was particularly disappointing because early on, Willkie had used harsh language in criticizing FDR's foreign policy. Willkie was deemed a decent candidate for president—far abler, more forceful, and more attractive than Thomas Dewey. But Wendell Willkie faltered, and then fell into the hands of the powerful internationalists who ran the most prestigious newspapers and waved the big money bags of the East Coast establishment. These were his friends and they had won him the Republican nomination. He felt obligated to them. But that sense of obligation also cost him the general election.

General Hugh Johnson put the issue in its proper context in the Scripps-Howard newspapers (10/5/40) when he wrote:

> It is peace or war. If the President, Governor Lehman, and Mr. Wallace want to whistle that air, why don't they play the whole tune? Surely on so terrible an issue this country has a right to know what is intended, and to vote on it is the only chance they will have in four years time—perhaps the very last chance.
>
> They don't play the whole tune because they don't dare. This country is 8 to 1 against war involvement. Only a vociferous minority on the Eastern seaboard wants war. Most of America lies west of the Allegheny Mountains. Yet the same little tail wagged the same great trusting dog into the last war. That Administration didn't dare make that issue out West either. Its slogan was: "He kept us out of war." This Administration simply keeps silent on real issues and blabs about such fake ones. I know of no well-informed Washington observer who isn't convinced that if Mr. Roosevelt is elected he will drag us into the war at the first opportunity and that if none presents itself he will make one.
>
> I know of none who is not aware that if that happens we shall have a war dictatorship with "emergency powers" in the hands of men who have constantly sought ever increasing "emergency" powers at the expense of our political system—and who have never willingly surrendered a single one. They have used them all to perpetuate themselves. I know of none who is not aware that participation in a major war costs so much that it will bankrupt the United States.
>
> O.K., if that's what a majority wants that's what we shall do. But let's see if that's what a majority wants. Let's make an issue of it and vote on it in the

election. Let's not countenance any clever and furtive destruction of the peace of the United States. There is only one man who can pose that question squarely—make that issue plain. His name is Wendell Willkie and, if he doesn't do it, he is licked right now. If he does it clearly, completely and effectively, he will win. We don't want war.

The *Washington Times Herald* (7/8/40) also reflected on the lack of choice being offered the electorate:

> The Republican Party has just nominated for President Wendell Willkie, whose public utterances show him to be in sympathy with the interventionists—though it is unlikely that he will come out for an actual AEF II before election. On the Democratic side, the renomination of Franklin D. Roosevelt becomes more likely each day; and the President is an interventionist up to everything except men, which of course in the long run will mean up to everything including men.
>
> The American people, therefore, are on the way to being cheated of their right to choose for themselves. We're in the war up to our chests now; and shortly after next election day or next inauguration day, if the war goes that long, we can expect to be in it up to our necks.

President Roosevelt, much as I disagreed with many of his domestic and foreign policies, was, I admit, the all-time master political strategist who ever sat in the White House. He naturally sensed and knew the deep-seated sentiment of the American people for peace and against involvement in foreign wars, and feared that this underlying sentiment would burst forth on election day and produce his defeat. He decided to take no chances with the peace-loving American people. So, on October 30, 1940, at a Democratic mass meeting in Boston, just a few days before the end of the campaign, he electrified the voters by his definite promise to keep America out of war.

This was the death-knell of Wendell Willkie's vacillating, tweedledee, tweedledum campaign. The bottom dropped out, and overnight millions of American voters, believing in this peace pledge, boarded the Roosevelt bandwagon. It was too late for Mr. Willkie to change his policies, even if he had wanted to do so. He had made his bed with the handful of Republican interventionists, mostly on Park Avenue in New York City and Commonwealth Avenue in Boston, and with the out-and-out pro-British elements of the country. Now he was forced to lie in that bed, even when it spelled electoral defeat. By listening to Wall Street and international advisors instead of the public sentiment on Main Street, he ended up carrying only ten states with eighty-two electoral votes.

This presidential campaign reached a peak of insincerity and mass deception unparalleled in any former national election up to then. Both major political parties had adopted forthright and unequivocal peace planks in their respective party platforms. And on October 23, 1940, a week before his famous speech in Boston announcing his intent to avoid a foreign war, President Roosevelt spoke in Philadelphia, where he said:

> We are arming ourselves not for any foreign war. We are arming ourselves not for any purposes of conquest or intervention in foreign disputes. I repeat again that I stand on the platform of our party. We will not send our army, naval, or air forces to fight in foreign lands outside of the Americas, except in case of attack.

What about Roosevelt's shoot-on-sight orders? What about FDR's secret appropriation of $200 million on September 2, 1940 to establish eight army and navy bases in British possession in the Atlantic? What about the placement of American troops in Iceland and Greenland? What about— within six months of this speech—the construction of port facilities and barracks in Iceland and Scotland for American troops?

On November 2, 1940, at Cleveland, just prior to the election, the president again reassured the American people of his peaceful intentions by saying, "The first purpose of our foreign policy is to keep our country out of war." Mr. Willkie, speaking at Cumberland, Maryland, on October 30, 1940, said rather pathetically, "The interests of the United States would have been better served if the third-term candidate had been outspokenly for peace and non-participation [earlier] instead of waiting to pledge it in an election."

Mr. Willkie had been outmaneuvered by President Roosevelt. A trained and experienced politician, FDR gave a definite peace pledge and grabbed millions of peace voters, while the Republican standard-bearer was saying in Buffalo, "I favor aid to Britain short of war and I mean short of war"; or at St. Louis, "We do not want to send our boys over there again. We cannot and we must not undertake to maintain by force of arms the peace of Europe"; or at Cambridge, Massachusetts, "We can have peace but we must begin to preserve it to begin with. We shall not undertake to fight anybody else's war. Our boys shall stay out of Europe." At Chicago, on October 22, 1940, candidate Willkie again chased the peace votes when he said:

One difference [between my foreign policy and Roosevelt's] is my determination to stay out of war. I have a real fear that this Administration is heading for war and I am against our going to war and will do all I can to avoid it.

After the election, Wendell Willkie himself repudiated his campaign speeches by referring to them as mere "campaign oratory." The voters had been given the proverbial political runaround and flim-flam by both candidates, but President Roosevelt was the highest bidder for the peace votes and won easily. Wendell Willkie never had his heart in any noninterventionist campaign, because his influential friends were mostly internationalists, as was the newspaper of which he was the darling, the *New York Herald Tribune*, which in 1940 editorialized: "It is quite probable that the least costly solution, in both life and welfare, would be [for the United States] to declare war on Germany at once."

I voted for Willkie because I opposed any president running for a third term and because I knew that Willkie's "fear that this [Roosevelt] Administration is heading for war" was right. Willkie himself confessed after the election that if he had run as a strict noninterventionist he could have defeated Roosevelt handily. The issue of war or peace was the issue in the 1940 campaign, and it was the issue most bungled by Willkie.

In truth, Willkie turned out to be even more of an interventionist than Franklin Roosevelt. Within six months after the 1940 election, Willkie's true colors became manifest. He began making speeches for the Committee to Defend America by Aiding the Allies. On May 7, 1941, he called for "less talk and more action" in giving effective aid to Britain, whether or not it meant convoys. "The struggle is already upon us," he said. "We cannot close our eyes to it." On October 18, 1941, six weeks before Pearl Harbor, Mr. Willkie said that the "United States must abandon hope for peace." This from the candidate who had said, "I favor aid to Britain short of war and I mean short of war."

The campaign of 1944, in which Governor Thomas E. Dewey of New York was the Republican nominee for president of the United States, was a replica of the Willkie-Roosevelt campaign four years before, except that Wendell Willkie was a far more auspicious candidate. Mr. Dewey sidestepped and avoided criticizing Roosevelt's foreign policies. He shadowboxed the New Deal and me-tooed large chunks of it. He soft-pedaled attacks on the communists and made no constructive proposals because he knew nothing about either national or international issues. He had one commendable asset and that was his first-rate radio voice. But what is a voice without knowledge and convictions? His campaign arguments, mostly lukewarm, failed to please, placate, or satisfy Republicans, constitutional Democrats, interventionists, noninterventionists, New Dealers, anti-New Dealers, labor, or business. Only occasionally did his rhetoric please anyone—and they tended to be dyed-in-the-wool Republican farmers.

President Roosevelt did not exert himself, yet he carried every Eastern state except Maine and Vermont. One of the main reasons for nominating Dewey was that he was expected to carry New York, where he was governor, and his home state of Michigan. But Governor Dewey lost New York by 320,000 votes—about 100,000 more than Willkie did—and Michigan by 30,000 votes (the Republican governor of Michigan won by 200,000 votes). Republican governors and senators were elected in many states, including Illinois, Minnesota, Missouri, Massachusetts, Connecticut, and New Jersey, all of which Dewey also failed to carry.

I supported Dewey—as did many of my colleagues—in spite of his poor candidacy. But through his tactlessness, he alienated most of the Republican party leaders and Republican members of Congress. As Mrs. Kenneth Simpson, wife of the former Republican National Committeeman from New York State, said, "You have got to know him to dislike him." Prior to his candidacy, through his dictatorial methods and unbounded conceit, he had managed to antagonize many members of the New York State Assembly. They supported his campaign for president only to get him out of Albany.

As a former football player myself, I don't put much stock in "moral victories," and I certainly saw no moral victory in Dewey's failure to carry any state east of Ohio except for Vermont and Maine. This was no moral victory—it was defeat, pure and simple. With such a poor candidate, that defeat was probably inevitable.

Most of the Dewey votes were anti-fourth term, anti-New Deal, anti-Roosevelt, and anti-communist—not pro-Dewey. Dewey did win the votes of the noninterventionists in the Middle West and he carried my district in New York State, but he was not exactly grateful for the support of Senator Nye and myself. After the election, a spokesman for Dewey said that he "was glad that Senator Gerald Nye and Representative Fish were defeated" (Richard Smith, *Thomas Dewey and His Times*).

Dewey and I had exchanged some harsh words during the campaign, but mine were in self-defense. I was asked by a New York newspaper reporter to predict the outcome of the vote in New York City, and I predicted that the majority of the Jewish voters would vote for Roosevelt. This was a straight-forward and, as it turned out, accurate prediction. Congressman Emanuel Celler, himself a Jew, stated in a public speech that all the Jews in New York City voted for Roosevelt in 1944. That is undoubtedly an overstatement, but it certainly is well within the traditions of American free speech. Dewey, however, chose to leap upon my prediction and make a campaign issue out of it, charging me with making a religious or racial issue out of a political campaign, which was the farthest thing from the truth. It was an obvious political ploy on Dewey's part to gain votes—and I was to pay the price for this tactic. While the false charges did hurt me politically, the issue boomeranged on Dewey and cost him many votes. My record on black and Jewish issues was entirely beyond reproach. I was in the forefront of civil rights legislation to guarantee just protection to both groups and, indeed, to all Americans. When the cynicism of Dewey's ploy became apparent, voters abandoned him.

In closing this particular subject, I will say that I also supported Dewey for governor in 1946, something I thought I'd never do. But it was yet another choice between two evils. The communists and the American Labor Party, which was controlled by the communists, had endorsed the Democratic candidate for governor—so my decision was made for me. Whatever else Dewey was, he was not a communist, and I could not sit idly by and let a communist-endorsed candidate move into the state house in Albany.

Chapter Twenty-Four

My Farewell to Congress

I lost my bid for reelection in 1944 because FDR, with Thomas Dewey's assistance, succeeded in getting me redistricted out of three of my counties and putting a Republican veteran on the Democratic ticket to run against me. Although the voters in my new district did not know me, I lost by only a few thousand votes.

On Monday, December 11, 1944, I stood in the House of Representatives and delivered my farewell speech. Although obviously one of the saddest moments in my life, I took the opportunity to address some of the political issues with which I had long been involved as a congressman:

> Mr. Speaker, I have a disagreeable task to perform in saying farewell to my colleagues in the House, and to the House of Representatives in which I have served for almost twenty-five years. I would not be telling the truth if I did not say that I was disappointed in not being returned to Congress. On the other hand, I am reconciled because it may prove to be a blessing in disguise. For many years—the last twelve—I have been in the front lines fighting the New Deal, bucking up against its entrenched ramparts, and now that it is in power again both in Congress and the administration, I think probably it is for the best that younger and newer blood undertake that thankless and difficult task. I assure my friends on the Democratic side that I have no intention in the time allotted to me this afternoon to discuss the New Deal. If I had, it would take more than an hour or a day or a week to present my views adequately. . . .
>
> At the outset let me say that I believe the House of Representatives is the

bulwark and guardian of personal liberties, of individual freedom, and of the representative and constitutional government in the United States. If we surrender our legislative powers, prerogatives, and functions to the Chief Executive, then it is the beginning of the end of free government in America, and the advent of totalitarianism which our sons are fighting against all over the world. . . .

And let me say to my colleagues that although the Congress and the House of Representatives have been under attack steadily from various radical groups within and without the United States, from long associations with its Members on both sides, I say without fear of contradiction that I know of no group in America, whether they be lawyers, doctors, clergymen, business-men, wage earners, or farmers, that compare with the Members of Congress for ability, integrity, character, patriotism, and desire for the public welfare.

I would not say this today because I believe that congressmen have been corrupted by the enormous amounts of money floating around congressional offices in terms of staff and perquisites.

But that sad day, I went on to discuss why I had been attacked so violently in my campaign and how I had been defeated, sparing nothing:

I waged a hard campaign to win, expecting that a Republican majority would be returned to the House of Representatives, and would have been heart-broken had that occurred and I was not among them, as I had hoped to be chairman of the Committee on Rules and in a position to stop the march toward Communism and totalitarianism in the United States. In Orange County—the only one left of my old district and where my legislative record is best known—I ran much better than in 1940 and 1942, carrying the county by 7,000, which is about twice my previous majority. I also carried my opponent's home district by 85 votes, and the town of Newburgh where he lives by 600, and the city of Newburgh by 2,200, running ahead of Mr. Dewey there.

Although the Communists, fellow travelers, and Sidney Hillman's PAC in New York City, with a slush fund of several hundred thousand dollars, combined in the drive to purge me, and the New Dealers joined in with their funds and orators including FDR, Mrs. Roosevelt, and Henry Wallace, yet they were all only contributing factors. It took most of the New Deal administration, half of Moscow, $400,000, and Governor Dewey to defeat me. I am confident that I would have been able to overcome all these efforts to purge me if it had not been for Governor Dewey's intolerant and false statement denouncing me as un-American, and raising a religious and racial issue for merely predicting that a majority of the Jews in New York City would vote for Roosevelt and the New Deal, which has never been denied by anyone—Jew or gentile.

Mr. Dewey asked for it, and here it is.

I am convinced that his stupid and colossal blunder, for selfish political purposes, was the direct cause of my defeat, as well as his own, and may have kept the Republicans from electing a majority in the House of Representatives. By his unprovoked attack on me he lost at least a million Democratic votes and a million Republican votes, which would otherwise have been cast for him for president, and a majority of them for Republican candidates for Congress. In spite of this I supported him, as I was against a fourth term and the New Deal fellow-travelers and their efforts to control the administration and to set up a one-man and one-party government. My opponent who was a Republican, and—defeated for Congress in the primaries by me—ran on the Democratic ticket with the Communist American Labor Party and Pink Liberal party support, and spoke every night for Dewey, stating that he (Dewey) was against me, which lost me enough Republican votes in the three new counties to bring about my defeat by 7,000 votes out of 130,000 cast.

I bitterly resent Governor Dewey's characterizing my remarks that a majority of the Jewish people would vote for FDR and the New Deal as un-American and raising a racial and religious issue. . . . Since when is it un-American to tell the truth or to mention the word "Jew," any more than the words "Christian, Irish, Italian, Pole, or Negro"? If it is, then free speech, the essence of Americanism ceases to exist and the inalienable and constitutional right of every American is placed in jeopardy.

It was Governor Dewey, not I, who raised the racial and religious issue—and for votes—as everyone knows. I have never been anti-Semitic in my life. I happen to be the author of the Palestine Resolution adopted in 1922 and incorporated into the Republican platform of 1944, on which Governor Dewey was supposed to stand. By what right has Governor Dewey to call me un-American, even by inference? I do not remember ever having heard of his serving a day in our armed forces or risking his life fighting the Germans, although he was in his thirties when World War number two started. No wonder he lost the soldier vote by two to one in New York State and elsewhere. . . .

I then began a long and detailed discussion of issues relating to the Second World War—a discussion it is not necessary to retell here—before beginning an extended peroration on the war's most serious consequence, the spread of communism.

Many people then and now might have thought my warnings about the spread of communism extreme and uncalled-for. But as I noted in my speech, communism was a very real threat to the American people, not just abroad but at home as well. In New York alone, in the 1944 election, the communist-dominated American Labor party cast 498,000 votes. The Liberal party, of pinker shade, composed of fellow travelers and radicals, received 320,000 votes. Communism, at least in New York State, was not to be laughed off or ignored.

Today, though communist groups are no longer much of an electoral threat to the nation, woolly-minded, decidedly left-wing professors in our colleges and universities are more dominant than ever and are doing everything possible to wreck our education system. How this could be so when communism is in such tatters is a matter for the professors to explain for themselves. But one reason might be that communism provides a ready dogma of beliefs, and that professors, for whatever reason, find these false and harmful beliefs attractive.

Communism may be in remission, but it is still a living, breathing ideology—alive, in fact, in the second greatest military power on the globe, and, as mentioned, in our influential colleges and universities. It is important, therefore, for Americans to remember what it is that the communists stand for and just what sorts of threats they pose to the most basic institutions of our society. The following are passages from Karl Marx's *Communist Manifesto*, given as I read them on the floor of the House of Representatives:

"The immediate aim of the Communist is the same as that of all the other proletarian parties: Formation of the proletariat into a class, overthrow of bourgeois supremacy, conquest of political power by the proletariat.

"In this sense the theory of the Communist may be summed up in the single sentence: Abolition of private property. You must, therefore, confess that by 'individual' you mean no other person than the bourgeois, than the middle-class owner of property. This person must, indeed, be swept out of the way, and made impossible.

"Abolition of the family. Even the most radical flare up at this infamous proposal of the Communist.

"On what foundation is the present family, the bourgeois family, based? On capital, on private gain. In its completely developed form this family exists only among the bourgeoisie.

"The bourgeois claptrap about the family and education, about the hallowed correlation of parent and child, becomes all the more disgusting, the more, by the action of modern industry, all family ties among the proletarians are torn asunder, and their children transformed into simple articles of commerce and instruments of labor.

"The working men have no country. We cannot take away from them what they have not got.

"But Communism abolishes eternal truths, it abolishes all religion, and all morality, instead of constituting them on a new basis; it therefore acts in contradiction to all past historical experience."

The beliefs expressed in these quotes show that communist ideas are both incredibly destructive and still lurking about in the world in general and in certain movements in the United States in particular.

In my speech, I counted the communist gains coming out of the Second World War, pointing to the human cost of the sweep of the Red army through Estonia, Latvia, Lithuania, Poland, and other nations throughout Eastern Europe, the subsequent liquidation of the middle class, the crushing of the brave heroes who had resisted the Nazi scourge only to fall prey to the Soviets, the deportation of tens of thousands of Eastern Europeans to prison camps in Siberia, and the severe persecution of Christians, which I likened to Hitler's persecution of the Jews.

Those were precarious times in Europe. It appeared at times as if communism were about to engulf far more of Europe than it already had. Communist partisans in Yugoslavia were consolidating power. Greece, Italy, and even France faced challenges from armed bands of communist partisans attempting to wrest power from fledgling postwar governments. Yet, I warned, anyone who attempts to expose or denounce the march of communism must be prepared to be called pro-Nazi or pro-fascist:

That is the typical smear that will be hurled at every friend of democracy or free government in Europe by Red agitators and propagandists, as they have already done against me.

If you are against the Communists swallowing or destroying democratic governments one by one either by armed force or political infiltration, then you will be denounced in the Red press as playing Hitler's game, and being a Nazi stooge or anti-Semitic—one as meaningless as the other.

There can be no compromise between Americanism and Communism. We do not propose to let the Communists or Sidney Hillman Sovietize us. Let us have faith in America and its glorious destiny under our own free institutions and constitutional and republican form of government. Let us rise above party affiliations and unite in an effort to save America from its enemies from without and within.

I then ended with words that have become my trademark in years since:

If there is any country worth living in, fighting for, or even dying for, it is the United States of America. Let us follow the example of Winston Churchill, Prime Minister of Great Britain, who always places the interests of the British Empire first, and even of Marshal Stalin who does the same for the Socialist Soviet Republics. Let us have faith in America, the greatest, richest, most powerful, and freest nation on earth. Let us follow the example of our allies and put the interests of America first and keep them uppermost all the time, for if we do not do it no other nation will do it for us.

I shall never despair of our free institutions, constitutional government, and the glorious destiny of our country as long as the elected representatives of the people in Congress maintain their constitutional power to legislate and resist all usurpations upon it. I expect to be more active in State and National politics than I have been in recent years past. I am enlisting in the fight to save America.

Thank God for the Congress of the United States, and more power to you, and especially the House of Representatives, which is the guardian and palladium of the freedom and liberties of the American people.

God bless and preserve America!

Chapter Twenty-Five

The Long, Tangled Roots of Our Involvement in Vietnam

If this book seems focused on the events that led up to the Second World War, it is because much of the shape of our modern world is the result of the mistakes, misjudgments, and plain chicanery of the prewar years. The Vietnam War—another war in which we should not have been involved and one that we entered without a declaration of war by Congress—is a case in point.

America's tragic involvement in Vietnam can be traced to the disastrous ultimatum President Roosevelt issued to the Japanese in November 1941 ordering them out of their conquered territories. This created a precedent of unbridled presidential authority and virtual war-making power that was later used by Presidents Kennedy and Johnson to involve the United States in yet another unnecessary and costly war.

John Foster Dulles—President Eisenhower's secretary of state—played a major role in prodding the United States into this mistaken adventure. Although Eisenhower was a fine president during both his terms in office, with eight years of peace and prosperity to his credit, he blundered severely when he appointed John Foster Dulles. Not only was Dulles a committed interventionist and a war hawk, but he was almost totally inept, making him the worst secretary of state the United States has ever had. Winston Churchill held Dulles in particular disdain, claiming that he was one of the stupidest men he had ever met. Churchill was fond of deliberately mispronouncing Dulles's name, lisping it to sound like "Dullith." Told that Dulles's brother Allen had been appointed to head the CIA, Churchill, in typical fashion, sardonically commented: "They tell me that there is another Dullith. Is that possible?"

Between 1953 and 1955 Dulles worked himself into a frenzy attempting—to no avail—to create an American, British, and French alliance to use military force against the coastal regions of China and Vietnam itself. Fortunately, the British and the French decided they had enough fighting to do in Asia without joining the United States in unnecessary skirmishes. If the British and French hadn't begged off, the United States would have been bogged down in Vietnam a decade earlier.

In January 1954, in my *Junius Americanus* newsletter, I wrote that "the greatest obstacle to peace is our own Secretary of State John Foster Dulles. He issues threats of reprisals or war at his breakfast table. He talks recklessly and too much." He provided an example of this on the eve of an armistice to end the Korean War when he complained that he did not "think we can get much out of a Korean settlement until we have shown— before all Asia—our clear superiority by giving the Chinese one hell of a licking."

This should have been sufficient cause for dismissing Dulles. But if Eisenhower had a weakness, it was his inability to fire subordinates, even when he realized or suspected that they were incompetent. Still, Eisenhower did remind Dulles who was in charge. Angered by Dulles's bellicosity, Eisenhower retorted: "All right, then. If Mr. Dulles and all his sophisticated advisors really mean that they cannot talk peace seriously, then I am in the wrong pew. For if it's war we should be talking about, I know the people to give me advice on that— and they're not in the State Department."

But even this rebuke from Eisenhower did not deter Dulles and likeminded internationalists from seeking other methods to involve the United States in an Asian war. Just before the 1955 Geneva Conference, which temporarily halted the fighting in Vietnam, Dulles spearheaded efforts to create the South East Asian Treaty Organization (SEATO). On September 8, 1954, eight nations—Australia, Great Britain, France, New Zealand, Pakistan, the Philippines, Thailand, and the United States—

met in Manila and signed the pact, each nation pledging joint action against aggressor nations.

Significantly, the pact was not signed by Vietnam, Cambodia, and Laos despite this and the further fact that the Geneva Agreement explicitly prohibited them from joining the new organization. Dulles nevertheless insisted that SEATO covered those three nations. Almost simultaneously with American entry into SEATO, John Foster Dulles gave his approval to acts of sabotage in Vietnam carried out by the CIA and directed by the head of that agency, his brother Allen. These operations achieved nothing but to plant the seeds from which America would reap the bitter harvest of full-scale military intervention.

I testified before the Senate Foreign Relations Committee on January 19, 1955, on the subject of the Southeast Asia Collective Defense Treaty. Besides having served more than twenty years on the House Foreign Affairs Committee, I was, in 1955, president of the American Political Action Committee, a nationwide nonpartisan political committee to combat communism, socialism, and superinternationalism. I think the reader will find that my comments shed enormous light on the perennial foreign policy questions that face this country. They also illustrate how predictable was our disaster in Vietnam:

Our committee considers the pending treaty as the worst and most dangerous type of one-worldism and interventionism ever presented to the Congress. It is a clear-cut example of superinternationalism that would inevitably drag us into a jungle war 10,000 miles away and actually play into the hands of the Communists.

It is not even based on our own security or self-defense except in words, platitudes, and generalities.

How can Cambodia and Laos in any way threaten our security, or even Vietnam or Thailand, if the islands off China do not threaten the security and defense of Formosa, only a few hundred miles away?

I thank the committee for this open hearing and for listening to my views in opposition to the so-called Southeast Asia Defense Pact. I use the word "so-called" advisedly, as it does not include the four largest Asian nations, India, China, Indonesia, and Burma. Furthermore, we own no territory in the Far East, and France will soon have none. Besides, both France and Britain are regarded as predatory colonial powers in the Far East.

I plead for an extended hearing and debate so that the American people will know all the facts and the inevitability of war involved in this pact. I plead that ample time be allowed the American people to read, learn, and thoroughly digest the warmaking provisions of this treaty before it is too late. At the present moment the American public, and including most Members of Congress except this committee, have not the faintest idea of the extreme war commitments made in this treaty. The fact is the American people have almost no knowledge of even the existence of such a hazardous warlike treaty. . . .

If I could but call up the spirits of Washington, Jefferson, Jackson, Lincoln, and many other great Americans of the past, they would, in no uncertain language, warn the American people that they are being betrayed into perpetual wars through foreign entanglements, alliances, and treaties that provide for sending American boys to fight and die in every swampland, jungle, and ricefield on the mainland of southeast Asia. This Southeast Asia Defense Treaty is more than a meaningless scrap of paper; it well may be the death certificate of a million or more selected youth of America in the bloody jungles of Indochina, Cambodia, Laos, and Thailand.

The danger is that the United States Government may now be able to make war without a declaration of war, and may feel it is duty-bound to react in a retaliatory or military way to any form of Chinese interference or aggression, direct or indirect. Then the fat is in the fire. But there is not likely to be war unity for such a jungle war on our side as there will be between China and Soviet Russia.

The time has come for a general public debate before the American people whether they favor this new brand of superinternationalism that causes us to virtually police the entire world singlehanded with American blood and treasure, and at our own instigation. The American people were never consulted about sending their sons to fight and die in Korea with only token support from the UN forces. But South Korea, surrounded on three sides by the ocean which we controlled, was incomparably better fighting ground than the malarial swamps and jungles of Southeast Asia. At least, we had a moral obligation to the South Koreans, but we have absolutely none on the mainland of Southeast Asia. . . .

If the treaty is ratified Uncle Sam will again be holding the bag and doing all the fighting, dying, and paying. This will not appeal to the American people once they know the facts. I propose, in my limited way, to help give them the facts and the awful truth as it affects the lives of their sons. I hope that I may be able to influence some Senators to come out fighting against the program of military intervention in Southeast Asia before it is too late. This treaty, if ratified, will confront the United States with a war crisis in a hydrogen age.

The fearless, outspoken leadership of Senator [Robert A.] Taft against military intervention in Southeast Asia is tragically missed. He would have inspired and rallied the Congress and the American people to violent protests against this treaty requiring military intervention in Indochina, Thailand,

Cambodia, and Laos. He would have warned the American mothers and fathers that it meant their sons would do the fighting and dying and not British or French or UN forces. He would have repeated his protest against sending a single American soldier to the mainland of Asia. From the grave comes the sound logic and practical reasoning of Senator Taft, a great American statesman who, shortly before his death, in a speech delivered by his son at Cincinnati, May 26, 1953, said: "I believe we might as well forget the United Nations as far as the Korean War is concerned."

I think it is only fair to Senator Taft, as long as I quoted him, that I read the full quotation: "I think we are bound to the policy of preventing Communist aggression where it occurs and where it is in our power to stop it. I have never felt that we should send American soldiers to the Continent of Asia, which, of course, includes China proper and Indochina, simply because we are so outnumbered in fighting a land war on the Continent of Asia that it would bring about complete exhaustion, even if we were able to win. . . ."

If this treaty is ratified it will be an evil day for America. It would inaugurate a ghastly and tragic policy for which we will pay in blood, sweat, and tears for generations to come. Why not consult the American people before making any binding war commitments? Not one American in ten would favor our entrance into war in Vietnam, Cambodia, Laos, Thailand. Nothing would be more unpopular. We cannot afford to squander our wealth, resources, or manpower all over the world without weakening our own economy and national defense, a condition which Moscow ardently desires. We must keep out of wars especially selected by Moscow and Peking for us, irrespective of our sympathies. We must stop our ceaseless campaign of rampant internationalism, one-worldism, and military intervention all over the entire world.

In conclusion, I am opposed to any military commitments that will involve us in a frightful jungle warfare in Indochina or Southeast Asia which would keep us tied down for years, provided we were not driven out by the Red hordes from China. We must not forget that Western Germany is the decisive battleground. We cannot police the world alone or act as military protector for either French or British imperialism in the Far East or elsewhere. We should concentrate our Armed Forces in Western Germany and Korea, arm the Japs, and choose our own battleground whenever necessary and not be committed by treaty to be drawn into jungle booby traps in Southeast Asia.

If the Eisenhower-Dulles-Stassen policies involve us in a jungle war on the Asian mainland there will be a political revolt such as has never been seen in this country. One hundred million Americans or more would resent it bitterly if a small handful of rabid interventionists, internationalists, and one-worlders succeeded in dragging us into a bloody, costly, and disastrous jungle war in Asia.

Having delivered this speech, I answered questions from the committee during the course of which I pointed out how different Australia, New Zealand, the Philippines, Formosa, and Japan were from the mainland of Asia. The former, being islands, were defensible; a mutual defense pact with these countries made some sense. Our fleet and the British fleet would be of significant use in helping our land forces defend these islands. But the mainland of Asia was an entirely different matter; a war there would bog down a vast number of our armed forces in circumstances where our naval forces would be of limited use and the enemy's manpower reserves would be overwhelming. This, it seemed to me, was playing directly into the hands of the Soviets—and I did not want us to get lured into such a conflict because of a revolution in Thailand, Laos, or Cambodia, or because of some other twist or turn in the domestic politics of those countries.

Along with Senator Taft, I was in favor of the North Atlantic Treaty Organization. I saw the need to erect a staunch military barrier to communist expansion in Europe. But the situation in Asia did not strike me as being in any way analogous. Though the communist threat in Asia was real—indeed I recognized that Indochina was doomed to communist-inspired war—there was an obvious limit to our defensive military capabilities, a limit that defending the Asian mainland surpassed.

I also understood that the president did not have the constitutional right to engage the country in hostilities without a declaration of war from Congress. But because of the expansion in presidential power under Franklin Roosevelt, I felt it necessary to point out in a reservation that the treaty should not be used as an excuse to drag the United States into war without the consent of Congress. But Congress did not add my reservation to the treaty and thereby paved the way for Presidents John F. Kennedy and Lyndon Baines Johnson to deepen American involvement in Vietnam without a declaration of war. Acting in ways so reminiscent of their idol, Franklin Roosevelt, Kennedy and Johnson ordered covert military operations that had the intent and the result of making *the* war in Vietnam *our* war in Vietnam.

On August 4, 1964, the United States destroyers *Maddox* and *Turner Joy* claimed they had been fired upon while off the North Vietnamese coast in the Gulf of Tonkin. Three days later Johnson asked for congressional approval to adopt more forceful military measures against North Vietnam under the provisions of the SEATO treaty. Congress, much to its later regret, gave its approval in the form of the Tonkin Gulf Resolution, effectively giving Johnson a blank check to wage war.

On February 16, 1966, I wrote to the *New York Herald Tribune* criticizing President Lyndon Johnson's role in dragging the United States into an unnecessary war in Vietnam:

> The American people have been virtually brainwashed into believing that they must support the President in the unwanted, unnecessary, and undeclared war in South Vietnam. President Johnson was elected in a campaign in which he excoriated Senator Goldwater as war-like and trigger-happy. This resulted in millions of Republican voters supporting Mr. Johnson. But almost immediately after the election he began to escalate the war. For every Communist we kill, hundreds join the Communist cause throughout Asia and the world. Johnson's war in South Vietnam has been the biggest shot in the arm to world Communism since the conference at Yalta. It solidifies, unites, and strengthens Communism everywhere. We should do everything we can to bring about a negotiated and honorable peace.

As Lyndon Johnson led the nation deeper into the morass of Vietnam, he began to lose the support of members of his own party. Senate Democratic Majority Leader Mike Mansfield publicly denounced Johnson's handling of the Vietnam War:

> If we would have peace, in my judgment, we must be prepared to spend political face for the purpose of saving lives. If we would have peace, we must act on the premise that this nation's proper interests do not lie in the prolongation of its deep military involvement on the Asian mainland. Others may indulge in pietism and pomposities on Vietnam and Asia. As Democrats we cannot. Ours is the responsibility for getting in. Ours should be the responsibility for getting out.

The difficult job of getting out of Vietnam, however, was left to a Republican president, Richard Nixon. When Nixon took office in 1969, there were more than 500,000 American soldiers actively engaged in fighting the ugly war in the teeming jungles of Vietnam. He gradually reduced the number of American troops so that by 1973 we had brought virtually all our soldiers home. Unfortunately, the communists succeeded in toppling the South Vietnamese government in 1975—a sad and tragic outcome, but one that all our years of intervention could not stop, leaving us with 55,000 Americans dead, 300,000 Americans wounded, a bill of hundreds of billions of dollars, and a nation embittered and divided over this tragic experience.

It was with saddened pleasure that I read the praise that Senator Claiborne Pell, Democrat from Rhode Island, had for me on June 17, 1970, when he reminded the Senate of the prescience of my testimony before the Senate Foreign Relations Committee almost fifteen years before. He said, in part:

> Hamilton Fish during his years of public service became known as an isolationist.
>
> In truth, and in the light of history, however, I think he would best be described as a noninterventionist. He saw, before many others, the limits of national power of even the most powerful nation on earth. Although strongly anti-Communist, he saw that the United States would not prevail in a world struggle by attempting to police the world with its own men and arms. And he had the vision to see that Southeast Asia was not vital to our national interests, but was a booby trap that would weaken and divide our country.

It is commonplace now to talk about the lessons of Vietnam, but the lesson today is as clear as it was when I spoke against the SEATO treaty in 1955: the United States must be the jealous guardian of its own national interest and not be drawn into endless conflicts all around the globe.

As I warned in Congress when Franklin Roosevelt was arrogating warmaking powers, so I warn the American people today that we must be vigilant in our efforts to prevent a future president from involving our nation in unnecessary wars far from our shores. We must always guard against becoming involved in foreign entanglements that are not in the national interest, but benefit only international economic interests whose allegiance is to the profit ledger, not to the flag.

We must, however, also always take care not to allow communist subversion in our own hemisphere. Even President Kennedy stated three days after the failed Bay of Pigs invasion of communist Cuba: "We must never tolerate another communist state in the American hemisphere." It was not until the end of President Reagan's administration and the beginning of George Bush's that communist gains in Central America were put into almost total retreat. Most communist guerilla movements are now almost completely defeated; the communist Sandinistas—still in powerful positions in President Chamorro's democratic government—were voted out of office in amazingly free elections in Nicaragua. To its discredit, Congress was not of much help to Presidents Reagan and Bush in achieving this outcome, but all Americans should remember the importance of enforcing the Monroe Doctrine for our own safety and for the security of the region.

Chapter Twenty-Six

The Nuclear Age

Another legacy of the Second World War is the atomic bomb. Over forty years ago, Bernard Baruch, a very close friend of mine, was appointed by President Harry Truman to present to the United Nations Energy Commission a plan that would have led to the total abolishment of all nuclear weapons. On June 14, 1946, Baruch told the commission that the issue of nuclear weapons was so threatening to the safety of the world that the United States and the Soviet Union had to choose between the "quick and the dead." Either every nation would renounce nuclear warfare or an insane nuclear arms race would ensue and would eventually end in a nuclear catastrophe.

Baruch's plan to abolish nuclear weapons was the first and one of the best opportunities the nations of the world had to abolish these fiendish weapons. Unfortunately, the Soviets rejected Baruch's proposal, embarking on an all-out program to build an enormous nuclear arsenal that in sheer numbers has long since far surpassed the arsenal of the United States.

Communism is on its way out in the Soviet Union and will probably fade away everywhere—except in the especially hard-line communist prison-states of China, Cuba, and North Korea—because people want freedom, democracy, and religion. Communism's failure to provide these has spelled its doom. But we must remember that the Soviet nuclear arsenal is still much larger than our own and that there are still communists in the Soviet Union who adhere to the tenets of Lenin and Stalin.

It is no waste of time, then, to refresh our memories with what these dictators stated publicly about their aims.

Lenin said: "It is necessary for Communists to use any ruse, cunning, unlawful methods, evasions, and concealments of truth in their war for world Communist dictatorship." He also predicted that communist states would surround the United States and destroy our country if it resisted their aggression.

In 1931 Professor Dimitri Manduilski, at the Lenin School of War in Moscow, stated a position that was reaffirmed in 1959 by the Soviet military. He declared:

> A war to the finish between Communism and Capitalism is inevitable. We are today naturally not strong enough to attack. Our opportunity will come in twenty or thirty years. To win, we will need the element of surprise, the bourgeoisie must be lulled to sleep. We will therefore begin by launching the most spectacular peace movement that ever existed. There will be electrifying proposals and extraordinary concessions. The stupid and decadent capitalistic countries will gladly cooperate in their own destruction. They will jump at a new chance for friendship. As soon as their guard is lowered WE WILL CRUSH THEM UNDER OUR IRON FIST.

One does not expect this sort of rhetoric from Mikhail Gorbachev. Nevertheless, the Soviets continue to build nuclear weapons at a rapid rate, and only yesterday they were sowing revolution in Central America, invading Afghanistan, and exporting Cuban troops and Russian officers to Africa. Gorbachev's government, moreover, is still filled with communists—the very same communists who under Lenin, and more grossly under Stalin, killed tens of millions of their own people in political murders.

The vast military power of the Soviet Union is so enormous that we cannot risk pushing them too fast in the direction of reform. And we must also keep our guard up—as long as the Soviets maintain their vast nuclear stockpile, we are a nation at risk.

Our nuclear weapons are relatively small; our biggest missiles carry five megatons. The Soviet armory is full of monstrous twenty-five megaton missiles. Just one of these would create a fireball of one-and-a-half miles in diameter, radiating a temperature of between twenty million and thirty million degrees Fahrenheit, killing everyone within seven miles of the center of the explosion and severely burning others within another seven mile radius. Buildings would disintegrate, food and water would be contaminated, and a crevice two hundred feet deep and several miles long would be carved out of the ground. In biblical terms, it would be Hell on Earth.

How could our common defense have become so imperilled, our nation and civilization so threatened? The blame can be attributed chiefly to two people: former Secretary of Defense Robert MacNamara and former President Jimmy Carter; the latter, judged on his record, has to be considered among the worst presidents in our history.

During the 1960s MacNamara believed that if we scrapped our large nuclear weapons, the Soviets would follow our example, and that if we stopped building nuclear weapons, the Soviets would do likewise after reaching a rough equivalence with us. MacNamara was wrong on both counts. Between 1965 and 1975, the Soviets built hundreds of twenty-five-megaton SS-18 missiles; and once they surpassed us in nuclear weapons, they kept building and never looked back.

To make matters worse, President Carter signed the SALT II treaty with the Soviet Union, limiting the size of our nuclear weapons to no more than five megatons, but allowing the Soviets to maintain their 308 twenty-five-megaton missiles. And he did it without submitting the treaty to the Senate, knowing it would have been rejected. SALT II was a highly effective blow to our deterrent capability, which was already being jeopardized by the Soviets' sheer numerical superiority, their improvements in the accuracy of their missiles, and their hardening of their missile silos. This latter greatly minimized the damage our smaller missiles could inflict on them. By the time President Carter signed SALT II, the United States, which in 1960 had a five-to-one nuclear superiority over the Soviet Union, was reduced to a nuclear inferiority on a scale of two-to-one. Today, incredibly but true, Soviet superiority in nuclear missiles is on the order of at least six-to-one.

If Carter had been serious about limiting the threat of nuclear weapons he should have sought the simple solution—abolishment of all nuclear weapons under a mutually verifiable treaty. Unfortunately, the Soviets were quick to realize that Carter's meek acquiescence to their demands gave them a golden opportunity to accelerate their build-up of armaments and expand their superiority over the United States—all with the seeming endorsement of an American president who had as one of his main objectives the banishment of what he regarded as America's unwarranted fear of the Soviet Union. This, of course, was before President Carter was taken aback by the Soviet invasion of Afghanistan.

The SALT II treaty was, in my opinion, the most shocking action taken against the best interests of the American people by any American president. Though Franklin Roosevelt had maneuvered us into a horrible and destructive world war, President Carter put America's entire existence at risk for the sake of a treaty that he considered a personal diplomatic triumph.

Since 1945, I have devoted my life to doing everything in my power to eliminate nuclear weapons from the face of the earth. I have made countless speeches to veterans groups and other public gatherings about the absolute necessity of abolishing all nuclear weapons. And the best way to this end is to negotiate with the Soviets from a position of strength.

At a convention of more than ten thousand veterans at the New York State American Legion Convention at Lake Placid in 1986, I introduced a resolution that proposed:

> . . . to abolish all nuclear weapons in every nation within the next four years on the basis of twenty-five percent reductions each year under strict mutual inspections.
> . . . [that since] the United States created this fiendish device and used it against two Japanese cities. . . [it] now should take the leadership in restoring peace throughout the world by abolishing all nuclear weapons, which, if they are ever used in a future war, would cause nearly total destruction of most of the civilized world.
> . . . [that] total abolishment of nuclear weapons by all nations will promote world peace and will save the human race from ultimate extinction.

Having gotten the support of the New York Legion, I traveled to the national convention in Texas in 1987. Unfortunately, three members of the U.S. State Department who were in attendance as distinguished guests had a negative reaction to my resolution, which they helped to block. The convention delegates who would have overwhelmingly supported my resolution were never allowed to vote on it. Why did the three State Department members take such efforts to silence me? I believe it was because George Schultz is a one-worlder internationalist for whom nuclear weapons are of no great importance.

I wrote a number of letters to President Ronald Reagan on the necessity of ridding the world of nuclear weapons, and I know that Reagan's instincts on this issue were sound. But he was frequently given bad advice by men like George Schultz and Howard Baker—one of the Republican senators who, during the Carter administration, voted to give away the Panama

Canal. The Intermediate Nuclear Forces treaty that Schultz negotiated for Reagan was another fiasco—eliminating an entire class of short-range missiles that were a key component of our deterrent capability. That Reagan allowed this to pass was surprising, given that he had in 1981 stated that "No nation that placed its faith in parchment or paper while at the same time gave up its protective hardware ever lasted long enough to write many pages in history. . . ." How right he was, and how wrong was his INF agreement.

But the United States has been lucky. The Soviet Union's crippling domestic problems have at least temporarily put it into retreat in international affairs and have distracted its attention from spreading world revolution. Still, we must negotiate with the Soviets to get them to join us in the complete abolition of nuclear weapons. I would endorse proposals that we negotiate away our Strategic Defense Initiative—or Star Wars—*if* it will bring the Soviets to an agreement to render useless our mutual nuclear stockpiles. However, I do not believe that SDI is without value. The Soviets were very much against our continuing research in this technology. I must credit President Reagan's push for this program as a contributing factor which persuaded the Soviets to begin the reforms that ultimately resulted in Germany's reunification and the collapse of the Berlin Wall.

I also believe that more heed should be given to proposals put forth by the Union of Concerned Scientists, a group of hundreds of scientists who know far more about this issue than anyone else. The Union of Concerned Scientists (USC) has long called for total abolishment of nuclear weapons, and their calls have been endorsed by other groups—notably by America's Catholic bishops. The objective of our negotiations should be, as the USC has stated, "to create a situation where nuclear weapons become increasingly insignificant to the relationship between the U.S. and the USSR. Other nations—Great Britain, France, China, and other nations that may have a nuclear capability—must also be brought into multilateral negotiations so as to achieve worldwide stability."

Israel would be one such nation. It would be reluctant to surrender its supposed nuclear arsenal—with good reason—because it is surrounded by hostile Arab nations that are continually threatening to attack. With this in mind, the United States and the Soviet Union, along with Great Britain and West Germany, must agree to stiff guarantees that Israel's right to exist as a free and democratic nation be upheld. These negotiations would have to be held concurrently with the nuclear disarmament discussions. Once Israel's security was guaranteed, it too would have to abolish its nuclear weapons.

We cannot let the current euphoria about the collapse of communism allow us to forget the nuclear payload the Soviets still have pointed at us. As Norman Podhoretz, the editor of *Commentary* magazine, has noted:

> With each disillusioning shock, we have awakened briefly to the reality of the Soviet threat, only to be driven by fear into a new period of denial. But never before has our denial gone so deep as it is going today.
>
> Thus, just as we are to hurl ourselves into a strategic situation whose logical outcome is a Soviet-dominated world, our secretary of state tells us that "we are on a roll," and our leading political commentators declare that we have won the ideological struggle against communism.

That was written several years ago, but Podhoretz's warning remains pertinent. The Soviet Union has gone through dire domestic straits many times before, but it has always reemerged to spread its tentacles as far as they can reach. Despite its inevitable economic calamities, which are a continuing testimony to the failures of communism, the Soviet Union is still a militarily potent threat to the United States.

President Ronald Reagan's administration was very successful in preserving peace and encouraging economic prosperity. But he did not succeed in ridding the world of nuclear weapons. This is a task that his highly competent successor George Bush should undertake. The mutually verifiable abolition of nuclear weapons would still leave the Soviet Union with by far the largest army in the world, with the greatest number of tanks, artillery pieces, and aircraft, as well as a navy much larger than our own, having twice as many submarines. Surely this provides the Soviets with more than adequate security for their national defense.

Abraham Lincoln once said that "To sin by silence when you should protest makes cowards of men." We Americans live in a free nation under a government that is derived by the consent of the governed. It is our right, our obligation, and our duty to demand that our public officials bring the Soviet Union to the negotiating table and do what is necessary to rid our nation and the world of the ever present threat of a nuclear holocaust.

Chapter Twenty-Seven

Trading with the Enemy

Lenin once said—in a now famous quote—that the capitalists would sell the communists the rope with which to hang them. This prediction has frequently contained more than a grain of truth. Our government has often operated under the delusion that we can bribe our way into friendship with our enemies by using taxpayer money for trade and aid agreements. Just as Franklin Roosevelt thought he could make Stalin a friend of the United States by letting the communists seize vast portions of Europe, so too Roosevelt's followers have thought to encourage reforms in communist governments and gain their support by showering them with aid and trade concessions. This policy was always idiocy. We merely supported the governments—and the governmental corruption—that oppressed the peoples of Eastern Europe. Only the forcible efforts of the peoples of Eastern Europe to oust their communist masters finally tore down the Iron Curtain, not our foolish trade policies.

And it is not just the communists that we have aided, but our other enemies as well, including the regime of Saddam Hussein in Iraq, and other unappetizing Third World dictators.

As long as the communists control the levers of power in the Soviet Union, they will work to destroy capitalism, free enterprise, and democracy anywhere they can, because that is what it means to be a communist; that is what communists hope for; that is what they try to achieve.

Every communist leader has held the same conviction as Lenin, who

177

said in a speech to the Moscow Communist party in 1920: "As long as
Capitalism and Socialism exist we cannot live in peace. In the end, one or
the other will triumph. A funeral dirge will be sung either over the Soviet
Republic or over world Capitalism." Stalin blamed the First World War on
"the Capitalist world economy" and the Second on "monopoly Capitalism." Others, of course, might be inclined to blame the First World War on
the fractious nations of Europe who have always been at each other's
throats; and they might blame the Second World War on people like Hitler
and Stalin who were one-time allies. Far from being a war of monopoly
capitalism, the Second World War was more accurately a war waged by
national socialist Germany and communist Russia against the free, democratic, capitalist West.

The communists consciously see their model of society as being in
competition with the free market, capitalist model of society. Though our
triumph seems absolute, one has only to look at communism's continuing
power in the Soviet Union and in China—two massive countries with
enormous populations—to know that the competition is not over. Indeed,
the capitalist model still has not won the hearts and minds of America's
numerous left-wing academics.

We will not bring the Soviets and the communist Chinese onto the road
to democracy by extending diplomatic and financial appeasement. These
policies have been tried and they have failed, because they strengthen the
wrong hands—the same hands that bloodily crushed the Chinese student
uprising for freedom in Tiananmen Square.

Trade with and loans to communist and Third World dictators serve only
to promote the employment of slave labor in these countries—perhaps
helping to build more munitions plants or chemical and biological warfare
facilities or some other power-driven venture to use against us or against
their own populations if they rise up crying out for freedom. Is this what we
want?

The United States has been involved in a cold war with Soviet Russia
since the end of World War II. The cold war has been a very real war and
has cost us more than any hot war in history. The United States has spent
over a trillion dollars in this war to counteract and combat world communism and it has sacrificed the lives of tens of thousands of American
men in the icy hills of Korea and steaming jungles of Vietnam. Yet while
the United States government was spending billions on fighting communism, it was also spending billions in direct military and economic aid to

communist nations. Fighter planes were sold at hugely discounted prices to the communist dictator Tito of Yugoslavia; we supplied nuclear reactors to the communist government of Czechoslovakia, railway equipment to Bulgaria, chemical plants to Yugoslavia, and synthetic rubber plants to the Soviet Union; we gave the Soviets the machinery to build ball-bearings (which can be used in guided missiles); and we built a highly automated steel finishing plant for the communist government in Poland. Even Fidel Castro, the communist dictator of Cuba, received a grant of $1,157,000 from the United Nations Special Fund headed by Paul Hoffman, an American, for the Communist Cuban Agricultural Program (Hearing Subcommittee on Foreign Relations, U.S. Senate, 88th Cong. 1st Sess., February 18, 1963, "UN Special Fund"; *Washington Post*, May 4, 1963, "UN Pact To Aid Cuba Is Signed"). How many countries have been so foolish as to aid their enemies while fighting them? Isn't giving aid and comfort to the enemy an act of treason?

Many people say that we have won the cold war. To them I say, maybe we are winning it, but the war is not over. To sink American dollars into the rotten regimes in communist China and Soviet Russia is not only to throw our money away but to disgrace the sacrifices we have made and the suffering that the peoples under these regimes have endured. It also undermines our credibility as the guardian angel of the free nations of Europe and the shining beacon of liberty to the other nations of the world. How can we inspire the Europeans if we trade with the enemy? How can the oppressed peoples of the world respect us if we trade with their oppressors? To trade with the new, free government of Poland and with the newly unified Germany is one thing. To trade with the butchers of Beijing and the tank commanders cutting their bloody swath through the streets of the Baltic States is quite another.

What is the purpose of trading with the Soviet Union? Mr. Edwin Marks, who was president of Karl Marks and Company, a dealer in foreign securities, once said: "The Russians are seeking to buy turn-key operations, not commodities or goods. They are interested in buying the tools of production for petroleum, chemical, and other manufacturing facilities . . . not in buying American products."

It makes sense for the Soviets to enrich their economic and industrial power, but does it make sense for us to help them do it? Is it to our advantage to establish modernized factories in the Soviet Union that will compete with American goods throughout the world on a much lower wage scale, with the profits going into the pockets of communists who manage an enormous war machine that blatantly wishes us harm?

The words of Senator Everett Dirksen hold as true today as they did when he uttered them against President Lyndon Johnson's efforts to expand our trade with and economic bridges to the Soviet Union. Dirksen asked if President Johnson's plan would not "become a structure for the conveying of our bounty and treasure to the unfriendly and uncooperative nations without any value whatever received in return." He went further:

> What justification can be cited for the Administration's persistent effort to liberalize and extend terms—tantamount to aid to the Soviet Union and Communist Governments of Eastern Europe—while these nations are supplying most of the guns and missiles that are killing American soldiers and shooting down American planes in Southeast Asia? The answer to all this is a clear one; more attention to the conservation of our own strength and resources and less to those nations of the world who regard us as an amiable, venerable Santa Claus who can be slurred at will and cuffed with impunity. The international bank of good will shows a mounting deficit where our external relations are concerned. . . . We are determined that our well-being shall to a greater degree be directed towards the well-being of the American family and of the American nation. . . . For the beneficences we have showered on this world, we deserve something more than the ungrateful cry, Yanqui, go home.

Wrapped up in the matter of trade and aid is the matter of Soviet diplomacy. The Soviets have always considered their diplomats abroad to be actual spies. Unfortunately, even with the appearance of glasnost and perestroika, there is plenty of evidence that Soviet espionage is as active as ever in Europe and the United States.

As Americans, we bear no hatred for any peoples since we are a nation made up of all peoples. We have no grievance with the Russians, but we have a very large grievance with the Communist party of the Soviet Union, with the communists in Red China, and with any other dictators who seek to overthrow our democratic, constitutional form of government and replace it with their tyranny.

Though we must, of course, wish the reformist movements in these countries every success, we must, on the one hand, guard against encouraging them to move faster than is safe and, on the other hand, not allow ourselves to be lulled into a contented sleep in which we do not notice the continuing activities of communist spies, the continuing build-up of communist arms, and the continuing diplomatic rivalry they insist on pursuing against the existence of democratic, free market societies.

I hope that one day the Russian people, who have contributed so much to the culture of the world, will truly free themselves from the most barbaric government Europe has ever known, pursue their country's own best interest, and forgo seeking to destabilize the free governments of the Western world. Until that time comes, however, we must be as vigilant as we have ever been to secure and protect our liberties, as the preamble to the Constitution says, for ourselves and our posterity.

Chapter Twenty-Eight

The War-making Powers of Congress

All Americans—and certainly all Americans who are elected officials— must hold allegiance to the Constitution. It is the law of the land by which our liberties are defended and the role of our government defined. Many of my disagreements with Franklin Roosevelt stemmed from his irresponsible and dangerous belief that he could dispense with the Constitution when it suited him. That way lies tyranny.

Roosevelt's actions established a precedent of executive supremacy over the Congress that his successors have attempted to widen and exploit. Many political activists who call themselves conservatives and profess to believe in the Constitution seem just as willing as liberals to grant extraordinary powers to the president—it depends on whose ox is being gored.

The issue of the separation of powers is especially vital when we talk about peace and war. Quite simply: The Congress has the sole and exclusive power to declare war. It was expressly given that power by the Founding Fathers to prevent the president from making war at his personal discretion. The Founders were well aware of the danger of placing such power in the hands of one individual—whether king or president. They realized that our existence as a free people demanded that proposals for war be debated, and accepted or rejected, by the elected representatives of the people.

Hamilton Fish with his Harvard roommate, Peabody Gardiner, who became a world famous tennis player.

Hamilton Fish, captain of Harvard's undefeated football team in 1908. Fish was twice chosen for Walter Camp's All-Time All-America Football Team and was honored in the College Football Hall of Fame in King's Island, Ohio for his football prowess.

Hamilton Fish as a member of the New York State Assembly, his first elective office.

Hamilton Fish working in the coal mines of Calgary, Canada, during a Harvard summer vacation.

Hamilton Fish in an army camp during World War I.

Captain Fish and his famed "Harlem Hellfighters"—the 369th Regiment. The entire regiment was awarded the French *Croix de Guerre*.

Hamilton Fish during a leisure moment somewhere in France during World War I.

Hamilton Fish visiting nephews Hamilton Fish Breese and William Lawrence Breese, Jr., in Paris at the end of World War I. The boys' mother was Fish's older sister Julia Kean Fish. Their father was killed during the war while serving in the British Army. William Jr. lives in Washington, D.C. His brother died at age 10 and is buried in England along with his father.

Hamilton Fish as a U.S. congressman in 1939.

Hamilton Fish playing tennis at the Chevy Chase tennis courts in Washington, D.C., while a U.S. congressman.

Hamilton Fish, third from the left, following a charity ball game in Washington, D.C., while a U.S. congressman.

Hamilton Fish posing with Gen. and Mrs. Douglas MacArthur after having presented the general with the Order of Lafayette Freedom Award in 1961. Fish was president of the Order of Lafayette.

RIGHT: French Undersecretary of Defense Gerard Renon, decorating Hamilton Fish with the French Legion of Honor Medal Award aboard U.S. aircraft carrier *Jeanne D'Arc* in April, 1987. Fish and his 369th Regiment fought side-by-side with the French army on the Rhine.

Hamilton Fish, age 100, and wife Lydia at the Inauguration of President George Bush, January 1988.

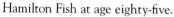

Hamilton Fish at age eighty-five.

ABOVE RIGHT: Hamilton Fish at the
Arlington National Cemetery in
1987 after placing a wreath at the
Tomb of the Unknown Soldier.
It was Fish who introduced the
legislation calling for the Tomb
of the Unknown Soldier.

Hamilton Fish waited many years to
lead the Harvard Alumni Parade as
the oldest alumnus. He finally got
his chance at his eightieth class
reunion.

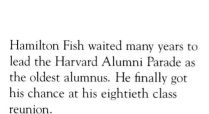

Hamilton Fish, at age 100, waves a salute at the Pearl Harbor Memorial Ceremony at Port Jefferson, New York in December, 1988. (Photo by Tom Koeniges/*Newsday*)

The controversial War Powers Act is a legislative version of putting the cart before the horse. The role of the Congress is not to interfere with the decisions of the president—the country's commander-in-chief—once war has started, but to decide whether or not the country should be at war in the first place. Unfortunately, and typically, the present members of Congress would rather pass the decision on making war over to the president and then, after the fact, argue whether or not to support him. This is a supreme dereliction of duty.

Once a war is entered upon, the president as commander-in-chief acquires enormous authority to conduct all military operations. In the extraordinary circumstances of war, it is essential that the command of our armed forces be unified in this way. The role of Congress is crucial, because it is the body that declares war and makes the president commander-in-chief. In this role, Congress can be a powerful restraining influence for the preservation of peace. It is easier to get into a war than to get out of one; and given the speed with which congressmen can travel nowadays, Congress's war-making powers are on a sounder footing than ever before, because Congress can be reassembled at a day's notice. Only an unannounced nuclear attack would make the Constitution's provisions impractical.

The dangers of a president taking the decision on war into his own hands are enormous. For example, on April 25, 1954, President Eisenhower, Secretary of State Dulles, and Admiral Radford agreed—without the consent of Congress or the American people—to send American air and naval power against the Vietnamese in defense of the French colonial forces trapped at Dien Bien Phu. Only the strong opposition of Great Britain's Prime Minister Winston Churchill and his cabinet prevented this folly. Even as responsible, courageous, and effective a president as Eisenhower was prepared—under the bad advice of John Foster Dulles—to violate the Constitution in order to intervene on behalf of the interests of a foreign power.

Any president who deliberately orders an attack on a foreign nation without the consent of Congress can be and should be impeached. To turn Congress into a rubber stamp on the war issue would be a tragic rending of the document that establishes our free government and rule by law. It would place total and dictatorial war-making authority in the hands of one individual to send our sons—and now our daughters as well—to fight in the far corners of the world. This power should never be given to any one individual, no matter who. All individuals are subject to impulse, anger, enmity, and the disabilities of bad health and old age. The authority of Congress is our Constitution's check on arbitrary power. Unfortunately, Congress itself seems happy to relinquish this role, preferring to backbite, to criticize, but not to act. Rudyard Kipling called power without responsibility the prerogative of the harlot throughout the ages. That's a pretty apt description of our present Congress.

The peace measures of Franklin Roosevelt were of course war measures; and the peace measures of all other internationalists are also war measures, because the road to peace for the internationalists is paved with wars and the deaths of uniformed Americans. Congress must be the defender of American interests, of the interests of the American people; Congress must not be cajoled into endless foreign adventures that lead us only into war, bankruptcy, and disaster. If the president acts without the consent of Congress, it is safe to assume that he is not pursuing American interests, but his own interests or the interests of internationalist advisors. If Congress is in agreement with the president about the need for war, then perhaps the heavy duty which our armed forces have lifted so often before does in fact have to be lifted again and carried on to final victory.

And if our troops are to achieve final victory, it will be on the basis of the wealth, power, and strength of the United States—three qualities that we continue to squander at will with foreign handouts. President George Washington warned us two hundred years ago about the danger of entangling foreign alliances and disabling foreign involvements. He was right.

It is impossible to buy friends, and if you do they will not be reliable. With the best of intentions we fought in two world wars, made numerous foreign commitments, and scattered hundreds of billions of dollars all around the globe. One wonders what we achieved. Our entry into the First World War might have prolonged a horrible conflagration and thereby helped topple the Russian czar and opened the door for the communist coup. Our victory in the Second World War was followed by the communist conquest of Eastern Europe. Our foreign handouts led only to foreign condemnation of us from the very countries we were aiding—followed by a demand for more money.

Wars are not profitable. And bribes and handouts win us no friends. America's business is America's own and we should apply that standard to the rest of the world. If other nations attended to their own business and we attended to ours, the world would be a better place. If a referendum were held, I'm sure the American people would vote five to one against foreign handouts. In this, as in many things, the instinct of the American people is at one with the Constitution. It is doubtful whether the Congress has the power under the general welfare clause of the Constitution to provide for huge foreign handouts. Unquestionably, the welfare clause was designed for the welfare of the American people, not for foreign nations.

Dollars make bad diplomacy, and our foreign policy should not follow our foreign handouts or the financial interests of our companies that invest abroad. During the Algerian War in the late 1950s, the French seized the Arab leader Ben Bellagh and four Arab chiefs in an airplane that they managed to divert either by trickery or treachery. The French claimed they found more than twenty-seven pounds worth of secret and incriminating papers, many of which showed that ARAMCO (the Arabian American Oil Company) had contributed money to stir up Arab uprisings in Algeria. The French had discovered a huge new oil field four hundred miles south of Algiers in the Sahara Desert, and now the French accused ARAMCO of plotting with the Arabs. The assumption was that the company believed it could cut a better deal with the Arabs than the French concerning the new find.

It does not take much imagination to realize the bitterness, anger, and indignation the French felt upon discovering that American money was being used to promote civil war and rebellion against their armed forces and civilians in an area the French believed was an integral part of France.

I believe that many of our government officials with responsibilities in this area knew little about this corporate adventure. I was told that our ambassador in Paris was dumbfounded when the captured documents were shown to him and that he flew immediately to Washington to make a report. But, then again, the oil companies had developed many friends in Congress and in the State Department.

The point of this story is not to disparage the oil companies, because I was in the oil business myself for several years and found it to be as honest a business as any other. The point is rather that Americans should not have to send their sons and daughters to fight and die for the business interests of ARAMCO or any other oil monopoly. I would not sacrifice the life of one American soldier for all the oil in Arabia.

Doubtless, all this talk of oil and war will lead the reader to wonder what I think of President Bush's deployment of American forces to Saudi Arabia in response to Iraq's invasion of Kuwait. I think very highly of President Bush, but I must say that I think this state of affairs would never have come to pass had President Reagan, with his forceful presence and unambiguous doctrine of peace through strength, been in office. I opposed the idea of going to war against Saddam Hussein unless it was absolutely necessary to stop him from committing heinous crimes against people we had pledged to defend. The situation in the Middle East is too volatile for me to comment further at this time, except to say that I proudly salute our troops in the Middle East and wish them well in their efforts to free Kuwait and to protect Saudi Arabia from further Iraqi aggression.

Epilogue: The Last Bull Moose

Hamilton Fish died January 18, 1991, at his home in Cold Spring, New York. He was 102 years old. For the last half of his life, right up until two weeks before his death, he remained active—writing, speaking, and attending various patriotic and political meetings. Though he never held public office after 1945, he was a politician all his life. His memoirs were intended as his last political testament, one final stump speech to carry his unchanging message to the American people.

"He was a political animal and he loved politics," says historian Tony Troncone, his friend and biographer. "Until the day he died, the man lived for politics. That's all he ever talked about. There were times when I would stay with him eight, nine, ten hours, and that's all the conversation was about."

Fish entertained more than a few hopes of capturing the Republican nomination for president in 1940 as a dark horse candidate. That year, the Republican convention in Philadelphia was expected to reach a deadlock between Senator Robert A. Taft of Ohio and Governor Thomas E. Dewey of New York. Fish attended with his family. "I remember seeing all those FISH signs on wooden sticks and materials and posters and such in a room ready to be brought out on the convention floor," recalls his son, Ham Jr., who was then thirteen years old.

The signs were never used. The expected deadlock occurred, but it was broken by Wendell Willkie. Late that night, as the family walked back to the hotel, Fish strode ahead a block or more. "We tried to trot along as fast as we could, but we kept falling further behind," his son adds. "He was obviously very, very disappointed."

According to Troncone, Fish never had a chance at the nomination. Fish was never liked by the businessmen who had taken control of the Republican party at the state and national levels. Troncone explains: "He was a progressive and he wanted to bring corporations under the rule of law, as did Theodore Roosevelt, and he opposed . . . the growth of the business wing of the Republican party."

It was not that Fish was unalterably opposed to the growth of the "business wing of the Republican party"; after all, he believed in the freedom of the marketplace and the individual's right to pursue his economic happiness. But, like other progressives, it was that he feared the political power that accompanied that growth. Business had to submit to the state and recognize that power flowed upward from the "people"; that is, business could not subvert the rights of the people to its advantage.

Fish also remained suspicious of big businessmen, saying that many of them "were greedy and didn't give a damn about the country, only their pocketbooks." This underscored his insistence that individuals had to make sacrifices in the interest of promoting the common good.

In 1933, big business Republicans made common cause with Fish to fight the New Deal, but by 1940, the debate over the New Deal had ended. Big business had decided it could live with an expanded, semisocialist federal government. Besides, the burden of expanded government fell more heavily on smaller competitors struggling to survive in a free market, which progressives like Fish wanted to preserve, than to the bigger outfits.

Fish's political strength had always been in his district among the people who had known him since 1914. But his popularity declined steadily after Pearl Harbor, although not enough to force him out of office until 1944. "Had his district remained intact, he would have been reelected," says Troncone. Outside his district, he was popular with die-hard opponents of the war and the New Deal, but he had no base of support. Thus, when Dewey, as governor of New York, engineered the redrawing of Fish's district, Dutchess and Putnam Counties, where his popularity was still high, Fish was simply cut out of New York politics. It was, for Fish, like being thrown out of his own home.

Fish always felt extremely bitter toward Dewey, but he did not consider himself beaten. In 1946, he moved from Washington to the comfortable Forest Hills neighborhood of Queens, then a heavily populated Republican stronghold. From Queens, Fish hoped to launch a bid for the U.S. Senate in 1950. In the meantime, he embarked on several business ventures that he hoped would provide him the money he would need for his campaign. He renewed his association with the John C. Paige insurance firm in New York City and was involved briefly with a Studebaker automobile dealership in Cold Spring, just north of his hometown of Garrison. He also invested unwisely in a risky Texas oil venture with the Deep South Oil Company, persuading several of his friends to do likewise. The company found no oil, and Fish lost over $15,000.

In 1947, Fish bought an anti-communist opinion magazine called *Today's World*—"The Magazine that Dares to Tell the Truth." Fish was editor and publisher and frequent contributor. His columns often appeared under the pseudonym "Junius Americanus"; the use of Latin pen-names was practiced by early American patriots, such as Alexander Hamilton, when writing to warn of dangers to the Republic.

Before selling the magazine in 1948, Fish used it to promote Robert A. Taft and Douglas MacArthur as presidential candidates, and to lash out at Thomas Dewey, big business Republicans, New Deal Democrats, and communists of any shade.

Dewey was a favorite target of Fish's. In one of its issues, the magazine reprinted an article Fish had written for the *Chicago Tribune* entitled "The General and the Chocolate Soldier." The title referred to a remark by Alice Roosevelt, daughter of Theodore Roosevelt and longtime Washington socialite, that Thomas Dewey looked like a chocolate bridegroom on a wedding cake. On another occasion, Fish contrasted MacArthur's illustrious war record with Dewey's lack of military service. In later years, he went so far as to call Dewey a draft-dodger. Though Dewey was too young to enlist during World War I, he was just 39, and governor of New York, when the U.S. entered World War II; in Fish's opinion, Dewey's failure to resign from office and seek a commission amounted to cowardice. Along the way, in his many public speeches, Fish liked to amuse his audiences by saying, "Governor Dewey bought himself a farm in Dutchess County and got himself exempted on the grounds he was a farmer—but he never milked a cow in his entire life."

Fish's criticisms of Dewey no doubt contributed to Dewey's upset defeat by Harry Truman in 1948, but they also aggravated Fish's feud with the leadership of the New York Republican party. By refusing to adopt a more conciliatory approach, he threw away what little chance he had of securing the nomination for the Senate in 1950. And in fact, he would never again hold public office. For many years his participation in party politics was limited to serving as a committeeman for the city of Newburgh.

Fish remained in the public limelight for several years, speaking frequently across the country and writing articles for newspapers and magazines. His first book, *The Challenge of World Communism*, was published in 1946. Over the years, he authored several more books on his favorite topics: communism, Franklin Roosevelt, nuclear disarmament, and American history. Most were published by a vanity press.

During the Eisenhower administration, Fish sought an ambassadorship to Germany and would have been pleased to accept one to Belgium, the Netherlands, or Britain, but he was no friend of John Foster Dulles, Eisenhower's secretary of state. Among other sins, Fish had founded the American Political Action Committee, which actively opposed Eisenhower's foreign policy, specifically U.S. participation in the Southeast Asia Treaty Organization (SEATO).

Fish was out of the game for good. Yet, when all he could do was watch, world events seemed to make his case for him. Several high-level government officials were exposed as communists; an interventionism foreign policy committed the U.S. to another war in Korea and, fifteen years later, still another in Vietnam; and Stalin was revealed to the world as a beast. In frustration, Fish wrote to an associate in 1954, saying, "Wherever I go today almost everyone stops me and says: 'Ham, you and I were right, weren't we?' "

As the years passed, he busied himself writing letters to presidents, senators, governors, admirals, and generals, and anyone else he thought needed his advice. He donated much of his time to various patriotic organizations, serving as committee chairman for the Society of the Cincinnati, an association of the descendants of Revolutionary War officers, and as president general of the Order of Lafayette, an association Fish founded for American military officers who served in France during World Wars I and II.

In 1965, when Jo Anne Mecca began work as his secretary, the seventy-seven-year-old Fish was living in the Mansfield Hotel, a rundown establishment on West 44th Street in Manhattan. The Mansfield's advantage for Fish was that it was across the street from the Harvard Club, where he was a member and where he often ate lunch, and sometimes received mail. Fish also rented an office on the first floor of the Mansfield, back between the kitchen and the men's room. "It was a horrible office," Jo Anne remembers, "windows looking out at a brick wall, a sink and a stamp machine and two desks—that was it."

Jo Anne's job consisted chiefly in preparing correspondence for Fish and arranging the annual Freedom Award Dinner for the Order of Lafayette. The dinner was attended by many famous Americans, including former president Dwight Eisenhower, General Douglas MacArthur, Admiral Chester Nimitz, actor Jimmy Stewart, and former congresswoman Clare Boothe Luce. Fish lived for such occasions. "People would come up to him and say hello, and he loved that attention. He loved being recognized," says Jo Anne. "He was very social when I first met him—out every night for dinner."

The Order of Lafayette also made yearly pilgrimages to France to visit Lafayette's tomb and lay wreaths at the graves of American servicemen. Fish assumed regular responsibility for chartering the airplane for the trip, in return for which he received a free ticket.

Fish was never rich, despite his heritage. During the Depression, he struggled for years to support his family while maintaining his social and professional standing. On weekends he would be in New York moonlighting with the John C. Paige insurance company or in Chicago speaking to a convention for a $50 fee. As late as 1965, he was still paying on a loan he had received while in Congress from the Riggs National Bank in Washington. After Congress, he lived well enough on his congressional pension, a small pension for his service in World War I, and a pension from the state of New York for his three years of part-time employment as a state assemblyman. He also owned shares for many years in two major oil companies, which grew to sizeable holdings. Fish lived so long that, by the time of his death, his pension from New York State, though originally small, had grown to over $2,000 a month.

It comes as no surprise to anyone who knew Fish that his memoirs exclude nearly all mention of his personal life, his four wives, and his son and daughter and many grandchildren and great-grandchildren. For Fish rarely shared personal details with anyone. "He didn't talk much about his wives. He very rarely spoke about anything personal," recalls Jo Anne, his secretary for twenty-five years. His office was decorated with portraits of Lafayette and Nicholas Fish, a bust of Alexander Hamilton, and a stuffed marlin—but not a single photograph of anyone in Fish's immediate family.

In 1920, the year he was elected to Congress, Fish married Grace Chapin Rogers, daughter of Alfred Clark Chapin, a former member of Congress, comptroller of the state of New York, and speaker of the New York Assembly. Fish was proud of his father-in-law and used to comment that Chapin was the last Democratic mayor of Brooklyn before it became a Manhattan borough. Grace's first husband was William Beverly Rogers, a cousin of Hamilton Fish. Rogers died and left Grace with two children, Alfred Chapin Rogers and Susan LeRoy Fish Rogers. Young Chapin was eleven and Susan seven when their mother married Hamilton Fish.

Soon after moving to Washington, Hamilton and Grace Fish bought a new, four-storey, red-brick house on Ashmead Place, overlooking Rock Creek Park, in the District of Columbia. In 1922, Grace gave birth to Elizabeth Stuyvesant Fish, who soon acquired the nickname "Zevah," her childish rendering of Elizabeth. Four years later, Hamilton Fish, Jr., was born. Like his father, he would be called Hammy.

Through Grace's family, the Fishes also owned a large summer house at Murray Bay, a cluster of French Canadian villages one hundred miles north of Quebec City on the St. Lawrence River. Every summer, Grace and the children would move to Murray Bay to escape the heat of Washington for a month or two. Fish would join them in August for a week or two when he would compete in the local tennis tournament, but he rarely stayed longer. He was impatient with the leisurely life of Murray Bay and professed to prefer warmer climates to the cool, damp nights on the St. Lawrence.

Murray Bay was also the summer home of the Taft family. Martha Taft and Grace Fish were best friends, and their families often spent New Year's Day together, while Senator Taft was Hamilton Fish's closest political ally, if not his closest friend. Says Troncone of Fish, "He was never really close to anyone. His friends were political in nature."

In Washington, Hamilton and Grace Fish upheld the social responsibilities of a prominent and ambitious politician. They were frequently the guests of Washington's social and diplomatic community, and, in turn, often entertained important political allies or ideological friends, including the Tafts, the Coolidges, the Hoovers, and the Lindberghs. As a party leader, Fish's political duties were demanding. He was always busy and very often on the road. In 1936, while promoting Senator William E. Borah as a candidate for president, Fish visited 44 states in two-and-a-half months. His daughter Zevah remembers that when he was home, he was busy going over his papers or rehearsing his speeches. His children saw very little of him.

In the late 1930s, Zevah attended St. Timothy's boarding school for girls in Catonsville, Maryland, and in 1943, married Insley Pyne, a navy dive-bomber pilot during the war and a professor of electrical engineering at Princeton University afterwards. Hammy attended St. Alban's School for

Boys in Washington before entering the navy in 1944. Subsequently, he earned his bachelor's degree at Harvard and then entered the foreign service. After an assignment to the U.S. Embassy in Dublin, he received his law degree from New York University and began practicing law in New York City. Ham Jr. married a childhood friend whom he first met at Murray Bay.

In 1946, Grace stayed on at the house on Ashmead Place while Fish established residency in Queens to prepare his campaign for the Senate. For a few weeks each year, they would gather with Zevah and Ham Jr. and the grandchildren at Murray Bay. But when Grace became ill in 1960, Ham Jr. moved her to New York where she died in the Southampton Hospital, aged seventy-four, with her husband at her bedside.

Fish himself was seventy-two and still going strong in 1960. He was writing and speaking frequently, and keeping his finger on the political pulse of the nation while doing all in his power to bring about the end of communism. When his son decided to run for Congress from the Hudson Valley in 1966, Fish could barely be restrained from joining the campaign. "I often told him, 'You know, Pop, you don't have to come in here and campaign for me. You've done it,' " Congressman Fish relates.

People had even then begun to wonder about the source of his strength. "What a doughty, indestructible patriot you are," observed Clare Boothe Luce. "The mold in which you were cast seems long ago to have been broken." A doctor who had served as personal physician to President Eisenhower asked Fish if he could have his heart when he died so as to solve the riddle of Fish's longevity.

Even in his seventies, Fish was very much a lady's man, with his massive build, his gentlemanly ways, and his utter self-assurance. In 1967, at the age of seventy-nine, he married Marie Choubaroff Blackton, an aristocratic White Russian *émigré*, whom Fish had met through fellow anticommunists in New York. Marie was a beautiful and charming woman, full of old world elegance. She was very sociable and enjoyed the many fundraising dinners and award banquets they attended almost as much as Fish did. The couple also shared a fierce anti-communism and a love and knowledge of things French, often conversing in French.

Marriage to Marie substantially improved Fish's quality of life. From the Mansfield Hotel, he moved to Marie's much more commodious apartment on Park Avenue. Each year the couple would vacation at West Palm Beach, giving Jo Anne a chance to clean out his office, disposing of the year's accumulation of newspapers. Marie, who held a more fatalistic view of communism, encouraged Fish to ease up on his fight against it and enjoy life. He was very fond of her, and very saddened when, in 1974, she died from cancer.

In 1976, he married his third wife, Alice Curtis Desmond, a wealthy Orange County heiress and a direct descendant of William Bradford, governor of Plymouth Colony in 1620. Alice had known Hamilton Fish for many years and had sought his attentions after Marie's death. She lived on a large estate near Newburgh, New York, where she was attended by a full staff of servants and personal nurses. Fish moved in after their wedding but kept Marie's apartment on Park Avenue as an office, commuting to New York on Wednesday and returning to Newburgh on Friday.

In many ways, they were well matched. Both were proud of their distinguished lineage, and both spent much of their time writing. Alice authored twenty-two books during her lifetime, many of which were early American historical novels. In 1980, the couple financed the construction of the Alice Desmond and Hamilton Fish Public Library in Garrison, New York, now the repository of many of the Fish and Desmond family papers.

In other ways, they were not so well suited. Both were incorrigibly eccentric. Fish was extremely messy, so much so that the servants at the Desmond estate refused to clean up after him. Fond of wildlife, especially birds, he built a large coop on the property and stocked it with pairs of rabbits, quails, pheasants, pigeons, doves, guinea hens, and turkeys. The animals, who often fought, created a constant racket, and a mess that was never cleaned up.

Fish was also sometimes thoughtless. For their last Christmas together, Fish neglected to buy Alice a gift. "Alice loved to give presents, and of course everybody likes to get presents," says Jo Anne. "She had fifteen or twenty presents for him that she had her servants buy and wrap, and he had nothing, not a single present."

Three weeks later, in early 1984, Alice's lawyer notified Fish that he would have to move out of the house for the sake of her health and that a divorce was in order. Fish at first refused to cooperate with divorce proceedings, saying he did not believe in divorce, but eventually he gave in. He was embarrassed, but not heartbroken.

Alice Desmond lived until October 1990 and died at the age of ninety-three.

Throughout his life, Hamilton Fish was almost never sick. He had no medical insurance except Medicare, which he hardly ever used. He hated hospitals, refusing to stay in one overnight, and for many years had no regular physician. Only his dentist saw him regularly.

Fish ascribed his longevity to moderation. He ate simply, never smoked, and drank no more than one mixed drink a day. He was fond of bourbon sours and an occasional Presbyterian—a mixture of bourbon, club soda, and ginger-ale.

An athlete all his life, he kept himself physically fit through exercise, playing tennis until he was over seventy. While living in Manhattan, he always walked when he could and did not own a car for most of his later life. He credited his ability to avoid injury from the bumps and falls that tend to cripple the elderly to his training as a football player.

He rarely ever watched television, except baseball or football games; he was an avid Mets fan. Although he followed professional football, he never had a favorite team. His passion was reserved for college football, and his favorite team was, of course, the Harvard Crimson. Every week he would fire off a letter to Harvard's coach, telling him what he was doing wrong. Fish never missed Harvard's yearly match with Yale. When his sister died, he had the family reschedule her funeral so as not to conflict with that year's Harvard-Yale game. He also kept up with the prep school rivalry between St. Marks and Groton, quite as if he had never recovered from losing to Groton in his last year at St. Marks. And he encouraged youngsters to pursue sports, donating money to the Little Leagues in the Hudson Valley.

For many years, Hudson Valley schools held competitions for the Hamilton Fish DUSO League Football Trophy (Dutchess, Ulster, Sullivan, and Orange Counties) and the Hamilton Fish Americanism Award. While the DUSO trophy was recently retired, local sportswriter Bo Gill of the *Hudson Valley Morning and Evening News* is putting two new trophies into competition—the Hamilton Fish Football and Soccer trophies—in his memory.

A man of simple tastes, he was easy to please. Fish was as satisfied dining in the finest restaurant in New York as eating leftover chicken in the kitchen. "I never heard him complain," Jo Anne muses. "He wasn't a complaining man. He just made do. He was very adaptable."

Fish did not worry himself with unimportant matters—or matters he considered unimportant. Others were left to worry about filing income-tax forms or keeping financial records. He gave no thought to the clothes he wore, preferring to wear the same light blue shirt, same navy blazer, same old raincoat. Even in his prime, he was a notoriously sloppy dresser. During the congressional franking controversy, Fish was implicated by a witness who said he had seen a well-dressed man smuggling illegally franked mail out of a House office building. In his defense, Fish told his colleagues on the House floor that the culprit could not possibly have been he because nobody could describe him as a "well-dressed man." The House resounded with laughter.

Fish was likewise indifferent to his surroundings. Once when his grand-daughter suggested he repaint his apartment, he brushed the suggestion aside. "Oh, don't be bothered by that," he said. "I don't want to be bothered by that." At one time, his room at the Mansfield Hotel was condemned by city officials. It seems he was accustomed to feeding pigeons from inside his room and not accustomed to cleaning up after them.

His papers, his writing—they were what he considered important. He felt he had a mission to tell the American people about FDR, about nuclear arms, about the evil of communism, and he had the will to live for that mission. He would sit for hours at his desk, sorting papers, filing documents, poring over his manuscripts—never saying a word to his secretary in the same room. At such times, he would not bother to eat or exercise. Lydia, his fourth wife, tells how she "would have to come and say, 'You have to eat, you have to have something to eat.' 'Not now, five minutes,' and then we'd go ten minutes." Adds Jo Anne, "We would try to get him to sit in the sun or take a walk, and he'd say, 'Oh, no, too busy.' 'It's good for you.' 'Yes, you're right, but not today.' " When Jo Anne left in the afternoon, Lydia would take her place at the word processor, where at times he would keep her until eleven or twelve at night, dictating letters or his memoirs.

He kept himself so busy that he did not have time to get sick. For a centenarian, he was always busy. A month before his 102nd birthday, his schedule included attending a veterans' night dinner at a local Moose lodge on Saturday; riding in a Veterans Day parade on Sunday; seeing his doctor Monday; attending a dinner at a local American Legion post on Wednesday; traveling to Boston on Friday for the annual Harvard-Yale game on Saturday; and returning home Sunday for a dinner of the Putnam County Historical Society.

Fish continued speaking in public right up until his 102nd birthday. "He loved to get up and speak. That's all he wanted to do," Jo Anne relates. "Wherever he went, he got up to speak whether they wanted him to or not. . . . There was no stopping him." His favorite topic was nuclear disarmament, but in the course of any speech he could easily weave in references to his illustrious ancestors, his feud with FDR, and his fight against communism. He prepared his speeches beforehand to send to the press but he delivered them without notes or written text, and he rarely needed a microphone. Even in old age, his voice and delivery remained strong and confident. For emphasis, he would pound the podium with his fist, his stentorian voice rising in pitch and volume to finish each phrase or sentence with a climax, as if he were preaching to the Devil himself in the back of the room.

He was a master of a style of oratory that was common among politicians in the dramatic decades before World War II, but which, according to Troncone, disappeared after 1945. "He grew up in a time when there was no television, no radio. When you spoke, you had to rely on your words more than an image. It was your words that conveyed your meaning, not a television camera angle," says Troncone. "He had to rely on his body, his forcefulness to prove to the audience that he possessed the right stuff, prove to them that what he was telling them was the truth, prove to them that what he had was the message."

Every speech was an emotional appeal intended to rouse people to action, whether he was speaking to the local VFW post or to guests at his fourth wedding reception. The audience and the occasion made little difference— Ham Fish was going to tell them what he thought they needed to hear, and he was going to finish by virtually shouting the same words he used to end every speech: "If there is any country worth living in, any country worth defending, any country worth fighting for, or any country worth dying for, it is the United States of America. God bless America." And he would often add, "and God bless everyone in this room." Audiences unaccustomed to such forcefulness often responded with standing ovations.

It was a style of oratory currently found only in the pulpit, but, iron-ically, Fish almost never attended church. Only in his last years did he begin going and contributing financially to his parish church in Garrison. He was, nevertheless, a fierce defender of religious faith.

"I believe in God," he told interviewers in 1987. "I do believe in God, and I believe in religion. I believe in religion more for what good it does. It's the only morals we've got. If you wipe out religion, it's your own morals— good, bad, or indifferent—you can make it whatever you want. An atheist has no morals except his own, so I'm very much against atheism and against communism, and that's probably why."

He often talked about God and religion. He was inspired by the sacrifice of early Christian martyrs and he saw religious faith, like the desire for freedom, as an essential, irrepressible part of human life. Sometimes he condemned immoral acts as un-Christian. And he often pointed to the common ground between Judaism and Christianity. Though he was neither theologian nor biblical scholar, when he died, he left behind a 145-

page manuscript on monotheism—"the world's greatest spiritual force"—which was to be his next book after he finished his memoirs.

Although he always identified himself as an Episcopalian—"I'm an Episcopalian and I'll die an Episcopalian," he said in 1987—his allegiance to the church of his birth was more a matter of heritage than faith. The differences between Christian denominations did not interest him. Of his four wives, only Grace Chapin was an Episcopalian. Marie Blackton was Russian Orthodox, and Lydia Ambrogio is Roman Catholic. Alice Desmond was Unitarian, a suspect sect to Hamilton Fish, who often accused her of being an atheist and a humanist. "I'm against the humanists. They're the ones doing the damage," he remarked in 1987. "It's a direct attack on religion, and it leads to nothing but hatred of everybody."

More than anything else, Hamilton Fish was a Bull Moose Progressive, a lifetime admirer and disciple of Theodore Roosevelt. "The only president I still adore, the greatest president we ever had, was Theodore Roosevelt. There was a man of real courage and real Americanism," he stated in 1987.

Among recent presidents, the only one Fish admired was Ronald Reagan. In fact, he put him in a class with Theodore Roosevelt, for he considered Reagan a loyal American who believed in God and country, and he was gratified by the recurrence of patriotism that grew during the Reagan administration. He also liked to refer to his "football connections" with the president. In many public speeches to veterans, he would announce in his familiar ringing tones, "President Reagan is the greatest president since Theodore Roosevelt!"

According to Troncone, Fish, like Roosevelt, believed in the free market and the importance of competition. He was skeptical of man's ability to understand and control the market, but suspicious of large corporations with the power to restrict competition. Progressives like Fish wanted to bring big business under the rule of law, not in order to make business subservient to the state, but to make businessmen behave themselves. They believed that government and business could work in harmony for the betterment of the nation. Like President George Bush, they emphasized voluntarism on the part of businesses and private citizens, but were willing when necessary to apply the force of government to keep things running smoothly.

What really disturbed Fish and the former Progressives about the New Deal was the institutionalization of the Wilsonian notion that power flowed downward from the state to the people. That executive administrative agencies could create and implement codes and regulations governing the relationship beween the state and business, independent of Congress, was totally unacceptable to him. Regulatory authority concentrated in the executive branch threatened his ideas about balanced government, wherein Congress acted as the legislative mechanism for the people and the president served as their steward.

As a Progressive, Fish supported minimum wage laws, Social Security, and other early New Deal relief measures. In fact, in the first few months of the Roosevelt administration, Fish feared his voting record was so pro-Roosevelt that it would weaken his position in the Republican party.

But as the New Dealers moved toward ever-increasing control of the economy, Fish and his fellow Progressives recoiled in horror. The New Deal was a dramatic break, a movement in a wholly new direction, which both Progressives and conservatives feared would lead to state socialism. Roosevelt's "brain trust" presumed to know business better than businessmen, and they sought to control the economy through unelected regulatory agencies. To Fish and others, the New Deal presented a serious threat to a free and democratic society. It was as if the New Dealers were using the Soviet Union as a model, Troncone adds.

To combat creeping socialism, Progressives like Fish joined conservatives in opposing the New Deal and found themselves looking more and more like conservatives as the years passed and the political spectrum shifted leftward. In a 1956 farewell letter to a Newburgh party official, Fish wrote:

> I was known as a liberal conservative but, I must confess, that I have been driven by the socialism and squander mania of the New Dealers to be temporarily a conservative Republican ready to go forward with the times but not into socialism or foreign ideologies that have no place in America.

In recent years, Fish's reputation as an archconservative solidified as his differences with his son and grandson, Hamilton Fish III, began to receive public attention. In 1974, when Ham Jr., as a member of the House Judiciary Committee, voted to impeach President Richard Nixon, his father took out full-page ads in local newspapers to voice support for Nixon and to denounce the vote for impeachment. Fish thought Nixon was no more culpable than many Democrats—far less culpable than FDR—and that the Watergate scandal was blown out of proportion for the sake of partisan political advantage. He thought the same of the Iran-Contra scandal and was an outspoken defender of marine Lt. Col. Oliver North.

At least Ham Jr. was a Republican, although a rather liberal one. But Hamilton Fish III was a Democrat and a very liberal one at that. For ten years, he was publisher of *The Nation*, the leftist opinion magazine. His grandfather was scandalized. When Ham III ran for Congress in 1988, his grandfather denounced him on radio and in the newspapers as a "communist appeaser." Ham III, he told *Newsweek*, was "undermining and belittling a family tradition, betraying my father and my grandfather." Ham Jr. supported his son by stressing the family tradition of public service, no matter the party affiliation, but Ham Sr. would have none of it. As it turned out, his grandson's campaign did not survive the Democratic primary.

Despite the commonly held view, Hamilton Fish was not a knee-jerk reactionary crank. He had inherited from the era of Teddy Roosevelt a sophisticated, internally consistent political ideology, which he understood but could not articulate. Neither his ideology nor his rhetoric changed much in his 102 years, reports Troncone. Fish might have gone further if he had been the kind to set his sails with the prevailing winds, but he was not an opportunist. He could have given in on the New Deal, as many did. He could have been more conciliatory toward the business wing of the Republican party. No doubt this would have been difficult for a prideful man to do, but it was impossible for a prideful man for whom ideas mattered more than ambition. It was a measure of his fundamental honesty to himself and to his constituents that when it was no longer necessary to please the voters, he continued saying and believing the same things as before.

Throughout his life, Hamilton Fish remained true to his Bull Moose principles. Though proud of his wartime service with black troops and his sponsorship of antilynching legislation, he was not an active participant in the civil rights movement of the 1960s. He agreed with Martin Luther King that blacks should be judged on the basis of their character and not on the color of their skin, but he had reservations about the movement's tactics. "He believed in principle with the blacks' demand for greater civil rights, recognizing that they had gotten a raw deal," says Troncone, "but he objected to the existence of executive-branch enforcement agencies which operated largely independent of Congress in setting rules governing employment practices." Fish was also concerned over rumors that Martin Luther King was involved with communists who might lead blacks in the wrong direction—toward demanding special treatment rather than equal opportunity.

Fish remained sensitive to the charge of anti-Semitism all his life. Whenever the subject came up, he took the opportunity to emphasize his support for the state of Israel. At his hundreth birthday dinner in New York, Fish interrupted the program to deliver an impromptu speech to the Israeli ambassador to the U.S., who was present but preparing to leave early. Fish expounded for many minutes on his pro-Israeli record, citing his sponsorship of the American equivalent of the British Balfour Declaration and claiming to have done more to establish the state of Israel than any other man.

Though his critics often called him an "isolationist," he never was one. "I was never even a member of the America First Organization, but I was for America first, and am still for America first and always will be. If that be treason, make the most of it," he wrote in a letter to the *New York Post* in 1952. In 1987, he told interviewers, "I never met but one isolationist in my life. There was one congressman from New England, a Republican, who didn't want to do anything with any foreign nation."

Fish believed strongly in the Monroe Doctrine. He therefore opposed President Carter's Panama Canal treaty and supported the 1983 invasion of Grenada and the 1989 invasion of Panama. He was less sure of the proper course to take in response to Iraq's 1990 invasion of Kuwait. "Nobody really knows what's right or wrong at this point in time," he told a group of schoolchildren in late 1990. U.S. troops should be there, he said, "for defensive purposes, to protect from an attack by Iraq, but it's unnecessary at the present time to go to war." Later, after the start of the air war with Iraq, Fish declared his support for President Bush. The deciding factor, Troncone believes, was that U.S. intervention would discourage Soviet influence in the Persian Gulf.

Fish also supported U.S. participation in NATO because he thought it necessary to hold the Soviets at bay, but he opposed most other joint-defense agreements as impositions on the constitutional war-making powers of Congress and threats to American independence. He never missed an opportunity to denounce internationalists, especially those who called themselves "Trilateralists," for their desire to bring all nations under the rule of international law. These "one-worlders," Fish argued, would sell the U.S. into bondage to an international government dominated by foreign powers. He included in this category both Jimmy Carter and George Schultz, Ronald Reagan's secretary of state.

Fish thought highly of Reagan until Reagan and Soviet leader Mikhail Gorbachev agreed on a treaty to limit intermediate-range nuclear missiles in 1987. Fish was all for eliminating nuclear missiles, but he thought Reagan should have held out for a more inclusive ban. "He had an opportunity to abolish all nuclear war, and he didn't," said Fish.

Though staunchly anti-communist, Fish was always a proponent of arms control. In the 1920s, he was a enthusiastic supporter of the Washington Conference, which limited the size and number of warships countries could build and maintain. Near the Second World War's end, he was horrified that the atomic bomb had been used against heavily populated areas in Japan and became an early advocate of a ban on nuclear weapons. He opposed the Strategic Arms Limitation Treaties I and II only because they did not include restrictions on throw-weight. In his later life, every speech he gave warned of the dangers of nuclear weapons—included among his proposals: that all nuclear weapons be abolished in four years time, 25 percent each year; and that the U.S. and the Soviet Union limit their arsenals to fifty 25-megaton missiles each, all equal in throw-weight. Of course, he always stipulated that any arms control agreement must be bilateral and verifiable.

After his divorce from Alice Desmond in 1984, Fish returned to his Park Avenue apartment, which he shared with the sister of his second wife Marie. He was then 95 and still writing and speaking frequently, but in need of personal care and companionship.

In the summer of 1985, he was waging a protracted battle in the Letters section of the Newburgh *Evening News* over the record of Franklin Roosevelt. Fish had accused Roosevelt of having known in advance that the Japanese were planning to attack the United States, a charge for which he had no proof. Several readers had written letters to the paper defending Roosevelt and denouncing Fish in very personal terms.

One reader, a reporter for a rival paper, sympathized with Fish. Lydia Ambrogio, the daughter of Sicilian immigrants, had grown up in Queens, New York. Her maternal great-grandmother was a Medici, and her paternal great-grandmother a Birritera; a cousin of the same name was recently archbishop of Ribera, Sicily. Lydia herself, like her parents, had been a loyal Democrat until she learned of Roosevelt's ultimatum to the Japanese from published excerpts of Henry L. Stimson's diary. In 1985, she was well into her second career as a journalist, having retired several years earlier as a New York State corrections officer.

As an associate editor for *The Sentinel* in New Windsor, New York, Lydia could not write a letter for publication in the *Evening News*, so she wrote directly to Fish to express her support for Fish and her dislike of Roosevelt. Fish was charmed by her letter, and she was encouraged by his response.

After an exchange of letters, they met in late November and became fast friends. When he learned that Lydia had degrees in history and media studies from Mount Saint Mary College, he asked her if she would do research for him at the FDR library. Soon she was visiting Fish regularly at his apartment and filling in for his secretary as needed. In July 1986, she moved into the apartment as his full-time secretary and personal aide.

Lydia remembers Fish looking thin and unkempt when they met. After a year in her care, he was back up to 200 lbs. and dressing like a fashion plate. A doctor who examined Fish told her, "Whatever you're doing, keep it up."

In July 1986, Ham and Lydia began the first of their road trips with a drive to Lake Placid, New York, for the American Legion New York Convention. That October, they drove to Indianapolis for the Legion's National Executive Committee meeting. (In a future trip to Denver, they stopped in Chicago for the Veterans of Foreign Wars national convention.) On the way, they stopped off at Kings Island, Ohio, to visit the College Football Hall of Fame where Fish is enshrined.

The following year, they drove to the Legion convention in San Antonio and stayed at the Menger Hotel, where Fish's cousin Hamilton had enlisted in the Rough Riders nearly a century earlier. Lydia was responsible for identifying Sergeant Fish in the photograph in the Alamo archives. Their return trip took them through El Paso and Tucson to Las Vegas to visit Lydia's sister, and then up through the Virgin River Gorge in southern Utah. "The canyon walls just rose above you on both sides. . . . It was just awesome and he was really full of wonderment," says Lydia. Fish had traveled often in his later life, but only by plane. With Lydia he saw America as he had never seen it before.

They stopped in Denver and stayed a week with Temple Buell, a millionaire architect and longtime friend of Fish. Buell invited them to stay for his 92nd birthday celebration, but Fish had previously promised to visit another old friend on his hundredth birthday in Topeka, Kansas.

Fish's elder friend was Alf Landon, Republican stalwart and former presidential candidate, whom Fish had not seen in over forty-five years. Lydia remembers Landon saying over and over, "Oh, my God. Oh, my God. I haven't seen you in ages!" At one hundred, Landon was small and frail. "In fifteen minutes he was tired and had to be carried back up to bed, but my husband, as robust as he was, spent another hour talking to the newspaper and television people outside," says Lydia. Landon died not long thereafter.

Ham and Lydia returned to New York just in time for one of his son's annual steer-and-beer campaign fundraisers. "We just made it. We came in from Pennsylvania and still had the car packed," Lydia recalls. The elder Fish nevertheless stepped right up to deliver his usual rousing speech, ending with the declaration, "I left here a New Yorker and I came back an American!"

In April 1988, a magazine reporter asked Fish during an interview if he was planning to marry Miss Ambrogio. Ham conceded that marriage was a possibility. The possibility grew with other inquiries from the press and, in June, Fish announced their engagement at an American Legion meeting in Middletown, New York. They were married in September at the Denver home of Temple Buell, who combined the wedding with his ninety-third birthday party. The celebration was widely reported by the press and was featured on Charles Kuralt's Sunday morning TV show on CBS. Fish, as strong as ever at ninety-nine, delivered his usual speech against nuclear arms.

After the wedding, the Hamilton Fishes drove out through Wyoming to Salt Lake City—where Ham insisted on seeing the Great Salt Lake and Lydia went wading, to Ham's great amusement. "Ham's patience sometimes wore thin," Lydia remembers, "when I was constantly stopping to take pictures of the scenery or picking interesting rocks from the roadside. More than once he scolded me, saying, 'I think you're a little crazy.' And I would laugh and tell him, 'But look, Ham, you know how much I love you, so you ought to be kind and indulge my insanity just a little,' and that would get him smiling again."

Then across Nevada to San Francisco and down to Los Angeles, turning east through Death Valley, Las Vegas, and the Grand Canyon. By the time they returned home, they had traveled forty-four days and driven over eight thousand miles. Ham's beloved two-and-a-half pound poodle, Cheree, accompanied them, as she did on all their trips. "She was the most adorable little dog I've ever seen," Lydia says. "I never saw such fierce love and devotion as that little poodle had for her master."

Fish was always looking ahead to his next appointment, always planning for the future. At one hundred, he was talking of building a house in his home district. He had always intended to move back to Garrison where he was born.

In the spring of 1989, Ham and Lydia moved into a one-level house in Cold Spring, New York, just north of Garrison. The house had a large office with a big picture window looking out at the backyard, where they mounted several birdfeeders on stands and in the trees and bushes. Fish worked from an easy chair at a table by the window. When he wasn't shuffling papers or dictating letters to Jo Anne or Lydia, he was watching the birds at the feeders.

In his final years, he had everything a man of his age could want: a loving wife, financial security, the time and the health to enjoy life and to continue his crusade—to tell the American people the truth, as he saw it, about nuclear arms, communism, and Franklin Roosevelt. He continued to speak at every opportunity and write letters to newspapers across the country, sometimes mailing out the same letter to as many as three hundred newspapers. "He loved publicity. He loved getting his picture in the papers. He loved going to dinner. He loved getting his letters-to-the-editor published," says Jo Anne. "Fortunately for him, the older he got, the more publicity he got."

Fish also had the great satisfaction of seeing the beginning of the end of communism. Though wary of Mikhail Gorbachev's motives and intent, Fish welcomed the reform movement in the Soviet Union and the break-up of the Eastern Bloc. Tears of joy filled his eyes as he watched the television reports of the tearing down of the Berlin Wall. He was old enough to have seen the wall go up. He was old enough to have seen the Red menace first cast its shadow across a continent. And he lived long enough to see the shadow fade and retreat.

Fish took ill on January 3, 1991, just one month after his 102nd birthday celebration attended by 150 relatives and friends. For a man who had always been healthy, it was a sign that his end was near. He had been expected to visit Fort Dix to see his old regiment, the 369th, off to Saudi Arabia, but he was too sick to travel.

He spent his last few days at home under the care of his wife and nurse, enjoying visits from family and friends. Days before he died, he was still saying he wanted to live to be 110. His daughter Zevah heard him tell the familiar story of Eisenhower's doctor who had wanted to examine Fish's heart when he died. With great satisfaction, her father said, "I outlived him—and all the other doctors."

Two days before his death, Fish was alert, at times sitting up in his study or in the living room seeing the news on "Desert Storm" and receiving family members come to say their good-byes. On Friday, January 18, Ham Jr. arrived to be near his father; he was joined later by several grand-children and great-grandchildren. Fish, alert and conscious throughout the day and evening, talked on and off briefly until the last two hours when weakness overtook him. Lydia, who had been constantly at his side, held her husband's hand and talked to him. Like a true soldier, he was conscious to the end. Death came for him at 9:55 that night.

The following week, a memorial ceremony was held in the Cadet Chapel at West Point. More than seven hundred people filled the chapel. Among the nearly one hundred veterans of the 369th Regiment in attendance were Sergeants William Layton, who had served in Fish's Company K, and Clinton J. Peterson of Putnam County. The congregation sang "God Bless America." Congressman Hamilton Fish Jr. and Secretary of the Army Michael Stone, and Past National Commander of the American Legion Martin McKneally delivered eulogies. Stone's remarks included a reading from Fish's citation for bravery during World War I, for which he received the Silver Star. It was a revelation to Ham Jr., who had never heard his father speak of his heroism in the war.

Fish was buried with full military honors in the churchyard of St. Philips in the Highlands Episcopal Church in Garrison, where many members of the famous Fish family are also buried. He left behind his fourth wife Lydia, his son Ham Jr. and daughter Elizabeth, eight grandchildren, five great-grandchildren, and five stepchildren. To Lydia he left the charge of keeping his memory alive. To all Americans, he left his message of freedom and democracy in the American way.

                                                                B.P.M.

Harry Dexter White's War Ultimatum Draft, June 6, 1941

Memo for Secretary:
   Appended is a memorandum which I would like to have you glance at.
   It is a preliminary and incomplete draft which I can shorten, tone down, tighten up, and modify if you think that the general idea contained therein can be of any use to you.

HPW

I.

The Franco-British brand of diplomacy emulated by our own State Department appears to have failed miserably. Due to half-measures, miscalculations, timidity, machinations or incompetence of the State Departments of the United States, England and France, we are being isolated and we find ourselves rapidly moving toward a war which can be won by us under present circumstances only after a costly and bitter effort and only with a terribly dangerous aftermath. Granted the necessity for being optimistic about the outcome of a war in which before many years we alone may be fighting a victorious Germany (with Japan and Italy as her allies, and with the whole of Europe turning out equipment for them), it would be fatal to let such optimism obscure the difficulty of the task confronting us and prevent us from taking drastic steps to strengthen our position while there yet remains time.

It is becoming increasingly evident that diplomatic preparedness is as important an instrument of defence as is military preparedness. Military activity may win battles, diplomatic activity can make the fighting of these battles unnecessary; military victories can gain raw material and equipment and can weaken the enemy, diplomatic victories can do the same. Without major diplomatic victories Germany could not have attained her spectacular success. Had they not suffered major diplomatic defeats neither England nor France would be in their present predicaments.

But to be effective, diplomacy, like an army, must use modern equipment and employ modern strategy. An "all out" effort involves in diplomacy as in military strategy the fullest use of every economic and political advantage. In the field of diplomacy many opportunities for successful strategy are open to a country like the United States. A rich country can do things a poor one cannot; a democratic country, having no expansionist ambitions, has advantages a totalitarian country bent on aggression has not; a government that has never broken its international pledges has advantages that governments which have repeatedly done so cannot claim. These advantages must be utilized to the fullest in modern diplomatic activity if it is to have any chance of success, just as our military forces in preparation for defence or in actual warfare must make intelligent use of our geographical position, our rich resources, our vast labor power, technical equipment and democratic traditions.

In the light of requirements and possibilities of modern diplomacy, the efforts of American foreign diplomatic manouvering during this grave crisis in the world's history have been pathetic. It has consisted of a 19th century pattern of petty bargaining with its dependence upon subtle half promises, irritating pin pricks, excursions into double dealing, and copious pronounciamentos of good will alternating with vague threats—and all of it veiled in an atmosphere of high secrecy designed or at least serving chiefly to hide the essential barrenness of achievement. Our diplomatic maneuvering is proving as futile in strengthening our international position or in keeping us out of a difficult war as was the equipment and strategy of the Polish Army in the task of defending Poland.

Virtually surrounded by a world ablaze, and with the fire growing hotter, and nearer and more dangerous, our diplomatic machinery concerns itself chiefly with maintaining a facade of important goings-on, an appearance of assured and effective functioning, whereas behind that front is largely hesitation, bewilderment, inaction, petty maneuvering, sterile conversations, and diverse objectives.

Here and there, now and then progress is made but on a scale that is completely inadequate to the task in hand. Where modern diplomacy calls for swift and bold action, we engage in long drawn out cautious negotiation; where we should talk in terms of billions of dollars, we think in terms of millions; where we should measure success by the generosity of the government that can best afford it, we measure it by the sharpness of the bargain driven; where we should be dealing with all-embracing economic, political and social problems, we discuss minor trade objectives, or small national advantages; instead of squarely facing realities, we persist in enjoying costly prejudices; where we should speak openly and clearly, we engage in protocol, in secret schemes and subtleties.

We must cut loose from that outmoded and decayed pattern of diplomacy. We must substitute, before it is too late, imagination for tradition; generosity for shrewdness; understanding for bargaining; toughness for caution, and wisdom for prejudice.

We are rich—we should use more of our wealth in the interests of peace and victory. We are powerful—we should be willing to use our power before our backs are to the wall. We need no nation's lands—we should make full use of that fact. We keep our national pledges—now is the time that record of integrity should stand us in good stead. We are protected by two oceans—let us exploit that protection while distance is still a potent barrier. We are a democracy—let us take full advantage of the strength of open covenants openly arrived at, where such covenants are in the interest of people in every land.

The longer we wait the less chance will we have to use diplomacy as an aid to our defence. The patterns of relationship jell; plans become irrevocable; opportunities lost are gone forever. A nation committed irrevocably to a course of action loses the power to exercise choice, to accept offers and make conditions.

If ever there was a time when diplomacy could secure its most brilliant victories for the United States, now is that time!

The proposed program of diplomatic effort given below will be called naive and visionary. It will be laughed at by the professional diplomats, but their ridicule will not alter our desperate situation, nor will their traditional method of handling the situation lead to any better results than have the efforts of their colleagues in England and France.

I am convinced the proposal is workable and could be spectacularly successful.

I am equally convinced the particular proposal, or anything resembling it will not be adopted nor, I fear, even get a serious hearing unless pushed, in the beginning at least, by high officials outside the State Department, yet the stakes are so great I believe it is worthwhile making a strenuous effort to get a new diplomatic offensive started.

The proposal consists of two parts. Part I deals with our relations with Japan; Part II deals with our relations with Russia.

Each proposal is given below only in bare outline and in only enough detail to indicate the essential point. Obviously, if and when the proposal is given serious consideration each of the enumerated points must be elaborated carefully, with appropriate conditions spelt out, loopholes or evasion blocked, and adequate protective clauses added.

II.

United States and Japan

A.

Whereas: War between the United States and Japan would cost thousands of lives, billions of dollars; would leave the vanquished country bitter and desirous of revenge; would foster social disruption, and would not insure peace during our children's lives, nor permanently solve troublesome problems now standing between the two countries, and

Whereas: The United States is eager to avoid war, and is willing to go more than half way to settle peaceably the issues that stand in the way of more friendly intercourse between the two countries, and

Whereas: The United States recognizes that Japan, because of the special nature of its economy, is greatly in need of opportunities for increased foreign trade, and in need of capital to repair the ravages of four years of warfare, and

Whereas: The United States recognizes that injustice has been done to the Japanese people by our immigration laws, and

Whereas: The United States believes that in the long run the interests of both the Japanese people and the American people can best be served by establishing fair and peaceful conditions under which Japan and her neighbors can prosper, and

Whereas: The United States is, because of numerous circumstances, powerful enough to destroy Japan should the United States be forced against her will to take up arms against Japan, and

Whereas: The United States is rich enough in funds, raw material, equipment, and technical skill to build, if necessary, a Navy and air force ten times as strong as that which Japan can build, and

Whereas: The United States wishes so much to avoid unnecessary bloodshed and destruction that it will pay well to help Japan's economy back to a peaceful and healthy basis, and

Whereas: The United States wishes to help China maintain her independence and attain peace so that she may go forward in her political and economic development, so unfortunately interrupted in 1937, and

Whereas: The United States believes there is no basic obstacle to permanent and more friendly relations between the United States and Japan and believes that the Japanese people will welcome an opportunity to restore peace, to reconstruct Japan's industry and trade, and to promote friendly relations with her neighbors on a basis fair both to Japan's needs and the needs of her neighbors.
And finally—and of most immediate importance—

Whereas: The United States wishes to concentrate as soon as possible her naval force in the Atlantic so as to be prepared for any emergency against a potential enemy with whom there is no current basis for friendship.

The United States proposes to enter into an Agreement with Japan at once under which the United States and Japan will agree to do certain things, as follows:

B.

On her part, the United States Government proposes to do the following:
1. To withdraw the bulk of the American Naval forces from the Pacific.
2. To sign a 20-year non-aggression pact with Japan.
3. To recognize Manchuria as a part of the Japanese Empire.
4. To place Indo-China under the Government of a joint British,

French, Japanese and American Commission, which will insure most-favored-nation treatment for those four countries until the European War is ended, and which will govern the country primarily in the interests of the Indo-Chinese people.

5. To give up all extra-territorial rights in China, and to obtain England's agreement to give up her extra-territorial rights in China, and cede Hong Kong back to China.

6. To present to Congress and push for enactment a bill to repeal the Immigration Act of 1917 which prohibits immigration into the United States of Japanese, and place the Japanese and the Chinese on the same basis as other peoples.

7. To negotiate a trade agreement with Japan, giving her (a) most-favored-nation treatment and (b) such concessions on imports as can be mutually satisfactorily arranged, including an agreement to keep raw silk on the free list for 20 years.

8. To extend a $3 billion 30-year credit at 2 per cent interest, to be drawn upon at the rate not to exceed $200 million a year except with approval of the President of the United States. Half of the funds to be used to purchase the products of the United States, and the remainder to be used to purchase commodities of Latin American countries.

9. To set up a $500 million stabilization fund half supplied by Japan and half by the United States, to be used for the stabilization of the dollar-yen rate.

C.

On its part, the Japanese Government proposes to do the following:

1. Withdraw all military, naval, air police forces from China (boundaries as of 1931) from Indo-China and from Thailand.

2. Withdraw all support—military, political, or economic—from any government in China other than that of the national government.

3. Replace with yen currency at a rate agreed upon among the Treasuries of China, Japan, England and United States all military scrip, yen and puppet notes circulating in China.

4. Give up all extra-territorial rights in China.

5. Extend to China a billion yen loan at 2 per cent to aid in reconstructing China (at rate of 100 million yen a year).

6. Lease at once to the U.S. Government for 3 years such naval vessels and airplanes as the United States selects, up to 50 per cent of Japan's

present naval and air strength. Rental to be paid to be equal to 50 per cent of the original cost price per year.

7. Sell to the United States up to half current output of war material— including naval, air, ordnance and commercial ships on a cost-plus 20 per cent basis as the United States may select.

8. Accord the United States and China most-favored-nation treatment in the whole Japanese Empire.

9. Negotiate a 10-year non-aggression pact with United States, China, British Empire, Dutch Indies (and Philippines).

D.

Inasmuch as the United States cannot permit the present uncertain status between the United States and Japan to continue in view of world developments, and feels that decisive action is called for now, the United States extends the above offer of a fair and peaceful solution of the difficulties between the two countries for only 30 days. If the Japanese Government does not indicate its acceptance of the proffered agreement before the expiration of that time, it can mean only that the present Japanese Government prefers other and less peaceful ways of solving those difficulties, and is possibly awaiting the propitious moment to carry out further a plan of conquest.

In the event that Japan elected to reject the offer of peaceful solution under terms herein indicated, the United States would have to shape her own policy accordingly.

The first step in such policy would be a complete embargo on imports from Japan.

III.

United States and Russia

A.

Whereas: The United States is desirous of improving its relations with Russia to the mutual benefit of both countries, and

Whereas: There is no geographical area in which the economic interests of the United States and of Russia are in conflict, and

Whereas: The United States is desirous of increasing its trade with Russia and believes that Russia is likewise desirous of increasing its trade with the United States, and

Whereas: Russia produces some essential raw materials that the United States needs and the United States produces goods that Russia needs, and

Whereas: The interests of the peoples of both countries are served by a restoration of world peace as rapidly as possible and the maintenance of that peace as long as possible, and

Whereas: The interests of both countries are especially served by maintenance of peace in the areas bordering the Pacific Ocean, and

Whereas: Both countries can maintain powerful military forces which can effectively supplement each other in the interests of preserving peace or checking aggression—the United States chiefly in form of naval and air forces and Russia chiefly army and air force, and

Whereas: Both countries have a great enough degree of economic self-sufficiency so far as Europe or Asia are concerned to carry out a program of economic collaboration without any significant lowering of the standard of living of either country, and

Whereas: Both countries are eager to be able to devote more of their productive effort to improving the standard of living of the peoples and less of their effort to armaments.

The United States proposes the following agreement with the Government of the U.S.S.R.

B.

On its part the United States Government will do the following:

1. Permit Russia to purchase up to $300 million a year in the United States of any kind of raw or finished material she may wish—with certain exceptions noted in the appendix.

2. Permit Russia to maintain up to 5,000 technical men in the United States as students or experts in our industries.

3. Permit Russia to maintain 50 military and naval attaches who shall be permitted to participate in our military and naval maneuvers.

4. Extend to Russia a 10-year credit of $500 million to be used at the rate of not more than $100 million a year, except with the approval of the United

States. The credit to be applicable only to purchases for her own use by Russia in the United States in any calendar year and not to exceed $200 million.

5. Enter into a 5-year Mutual Economic Assistance Pact under which the United States agrees to the following:

  (a) In the event of war between Russia and any major power, the United States will undertake to sell to Russia and to deliver to Russian ports military equipment or material out of current stocks such goods as Russia may desire up to $2 billion a year. The sale to be made on a cost-plus 10 per cent basis and $1/4$ for cash and the remainder for a 20-year credit at 2 per cent interest.

  (b) To place an embargo on any imports whose origin is a country with which Russia is in a state of war and to impose an embargo against any exports, the destination of which involves a country with which Russia is in a state of war.

  (c) To at once undertake to prohibit all exports to or from Germany or all countries which have been conquered by Germany.

6. Extend to Russia most-favored-nation treatment with respect to trade.

C.

The Russian Government on its part agrees to do the following:

1. Impose an effective embargo at once on all exports of any commodities to Germany or to countries conquered by Germany and also impose an embargo on all imports from those areas.

2. To prohibit the passage through Russian territory or waters of any goods, troops, or equipment under control of Germany or her Allies.

3. To sell to the United States up to $200 million of any commodities produced in Russia—with conditions noted in appendix.

4. To effectively prohibit the export, directly or indirectly to the United States, of all propaganda whether in the form of material, literature, radio or economic support.

5. To settle the outstanding debts of the Russian Government to Americans under terms similar to those offered in 1933.

6. To conclude a non-aggression pact with the National Government of China.

7. To permit up to 5,000 American professional or technical men a year to freely inspect, or study, in Russian institutions and industries.

8. To permit 50 United States military or naval observers to participate in the military maneuvers of the Russian forces.

IV.

The advantages of terms indicated above to the three countries are so great, and the disadvantages so small, that it is difficult to believe either the Japanese or Russian Government would hesitate to accept the offers.

The advantages accruing to each government are listed below:

A. *To the United States*

1. Our naval power will be greatly increased at once—both by the freeing of our Pacific fleet for duty elsewhere, and by the addition of Japanese ships leased to us.

2. We would be able to send more of our equipment to England without increasing our vulnerability to an attack from the East.

3. We will have stopped the war in China and have regained for her her freedom.

4. We will have paved the way for a substantial increase in trade of non-war materials.

5. We would greatly strengthen England's position vis-a-vis Germany.

6. We will have saved ourselves from a war with Japan with all its terrible social, political and economic consequences.

Appendix Two

Harry Dexter White's War Ultimatum Draft, November 17, 1941

TO   Secretary Morgenthau
FROM   H. D. White
SUBJECT   Suggested Approach for Elimination of United States-Japanese
          Tension

I.

It is becoming increasingly evident that diplomatic preparedness is as important an instrument of defense as is military preparedness. Military activity may win battles, diplomatic activity can make the fighting of these battles unnecessary; military victories can gain raw material, equipment and can weaken the enemy, diplomatic victories can achieve similar gains. Without major diplomatic victories Germany could not have attained her spectacular success. Had they not suffered major diplomatic defeats neither England nor France would be in their present predicaments.

But to be effective, diplomacy, like an Army, must use modern equipment and employ modern strategy. An "all out" effort involves in diplomacy as in

217

military strategy the fullest use of every economic and political advantage. Just as our military forces in preparation for an "all out" defense or in actual warfare must make intelligent use of our geographical position, our rich resources, our vast labor power, technical equipment and democratic traditions, so must diplomacy utilize those advantages to the full if it is to have any chance of success.

In the light of requirements and possibilities of modern diplomacy, the manoeuvers of American diplomacy during this grave crisis in the world's history have been pathetic.

Virtually surrounded by a world ablaze, and with the fire growing hotter, and nearer and more dangerous, our diplomatic machinery concerns itself chiefly with maintaining a facade of important goings-on, an appearance of assured and effective functioning, whereas behind that front is largely hesitation, bewilderment, inaction, petty maneuvering, sterile conversations, and diverse objectives.

Here and there, now and then, progress is made but on a scale that is completely inadequate to the task in hand. Where modern diplomacy calls for swift and bold action, we engage in long drawn out cautious negotiation; where we should talk in terms of billions of dollars, we think in terms of millions; where we should measure success by the generosity of the government that can best afford it, we measure it by the sharpness of the bargain driven; where we should be dealing with all-embracing economic, political and social problems, we discuss minor trade objectives, or small national advantages; instead of squarely facing realities, we persist in enjoying costly prejudices; where we should speak openly and clearly, we engage in protocol, in secret schemes and subtleties.

We must cut loose from that outmoded and decayed pattern of diplomacy. We must substitute, before it is too late, imagination for tradition; generosity for shrewdness; understanding for bargaining; toughness for caution, wisdom for prejudice, and strategy for tactics.

We are rich—we should use more of our wealth in the interests of peace and victory. We are powerful—we should be willing to use our power before our backs are to the wall. We need no nation's lands—we should make full use of that fact. We keep our national pledges—now is the time that record of integrity should stand us in good stead. We are protected by two oceans—let us exploit that protection while distance is still a potent barrier. We are a democracy—let us take full advantage of the strength just covenants openly arrived at.

If ever there was a time when diplomacy could secure its most brilliant victories for the United States, now is that time! The longer we wait the less chance will we have to use diplomacy as an aid to our defense. The patterns of relationship jell; plans become irrevocable; opportunities lost are gone forever. A nation committed irrevocably to a course of action loses the power to exercise choice, to accept offers and make conditions.

The proposed program of diplomatic effort given below will be called naive and visionary. It may be laughed at by the professional diplomats, but their ridicule will not alleviate the danger that confronts us, nor will their traditional method of handling the situation lead to any better results than have the efforts of their colleagues in England and France.

I am convinced the proposal is workable and could be spectacularly successful.

The proposal is given below only in bare outline and in only enough detail to indicate the essential point. Obviously, if and when the proposal is given serious consideration each of the enumerated points must be elaborated carefully, with appropriate conditions spelt out, loopholes or evasion blocked, and adequate protective clauses added.

The important thing right now is not a carefully worked-out proposal, but is rather the acceptance by the President and Secretary Hull of the worthwhileness of a different approach to the problem so that in the preliminary discussions with the Japanese emissary the negotiations can begin on a very different level than that likely to be the case if traditional methods are pursued.

If the President were to propose something like the appended agreement and the Japanese accept, the whole world would be electrified by the successful transformation of a threatening and belligerent powerful enemy into a peaceful and prosperous neighbor. The prestige and the leadership of the President both at home and abroad would skyrocket by so brilliant and momentous a diplomatic victory—a victory that requires no vanquished, a victory that immediately would bring peace, happiness and prosperity to hundreds of millions of Eastern peoples, and assure the subsequent defeat of Germany!

I fully appreciate the difficulty and possible resultant unpleasantness involved in your getting the President and Secretary Hull to give the proposal serious consideration—but isn't the goal worth the risk of being turned down?

United States and Japan

A.

1. War between the United States and Japan would cost thousands of

lives, billions of dollars; would leave the vanquished country bitter and desirous of revenge; would foster social disruption, and would not insure peace during our children's lives, nor permanently solve troublesome problems now standing between the two countries, and

2. The United States is eager to avoid war, and is willing to go more than half way to settle peaceably the issues that stand in the way of more friendly intercourse between the two countries, and

3. The United States recognizes that Japan, because of the special nature of its economy, is greatly in need of opportunities for increased foreign trade, and in need of capital to repair the ravages of four years of warfare, and

4. The United States recognizes that injustice has been done to the Japanese people by our immigration laws, and

5. The United States believes that in the long run the interests of both the Japanese people and the American people can best be served by establishing fair and peaceful conditions under which Japan and her neighbors can prosper, and

6. The United States is rich enough in funds, raw material, equipment, and technical skill to build, if necessary, a Navy and air force ten times as strong as that which Japan can build, and

7. The United States is, because of numerous circumstances, powerful enough to destroy Japan should the United States be forced against her will to take up arms against Japan, and

8. The United States wishes so much to avoid unnecessary bloodshed and destruction that it will pay well to help Japan's economy back to a peaceful and healthy basis, and

9. The United States wishes to help China maintain her independence and attain peace so that she may go forward in her political and economic development, so unfortunately interrupted in 1937, and

10. The United States believes there is no basic obstacle to permanent and more friendly relations between the United States and Japan and believes that the Japanese people will welcome an opportunity to restore peace, to reconstruct Japan's industry and trade, and to promote friendly relations with her neighbors on a basis fair both to Japan's needs and the needs of her neighbors.

And finally—and of most immediate importance—

11. The United States wishes to concentrate as soon as possible her naval force in the Atlantic so as to be prepared for any emergency against a potential enemy with whom there is no current basis for friendship.

B.

Because of the foregoing facts, the United States proposes to enter into an Agreement with Japan at once under which the United States and Japan will agree to do certain things, as follows:

On her part, the United States Government proposes to do the following:

1. To withdraw the bulk of the American Naval forces from the Pacific.

2. To sign a 20-year non-aggression pact with Japan.

3. To promote a final settlement of the Manchurian question.

4. To place Indo-China under the Government of a joint British, French, Japanese, Chinese and American Commission, which will insure most-favored-nation treatment for those five countries until the European War is ended, and which will govern the country primarily in the interests of the Indo-Chinese people.

5. To give up all extra-territorial rights in China, and to obtain England's agreement to give up her extra-territorial rights in China, and give Hong Kong back to China.

6. To present to Congress and push for enactment a bill to repeal the Immigration Act of 1917 which prohibits immigration into the United States of Japanese, and place the Japanese and the Chinese on the same basis as other peoples.

7. To negotiate a trade agreement with Japan, giving her (a) most-favored-nation treatment and (b) such concessions on imports as can be mutually satisfactorily arranged, including an agreement to keep raw silk on the free list for 20 years.

8. To extend a $2 billion 20-year credit at 2 per cent interest, to be drawn upon at the rate not to exceed $200 million a year except with approval of the President of the United States.

9. To set up a $500 million stabilization fund half supplied by Japan and half by the United States, to be used for the stabilization of the dollar-yen rate.

10. To remove at once restrictions on Japanese funds in the United States.

11. To use its influence to the full to attempt to eliminate sources of potential friction between Japan and her neighbors.

November 17, 1941

C.

On its part, the Japanese Government proposes to do the following:

1. Withdraw all military, naval, air police forces from China (boundaries as of 1931) from Indo-China and from Thailand.

2. Withdraw all support—military, political, or economic—from any government in China other than that of the national government.

3. Replace with yen currency at a rate agreed upon among the Treasuries of China, Japan, England and United States all military scrip, yen and puppet notes circulating in China.

4. Give up all extra-territorial rights in China.

5. Extend to China a billion yen loan at 2 per cent to aid in reconstructing China (at rate of 100 million yen a year).

6. Withdraw all Japanese troops from Manchuria except for a few divisions necessary as a police force, provided U.S.S.R. withdraws all her troops from the Far Eastern front except for an equivalent remainder.

7. Sell to the United States up to three-fourths of her current output of war material—including naval, air, ordnance and commercial ships on a cost-plus 20 per cent basis as the United States may select.

8. Accord the United States and China most-favored-nation treatment in the whole Japanese Empire.

9. Negotiate a 10-year non-aggression pact with United States, China, British Empire, Dutch Indies (and Philippines).

D.

Inasmuch as the United States cannot permit the present uncertain status between the United States and Japan to continue in view of world developments, and feels that decisive action is called for now, the United States should extend the above offer of a generous and peaceful solution of the difficulties between the two countries for only a limited time. If the Japanese Government does not indicate its acceptance in principle at least of the proffered terms before the expiration of that time, it can mean only that the present Japanese Government prefers other and less peaceful ways of solving those difficulties, and is possibly awaiting the propitious moment to carry out further a plan of conquest.

In the event that Japan elected to reject the offer of peaceful solution under terms herein indicated, the United States would have a clearer idea of what to expect and would therefore know better how to shape her own policy.

III.

The advantages of terms indicated above to the two countries are so great, and the disadvantages so small, that it is difficult to believe that the Japanese Government would hesitate to accept the offers. Certainly the bulk of the Japanese people would be enthusiastic about the offer.

The advantages accruing to each government are listed below:

A.   *To the United States*

1. Our naval power will be greatly increased at once by the freeing of our Pacific fleet for duty elsewhere.

2. We would be able to send more of our equipment to England and Russia without increasing our vulnerability to an attack from the East.

3. We will have stopped the war in China and have regained for her her freedom.

4. We will have paved the way for a substantial increase in post-war trade.

5. We would greatly strengthen the Allied position vis-a-vis Germany.

6. We will have saved ourselves from a war with Japan.

7. The money it would cost us would be a very small part of what we would save by not having to fight Japan, or by not having to be prepared for a two-ocean war.

8. A prosperous Japan and China can greatly help to restore our normal trade, and thus make easier our own transition to a peace time economy.

9. Insure for ourselves an increased supply of tin, antimony and wood oil and rubber from the Far East.

10. Handicap Germany in its present military campaign and at the same time give great moral encouragement to the British and Russian people.

11. Finally, military and naval experts who now fear a "two front" naval threat will be more enthusiastic about all out help to England and Russia. There will be much less cause to oppose the administration's foreign policy.

B.   *To Japan*

1. Instead of being confronted with prospect of a more serious war and certain defeat in the end, she can have peace at once.

2. She can proceed at once to shift from a war economy to peace economy and at the same time experience prosperity rather than a serious depression.

3. She can withdraw from the China incident without loss of "face".

4. She can strengthen her currency and reduce her public debt.

5. Her foreign trade will greatly increase.

6. She can devote her energies and capital to reconstructing Japan, building up Manchuria, and developing new trade possibilities at a time when other countries are engaged in war or preparation for war.

7. She will at one stroke have solved some of her thorniest problems in her international relations.

8. She will avoid the social disruption that is bound to take place in Japan after an expanded and prolonged war effort.

IV.

It would, of course, be necessary to obtain Congressional approval before making definite offers, but through preliminary confidential conferences with leaders of both parties and with appropriate committees, the ground could be quickly prepared so that negotiations could go forward.

A completed document could in a week or two be offered to the Japanese Government. The world, including the *Japanese people*, would know the motives and the contents of our offer. If the Japanese Government would not accept, it would have at least the great advantages of (1) clarifying our own policy and rallying support behind the President, (2) create serious division in Japan.

If the Japanese Government were to indicate its tentative acceptance in principle, the President could at once call a conference in Washington to be attended by Chinese, British, Russian, and possibly Dutch East Indian and Philippine representatives. Inasmuch as all the important concessions are to be made by United States and Japan, the participation of other governments in the conference need not complicate negotiations.

The one danger inherent in the proposed concessions is that if accepted by Japan it would provide her with a breathing space during which she could greatly strengthen her military and economic potential. She might then be a greater threat to us a year or two hence than she is now.

Against that possibility are the following factors:

1. Owing to the scarcity of many raw materials she will not be able to expand her navy and air force during the next year nearly as much as we can—particularly in view of the provision in the agreement that we can buy 80 percent of her current output of armaments.

2. The next two years are crucial for us. If we can obtain the release of the Russian, British and American forces now being tied up in the Far

East by Japan's continuous threatening, we will have done more to strengthen United Kingdom and Russia vis-a-vis Germany than we could with a whole year's output of planes and tanks and ships.

3. The Japanese people would be so relieved by the settlement of the China "incident", and the end of the threat of war with major powers, and would be so happy at the cessation of economic strangulation and the emergence of real prosperity, that it is hardly likely that any military clique could stir up significant trouble for years to come.

4. Finally, there would be nothing important left for Japan to threaten to fight for that she could hope to get if Germany were defeated. Japan would hardly dare invade China again soon—so long as the Chinese did not have civil war. Japan would certainly not wish to threaten the United States, the United Kingdom, or the U.S.S.R. if Germany were defeated. She also would not wish to interrupt the annual increments of loan to Japan, nor again jeopardize her markets and sources of raw materials.

Altogether, the likelihood of Japan's strengthening her position and re-entering the world scene as a belligerent aggressor in the next few years seems very slim—provided Germany is defeated.

Appendix Three

Morgenthau's War Ultimatum Memoranda to Hull and FDR, November 18, 1941

NOV 18 1941

Dear Cordell:

    I am enclosing copy of a
letter and memorandum which I
am sending to the President.

        Sincerely,

        (Signed) Henny

The Honorable,
    The Secretary of State.

Enclosures

Carbon to Mr. White
Sent by Secret Service 4:35
marked "Confidential"

HDW:ls
11/18/41

NOV 18 1941

My dear Mr. President:

I am sending you herewith for your
perusal a memorandum on the Japanese
situation which was submitted to me by
one of my assistants.

I realize that I do not know the
details or character of the current negotiations with the Japanese Government
and therefore do not know whether or
not the financial proposals, which are
a vital part of the program sketched in
this memorandum, will fit into your
plans. Nevertheless, I am taking the
liberty of sending it along on the chance
that you may find the suggestions helpful.

I am also sending a copy of this
letter and memorandum to Secretary Hull.

Faithfully,

(Signed) H. Morgenthau, Jr.

The President,

    The White House.

Enclosure

Carbon to Mr. White.

Sent by Secret Service at 3:35
marked "confidential"

HDW:dlm
11/18/41.

AN APPROACH TO THE PROBLEM OF ELIMINATING TENSION WITH JAPAN AND HELPING DEFEAT OF GERMANY

AN APPROACH TO THE PROBLEM OF ELIMINATING TENSION WITH JAPAN AND INSURING DEFEAT OF GERMANY

I.

Foreword

It is becoming increasingly evident that "all out" diplomatic preparedness is as important an instrument of defense as is adequate military preparedness. Military activity may win battles, diplomatic activity can make the fighting of these battles unnecessary; military victories can gain raw material and equipment and can weaken the enemy, diplomatic victories can achieve similar gains. Without major diplomatic victories Germany could not have attained her spectacular success. Had they not suffered major diplomatic defeats neither England nor France would be in their present predicaments.

An "all out" effort involves in diplomacy as in military strategy the fullest use of every economic and political advantage. Just as our military forces in preparation for an "all out" defense or in actual warfare must make intelligent use of our geographical position, our rich resources, our vast labor power, technical equipment and democratic traditions, so must diplomacy utilize those advantages to the full if it is to have any chance of success.

We are rich—we should use more of our wealth in the interests of peace and victory. We are powerful—we should be willing to use our power before our backs are to the wall. We need no nation's lands—we should make full use of that fact. We keep our national pledges—now is the time that record of integrity should stand us in good stead. We are protected by two oceans—let us exploit that protection while distance is still a potent barrier. We are a democracy—let us take full advantage of the strength of just covenants openly arrived at.

If ever there was a time when diplomacy could secure its most brilliant victories for the United States, now is that time! The longer we wait the less chance will we have to use diplomacy as an aid to our defense. The patterns of relationship jell; plans become irrevocable; opportunities lost are gone forever. A nation committed irrevocably to a course of action loses the power to exercise choice, to accept offers and make conditions.

If the President were to propose something like the appended agreement and the Japanese accept, the whole world would be electrified by the successful transformation of a threatening and belligerent powerful enemy into a peaceful and prosperous neighbor. The prestige and the leadership of the President both at home and abroad would skyrocket by so brilliant and momentous a diplomatic victory—a victory that requires no vanquished, a victory that immediately would bring peace, happiness and prosperity to hundreds of millions of Eastern peoples, and assure the subsequent defeat of Germany!

The proposal is workable and could be spectacularly successful, if Japan could be induced to accept the arrangement, and the great advantages it offers to Japan, and the fact that the likely alternative is war might induce Japan to accept the arrangement.

The proposal is given below only in bare outline and in only enough detail to indicate the essential points. What is most needed at this moment is not a carefully worked out program, but rather a decision to employ an all-out diplomatic approach in the current discussions with the Japanese.

II.

Self-Evident Propositions Concerning United States and Japan

1. War between the United States and Japan would cost thousands of lives, billions of dollars; would leave the vanquished country bitter and desirous of revenge; would foster social disruption, and would not

insure peace during our children's lives, nor permanently solve troublesome problems now standing between the two countries.

2. The United States prefers a just and peaceful settlement to war as a
    means of settling international difficulties, and is willing to go more
    than half way to settle peaceably the issues that stand in the way of
    more friendly intercourse between the two countries.

3. The United States recognizes that Japan, because of the special nature
    of its economy, is greatly in need of opportunities for increased foreign
    trade, and in need of capital to repair the ravages of four years of
    warfare, and in need of assured sources of basic raw materials.

4. The United States recognizes that our immigration laws have in fact
    unjustly discriminated against the Japanese people.

5. The United States believes that in the long run the interests of both
    the Japanese people and the American people can best be served by
    establishing fair and peaceful conditions under which Japan and her
    neighbors can prosper.

6. The United States is rich enough in funds, raw material, equipment,
    and technical skill to build, if necessary, and maintain a Navy and air
    force ten times as strong as that which Japan can build, and the
    United States is, because of numerous circumstances, powerful
    enough to destroy Japan should the United States be forced against her
    will to take up arms against Japan.

7. Should Japan force the United States to fight, Japan would have
    actively arrayed against her not only the United States but the British
    Empire, Netherlands East Indies, China, and probably Russia. In
    addition, the peoples of Indo China, Thailand, Manchuria and Korea
    would become much more difficult for Japan to control. In such a war
    victory for Japan would be impossible.

8. Defeat of Japan would bring bankruptcy, revolution and chaos in
    Japan. It would cost Japan her empire and her navy, and leave her a
    fourth-rate power with little chance of regaining her present world
    position for decades to come.

9. The United States wishes so much to avoid unnecessary bloodshed and
    destruction and to attain friendship between the Japanese and the

American people, that it will pay well to help Japan's economy back to a peaceful and healthy basis.

10. The United States believes there is no basic obstacle to permanent and more friendly relations between the United States and Japan and believes that the Japanese people will welcome an opportunity to restore peace, to reconstruct Japan's industry and trade, and to promote friendly relations with her neighbors on a basis fair both to Japan's needs and the needs of her neighbors.

11. The United States wishes to help China maintain her independence and attain peace so that she may go forward in her political and economic development, so unfortunately interrupted a few years ago.

And finally—and of most immediate importance—

12. The United States wishes to concentrate as soon as possible her naval force in the Atlantic so as to be prepared for any emergency against a potential enemy with whom there is no current basis for friendship.

III.

Proposed Agreement

Because of the foregoing facts, the United States proposes to enter into an Agreement with Japan at once under which the United States and Japan will agree to do certain things, as follows:

A. On her part, the United States Government proposes to do the following:

1. To withdraw the bulk of the American Naval forces from the Pacific.
2. To sign a 20-year non-aggression pact with Japan.
3. To promote a final settlement of the Manchurian question.
4. To actively advocate the placing of Indo-China under the Government of a joint British, French, Japanese, Chinese and American Commission, which will insure most-favored-nation treatment for those five countries until the European War is ended, and which will govern the country primarily in the interests of the Indo-Chinese people.
5. To give up all extra-territorial rights in China, and to obtain England's agreement to give up her extra-territorial rights in China, and give Hong Kong back to China.
6. To present to Congress and push for enactment a bill to repeal the

Immigration Act of 1917 which prohibits immigration into the United States of Japanese, and place the Japanese and the Chinese on the same basis as other peoples.

7. To negotiate a trade agreement with Japan, giving her (a) most-favored-nation treatment and (b) such concessions on imports as can be mutually satisfactorily arranged, including an agreement to keep raw silk on the free list for 20 years.

8. To extend a $2 billion 20-year credit at 2 per cent interest, to be drawn upon at the rate not to exceed $200 million a year except with approval of the President of the United States.

9. To set up a $500 million stabilization fund half supplied by Japan and half by the United States, to be used for the stabilization of the dollar-yen rate.

10. To remove the restrictions on Japanese funds in the United States.

11. To use its influence to the full to attempt to eliminate sources of potential friction between Japan and her neighbors, and to assure Japan access to the raw materials of the world on the same basis as now enjoyed by United States and Great Britain.

B.   On its part, the Japanese Government proposes to do the following:

1. Withdraw all military, naval, air police forces from China (boundaries as of 1931) from Indo-China and from Thailand.

2. Withdraw all support—military, political, or economic—from any government in China other than that of the national government.

3. Replace with yen currency at a rate agreed upon among the Treasuries of China, Japan, England and United States all military scrip, yen and puppet notes circulating in China.

4. Give up all extra-territorial rights in China.

5. Extend to China a billion yen loan at 2 per cent to aid in reconstructing China (at rate of 100 million yen a year).

6. Withdraw all Japanese troops from Manchuria except for a few divisions necessary as a police force, provided U.S.S.R. withdraws all her troops from the Far Eastern front except for an equivalent remainder.

7. Sell to the United States up to three-fourths of her current output of war material—including naval, air, ordnance and commercial ships on a cost-plus 20 per cent basis as the United States may select.

8. Expel all German technical men, military officials and propogandists.

9. Accord the United States and China most-favored-nation treatment in the whole Japanese Empire.

10. Negotiate a 10-year non-aggression pact with United States, China, British Empire, Dutch Indies (and Philippines).

C.   Inasmuch as the United States cannot permit the present uncertain status between the United States and Japan to continue in view of world developments, and feels that decisive action is called for now, the United States should extend the above offer of a generous and peaceful solution of the difficulties between the two countries for only a limited time. If the Japanese Government does not indicate its acceptance in principle at least of the proferred terms before the expiration of that time, it can mean only that the present Japanese Government prefers other and less peaceful ways of solving those difficulties, and is awaiting the propitious moment to attempt to carry out further a plan of conquest.

IV.

*Advantages to Japan and United
States of Such an Agreement*

The Advantages accruing to each government are listed below:

A.   *To the United States*
1. In the event that Japan elected to reject the offer of peaceful solution under terms herein indicated, the United States would have a clearer idea of what to expect and would therefore know better how to shape her own policy.
2. Our naval power will be greatly increased at once by the freeing of our Pacific fleet for duty elsewhere.
3. We would be able to send more of our equipment to England and Russia without increasing our vulnerability to an attack from the East.
4. We will have stopped the war in China and have regained for her her freedom.
5. We will have paved the way for a substantial increase in post-war trade.
6. We would greatly strengthen the Allied position vis-a-vis Germany.
7. We will have saved ourselves from a war with Japan.
8. The money it would cost us would be a very small part of what we would save by not having to fight Japan, or by not having to be prepared for a two-ocean war.
9. A prosperous Japan and China can greatly help to restore our normal trade, and thus make easier our own transition to a peace time economy.

10. Insure for ourselves an increased supply of tin, antimony and wood oil and rubber from the Far East.

11. Handicap Germany in its present military campaign and at the same time give great moral encouragement to the British and Russian people.

12. Finally, military and naval experts who now fear a "two front" naval threat will be more enthusiastic about all out help to England and Russia. There will be much less cause to oppose the administration's foreign policy.

B.   *To Japan*

1. Instead of being confronted with prospect of a more serious war and certain defeat in the end, she can have peace at once.

2. She can proceed at once to shift from a war economy to peace economy and at the same time experience prosperity rather than a serious depression.

3. She can withdraw from the China incident without loss of "face".

4. She can strengthen her currency and reduce her public debt.

5. Her foreign trade will greatly increase.

6. She can devote her energies and capital to reconstructing Japan, building up Manchuria, and developing new trade possibilities at a time when other countries are engaged in war or preparation for war.

7. She will at one stroke have solved some of her thorniest problems in her international relations.

8. She will avoid the social disruption that is bound to take place in Japan after an expanded and prolonged war effort.

Index